The Dawn of the Arab Uprisings

"In the last few years, *Jadaliyya* has established itself as an indispensable source dealing with the contemporary Arab world. This collection of its pieces on the Arab uprisings is perhaps the best introduction to the political movements that have shaken that region since January 2011. It offers a set of intelligent commentaries on revolutionary events in almost every Arab country, and their repercussions in the area and beyond. *Dawn of the Arab Uprisings* is essential reading for anyone wanting to understand the possible future developments of our uncertain world."

Talal Asad, City University of New York

"As contemporary reflections, these writings capture the unfolding of revolutionary events as they happened and convey the uncertainties, hopes and disappointments of collective worlds being remade. As the work of scholars and activists with a rich knowledge of the region's histories and political aspirations, the essays offer lasting insights into the forces shaping a new moment in world history."

Timothy Mitchell, Columbia University

"The outburst of the Arab Revolutions demands imaginative and novel perspectives on the Arab world, and *Jadaliyya* has managed to provide a unique forum covering the region with a fresh approach to its issues and problems. Its talented contributors, from the Arab world and beyond, combine objectivity with a progressive, humanistic engagement, and never shy away from sometimes explosive topics such as the world of oil and its despotic monarchies. Necessary reading on an Arab world in the throes of change."

Fawwaz Traboulsi, author of *A History of Modern Lebanon*

"Not since struggles for independence has the Middle East witnessed the kind of mass mobilization characteristic of recent Arab uprisings. The online journal *Jadaliyya* has been at the forefront of intelligent commentary, capturing the immediacy of current events with uncommon thoughtfulness. With an appreciation for the various genres expressive of politics, the journal has placed public intellectuals, activists, journalists, artists, and academics in conversation, enabling contentious debates and divergent analyses to reach multiple, global publics. A primer of importance not only to students of the 'Arab Spring,' but also to those concerned with protest more generally, this collection represents relevant writings from the early months of the uprisings. Registering both the exhilarating optimism and crushing disappointment of contemporary political life, this volume is recommended for anyone interested in the interrelationships among domestic, regional, and international affairs; it gives voice to some of the possibilities for and impasses to political transformation."

Lisa Wedeen, Mary R. Morton Professor of Political Science and the College, University of Chicago

"During the Arab uprisings, my first port of call every day was *Jadaliyya* to understand and interpret the events. The articles collected here are a very rare combination—scholarly but also accessible for a broad public. This book will be a much-treasured volume for undergraduate students, and its sophistication will also benefit postgraduates and academics. More importantly, an intelligent lay reader will also find the book immediately useful."

Dr Laleh Khalili, SOAS, University of London

THE DAWN OF THE ARAB UPRISINGS

End of an Old Order?

Edited by Bassam Haddad,
Rosie Bsheer and Ziad Abu-Rish

Foreword by Roger Owen

PlutoPress
www.plutobooks.com

First published 2012 by Pluto Press
345 Archway Road, London N6 5AA

www.plutobooks.com

Distributed in the United States of America exclusively by
Palgrave Macmillan, a division of St. Martin's Press LLC,
175 Fifth Avenue, New York, NY 10010

British Library Cataloguing in Publication Data
A catalogue record for this book is available from the British Library

ISBN   978 0 7453 3325 0   Hardback
ISBN   978 0 7453 3324 3   Paperback
ISBN   978 1 8496 4797 7   PDF eBook
ISBN   978 1 8496 4798 4   Kindle eBook
ISBN   978 1 8496 4799 1   EPUB eBook

Library of Congress Cataloging in Publication Data applied for

This book is printed on paper suitable for recycling and made from fully
managed and sustained forest sources. Logging, pulping and manufacturing
processes are expected to conform to the environmental standards of the
country of origin.

10   9   8   7   6   5   4   3   2

Designed and produced for Pluto Press by Chase Publishing Services Ltd
Typeset from disk by Stanford DTP Services, Northampton, England
Simultaneously printed digitally by CPI Antony Rowe, Chippenham, UK and
Edwards Bros in the United States of America

Contents

Acknowledgments

We would first like to extend our appreciation to the authors whose articles make up the bulk of these pages. Their willingness to share their research, experiences, and reflections vis-à-vis the Middle East in general and the Arab uprisings more specifically was central to *Jadaliyya*'s role in shaping academic and non-academic discourses alike. We would also like to thank *Jadaliyya*'s co-editors, contributing editors, and our many dedicated interns. They were all part of the solicitation, submission, review, editing, and posting processes that initially brought these articles to light.

The transformation of a disparate set of articles published on *Jadaliyya* into a coherent edited volume encapsulating the initial period of the Arab uprisings involved several individuals. Roger Owen's Foreword and Madawi Al-Rasheed's Epilogue are testaments of their commitment to supporting new projects and advancing critical interventions related to the production of knowledge on and solidarity networks in the Arab world. Thomas Sullivan was an invaluable resource in preparing the format and layout of the manuscript for submission. We are grateful for his copy-editing work and that of Adam Gallagher. Finally, we offer our appreciation to David Shulman and his colleagues at Pluto Press, both for their initial excitement about the project as well as their diligence in seeing it through to completion.

We dedicate this volume to Mohamed Bouazizi and the countless others who have given their lives in the struggle for dignity, justice, and freedom.

Foreword
Jadaliyya: Archiving the Revolution

The uprisings in the Arab world in the early part of 2011 clearly constitute a world historical event. Although the actual word "revolution" is somewhat imprecise, it has the great value of linking them to a long line of revolutionary activity, including the violent overthrow of the old orders in Paris beginning in 1789, as well as to the more peaceful "Velvet" revolutions in Eastern Europe following the withdrawal of the Soviet military forces in 1989–90. In the Middle East's own version of these mighty events, not only were a series of tyrants toppled but the strength of popular feeling, and the stubborn willingness of the demonstrators to sustain their challenge to those who remained, also sent shockwaves across the Arab world from Morocco to Kuwait.

The result: a return of the separate parts of the Arab region to the mainstream of world history after decades in which they had been largely sidelined by oppressive and inflexible regimes, some ruled by kings, others by presidents who acted like kings in their desire to perpetuate a stifling family rule at all costs. Whatever else may happen, it is pretty obvious that the old era of presidents-for-life ruling over a fearful people is now gone for good—even if the shape of the new, post-revolutionary political order still remains quite extraordinarily difficult to make out.

It is a natural human desire to want to record these remarkable events, to keep the experience of them alive, and to make the memory of the excitement they generated and the hopes they raised widely available to Arabs and non-Arabs alike. Hence the number of archival projects which have already sprung into existence. Some, like those run by the *Egyptian Committee to Document the 25 January Revolution* or the American University in Cairo's *University on the Square* initiative are concerned largely with just one country; others, like the *Jadaliyya* electronic archive, include the whole Arab world. In each case the task appears to be to collect as much as possible, of as great a variety of different official, editorial, and popular expressions as possible, and then to organize and to digitize it so as to make it easily available to the largest possible number of people around the world.

Similar projects have, of course, taken place with respect to previous revolutionary outbursts. It is thanks to them that we know so much about what it was like, for example, in the streets of Paris after the fall of the Bastille in July 1789. There is also much to be learned from similar efforts to collect objects, pictures, and other memorabilia connected with other great events like wars, on the one hand, and the everyday life of people living in more ordinary times, on the other. Each has its purpose, its own logic, and its own method for engaging the interest and the sensibilities of its putative audience.

Each of us knows, from our own particular experience, what it is we want from such collections and displays, and what it is that speaks to us most vividly about the lives and experiences of those whose activities are on display. For most, I suspect, it is the sense of the immediacy of a particular historical moment that we respond to the most directly, whether by hearing a song like Midan al-Tahrir's "*Sawt al-Hurriya*"[1] (Voice of Freedom) that captures the essence of a people tasting freedom for the first time, or looking at a picture of a man holding up a placard saying, "I used to be afraid. I became an Egyptian." We feel ourselves right in the square with the excited crowds, just as we recognize, what the demonstrators themselves could not know at the time: how ephemeral all such moments must prove to be.

Other signs are suggestive of a more complex political reality, like the indictment painted in white on the side of a burned out Syrian car, "*anta fi Banyas la fi Israel*," (You are in Banyas not in Israel) observed in April 2011; one piece in the jigsaw puzzle of a larger picture of sectional and sectarian struggle, the outlines of which we are even now only dimly aware. Here too, as elsewhere, we can also observe the spirited play on words directed toward those seeking to repress them: a request to the Syrian authorities for "*silmiyah* (with the 'm' underlined) *mou silahiya*" (peaceful, not armed); or a message to President Husni Mubarak in hieroglyphs as the only language a Pharaoh can understand.

That said, collection and dissemination, exciting though they may be, are just one aspect of the archival project. In what follows I would like to turn to the equally important questions of organization, definition, purpose, and use.

DEFINITION AND USE

Let me start with a simple proposition: archives such as that of the *Jadaliyya* project, must be conceived of, first and foremost, as constituting a vast data bank, many of the uses of which cannot be known in advance. Indeed, it might even be argued that there should not be too much conscious anticipation of what such uses might be, on the grounds that this might place limits on fruitful future possibilities. To take just one contemporary example: who could have imagined that the photos and artefacts collected by Berlin's Deutsches Historisches Museum about life during the Second World War—from busts of Hitler to the original clothes worn by concentration camp victims—would one day be used as the basis for a contemporary 2011 exhibition called "Hitler and the Germans—Nation and Crime," with the specific aim of addressing the question of how the Nazis came to power and how they achieved such power and influence over German people? Nor how the exhibits themselves might actually be one day presented, for instance by allowing curious visitors to access the pages of the Daily Visitor's Book of Hitler's Chancellery with the click of a mouse—and so turning it into a living indictment of the heads of state and other visiting dignitaries who continued to pay court to Hitler himself until well into 1944?

Nevertheless, some preliminary definitions are necessary in terms of scope and time. First, does the remit to collect "everything" actually mean everything? And where to draw the line in a world, particularly the Arab world, where everything is so closely interconnected with everything else? Also, how to do justice to events right across the Arab region where some regimes have fallen, others are engaged in armed resistance to the people's uprisings, and others again, as in often-overlooked Oman, have been trying, with some success, to find a way to disarm criticism without any surrender of real power?

Second, what to do about the information released by the revolutionary events as they relate to the practices of government—their use of force and fear, their cronyism and corruption—which not only characterized the previous era but were also in large measure responsible for the revolutionary challenges all came to face? When to do so immediately invites a detailed examination not just of the whole pre-history of Arab politics since independence but also of possible futures as well.

And then, third, there is the question of the time-span of the revolutionary process itself. In Egypt and Tunisia, for example, the holding of free elections and the drawing up of a new constitution may be considered to constitute the beginning of a new, post-revolutionary, political order. But revolutionary events elsewhere, in Syria and Yemen, in Morocco and Algeria, will surely continue to rumble on for many years, making the task of collecting data about day-to-day developments in those countries so much more onerous.

Lastly, how to maintain interest in the collections over time? History moves on, while collections have a way of reducing their once vibrant artefacts and memorabilia into a discrete set of lifeless objects once the context that produced and sustained them has disappeared. True, this is not quite the same challenge as that facing a conventional museum with its large cellars full of rarely displayed objects. But there are other pressing problems concerning their continued immediacy and relevance such as the challenge posed, for example, by Egypt's Mohamed Hassanein Heikal in May 2011 to the effect that the new political actors must get over the excitement of overthrowing, and then punishing, the Mubarak regime in the interests of confronting the insistent challenge of building a new economic and political order. In Heikal's case this would mean leaving judgment of the Mubaraks and their cronies to the elected politicians. It would also, so it seems to me, create a situation in which the day-to-day documentation of the revolutionary moment would all too easily be thrust aside by novelists, social historians, memoir-writers, collectors of photographs, and others determined, like a de Tocqueville or a Stendhal, to stamp their own personal and inevitably simplified vision on these large events.

QUESTIONS OF ORGANIZATION

Everyone will agree that archives should be well-curated, that is, organized in such a way that they are usable in terms of both accessibility and of revealing exactly what they possess via a comprehensible system of classification and cross-reference in terms of subject, time, place, and content. Fortunately there are many proven systems involving links, search engines, and key words to do the job. But this does not obviate the fact that the curators themselves have to choose what categories and what sub-categories they want in the first place—a difficult task. How to impose some order, for example, on the mountains of material generated by the intense national debates that broke out in Egypt and Tunisia concerning the political timetable as it related to elections—both popular and presidential—and to the mechanism for drawing up a new social contract enshrined in a new constitution? Or how to catalog the vast amount of rumors which revolutionary events generate? Or what to make of the evidence of popular recourse to what were often the wildest and most improbable conspiracy theories?

Then there is the question of finance. As a rule such collections get started as a result of the initiative of an enthusiastic organizer, or group of organizers, aided by a staff of equally enthusiastic but usually unpaid volunteers. Yet, if the effort is to be sustained, it can only be by finding money for a more permanent professional staff working in a permanent home, either by fund-raising or by marketing some of its collection for money.

Other important questions include how to publicize the archive beyond the confines of academia; how to cooperate with other, similar archives—particularly in the Middle East itself; and how to make the best use of the lessons to be learned from previous archival projects like that of the *Iraq Memory Foundation* with its aim of making knowledge of the crimes of the Saddam Hussein regime available to all the people of Iraq.

Last, but certainly not least, there is the need to be clear about the history of the archive itself: how was it conceived; how were the objects in it collected; how were criticisms met; and how were the various problems it faced addressed. Given that one of its most powerful aims must surely be to criticize the secrecy and the hypocrisy of the previous Arab information regimes, then it must obviously make sure that its own processes, its own logic and modus operandi, are freely on display.

QUESTIONS OF CONTESTATION

All great revolutionary events excite counter-revolutions from both inside and outside, and the Arab revolutions have proved no exception. Attempts have been made to contain, to resist or to undermine them by forces loyal to the *ancien régime*, sometimes in alliance with other Arab regimes (and their foreign allies) fearful that the demonstration effect might affect their own restive people. And this, in turn, has produced its own set of counter-discourses, as well as, on occasions, a set of practices ranging from outright armed contestation as in Libya, Syria, and Yemen, or armed intervention as in Bahrain, to more covert forms of repression and cross-border interference.

The collection of data relating to such a wide variety of counter-revolutionary activity all across the Arab world produces many extra archival problems, the more so as much of it is, and was, conducted in secret and can only be known via rumor or at second or third hand. Take, for example, the activities of the Syrian regime to confront its enemies both inside Syria and across its borders. Or, for instance, the situation in Tripoli, Libya where a special combination of confused speeches by members of the Qaddafi family and the direct but covert action taken against the rebels makes it necessary to collect information not only about the speeches and actions themselves but also about the various attempts by outsiders, exiles, and others to understand and interpret them as well. None of this data can in any way be described as neutral; most can only be understood in context and in terms of the reliability of whoever produced it in the first place.

Clearly, some preliminary guidelines are necessary, even if they are found to need amendment as time and experience goes by. At first sight, "revolution" and "counter-revolution" seem useful categories. But can they be separated, conceptually, for the purposes of classification? And can data classified as the latter itself be further classified in terms of its sources, its putative reliability, so on and so forth? Then, perhaps most important of all, can all this be done in such a way as to preserve both the "revolutionary" spirit of the whole archival project while preventing it from coming under serious attack from those who are threatened by the whole enterprise and who see it as an essential part of the war against them, their beliefs, and their place in the world?

A final thought: what about the lives of people affected by the great revolutionary events taking place in the Arab world but who remain either ambivalent about, or not directly concerned with, their outcome? Feelings of this type can range all the way from confusion and indifference, on the one hand, to opportunism and a kind of wait-and-see-ism, on the other. Not to speak of those who view politics in quite other terms: as a form of *fitna* (sedition) or a questioning of God's Holy law. Are their voices to be included in the archival project? Or excluded on the grounds of irrelevance?

QUESTIONS OF USE

Finally, there is the question of the multiple uses to which the new archives are to be put. For some they will be seen, primarily, as an important academic tool as far as future teaching and research is concerned. For others, they will be viewed in much more directly political terms, regarded not only as a record of certain kinds of political activity which aimed at, for example, a new kind of inclusivity—men and women, Christian and Muslim, rich and poor—but also as the foundation of a political program which aims to keep alive the hope and enthusiasms generated by each great revolutionary moment. One might propose, for example, that in both Egypt and Tunisia, the rights of certain sections of the population, those of women and of minorities, were perhaps better expanded and protected under the old dictatorships than they threaten to be under the new democracies. And there will be many who will want to return to the Tahrir or Casbah experience to prove this particular proposition wrong.

Then there is the more expansive project of creating a historical memory, not just for the Arab peoples directly involved, but also for those not yet born or still too young to understand what was going on all around them. Unlike the records of such salient events from the Egyptian popular resistance in Port Said to the Tripartite invasion by Britain, France, and Israel in 1956 or the revolutionary events in Baghdad in July 1958, these will not be locked up in inaccessible government archives but will be made freely available to anyone who wants to see them. Men and women will want to say that "this was our finest hour," as Prime Minister Winston Churchill told his British audience as they were about to fight what he called the "Battle of Britain" in the summer of 1940. Such moments form an essential ingredient of each people's national story, testimony to the best in them, to something of which they can be endlessly proud.

But there is still more to it than that. Most people would probably applaud the use of these same archives as a check against future dictatorial regimes, for example, by providing evidence in future trials concerning war crimes and human rights violations. But what if they were also employed, as they surely will be, by militaries to train their recruits in domestic policing and by security forces to identify possible troublemakers or to develop ways of containing and controlling the social media and of discovering how best to avoid international surveillance? Perhaps lawyers will be needed at some stage to guide the curators of these archives through such thickets, perhaps a board of "wise men?"

CONCLUSION

The creation of a new archive to record a set of world historical events is an exciting project, but also one that brings with it great responsibilities. It is the Arab people themselves who, after decades of neglect, took center stage, whether as participants or observers, victims or villains, each with his or her own set of memories, each with a stake in their own experience, each doing or saying something that is open for the later observer to marvel at and, perhaps also, to exploit, to judge or perhaps even to belittle. And it is the same "people" in whose name the new constitutional regime is being built, whether they took part in the vast, and mostly peaceful, national debate which took place in Tunisia and Egypt after the fall of the Ben Ali and Mubarak regimes, or the more muted ones in Jordan and Morocco—not forgetting the heated and violent exchanges which split the populations of Bahrain, Libya, Syria, and Yemen.

For those of us who live outside the Middle East, it is usually our lot to act as observers and commentators, not as actors in the events we witness and try to describe. The fact that some *Jadaliyya* editors are based in the region and most travel extensively back and forth, makes them direct observers and often participants, not just commentators. So it is a particularly exciting moment when a US-based institution with deep roots in the region can become home to such an eminently worthwhile project of collection and public memory as this. I offer it my warmest congratulations and my very best wishes.

Roger Owen
Harvard University
Fall 2011

Introduction

Bassam Haddad, Rosie Bsheer, and Ziad Abu-Rish

If in early December 2010 one had predicted the fall, in whole or in part, of four heads of Arab states and the prevalence of anti-regime protests across the Arab world, it would have been dismissed as wishful thinking. Indeed, in academic circles, such predictions would have been deemed analytically implausible, if not outright sloppy. Yet, what had seemed utterly improbable less than a year ago has become an enduring reality over a year after Mohamed Bouazizi immolated himself in Tunisia on 17 December 2010. Since then, three Arab countries have experienced fundamental transformation and two are on the brink of major change, or so it seems. The reverberations of the popular movements of the so-called Arab Spring have also been felt across the Arab Middle East and beyond.

Jadaliyya followed, analyzed, and archived the monumental developments, starting with the Tunisian case. We covered and tried to make legible nearly every dramatic juncture in a play-by-play fashion. We also published daily analysis on significant turning points, and their impacts on the lived experiences of people on the ground as well as on the future of academic and journalistic writings on the region.

The partial breakdown of regimes that survived well for decades, however, is no small feat. It is impossible to cover all aspects of such transformations, let alone detect all the ramifications, many of which remain to be revealed. As individuals and groups become increasingly more empowered and find avenues to share their experiences, clearer narratives of the anti-regime movements have, and will continue to emerge.

Analyzing the causes of these transitions, which remain in their very early phases, is less daunting than accounting for the timing of these uprisings, a task that will perhaps remain elusive. Suffice it to say that the wonder is not that these regimes began to crack, because they really did not do so on their own. After all, it was mass protests—and battle in the Libyan case—that compelled change. Rather, the question is how these regimes survived for so long, a more manageable explanatory task that some authors have started to revisit.

Many challenges remain ahead for people living in and from the region. It is one thing to break the psychological barrier of fear and go onto the streets en masse to demand the fall of a regime. It is another to rebuild more democratic and sustainable institutions that safeguard that which was won amid unending sacrifices. Out of all tasks ahead, the latter is the most germane and critical. The array of factors and forces for change and some form of revolution is matched locally, regionally, and globally by another that seeks either a restoration of the status quo or the mitigation of change. Not only do the popular Arab movements have to mobilize against the entrenched and brutal regimes in power, they also have to resist a multi-pronged, ruthless counter-revolution spearheaded and financed by Saudi Arabia, Qatar, and their allies. Bahrain and Yemen are two cases in point where the uprisings were either quelled or temporarily muted by a cosmetic transfer of power at the very top.

Yet, we also find that some cases are more complex than others, namely, that of Syria. After more than a year of constant uprisings, notably in the countryside and smaller cities, there seems to be no end in sight. With more than eight thousand dead, and many more who have been arrested or have disappeared, this particular uprising is turning into a battle between the regime and an increasingly militarized opposition, in a charged regional and international context. In fact, whereas some thought that Libya would be the case that would halt further uprisings, we are now witnessing the Syrian case playing that role. Located at the heart of various conflicts and causes, the Syrian case has come to represent far more than itself: beyond similarities with other cases, it represents the battle between the pro-"resistance" camp and the conservative Arab status quo as well as its Western allies; it also represents a pivotal element in the regional balance of power, with Iran and Hizbollah at its side, opposing most other states in the region. Finally, it also represents a further power-play between the United States and Russia (and China to a lesser extent). Hence, we are likely to witness the continuation of a stalemate for some time to come. At the time of publication, it does not appear that we will witness a flaring up of ubiquitous mass protests in other Arab countries for some time, barring the continuing struggle for capitalizing on the gains of the revolutions elsewhere. However, in countries like Egypt and Libya, the path to realizing the fruits of last year's transformations is proving far more rocky than expected, with potential for reversals.

More than a year on, it has become fairly evident that we should avoid addressing the regional protests as a singular unit of analysis. Commonalities exist, but they are limited. The recurring theme across these Arab countries is that they are experiencing (or have experienced) high levels of mass mobilization on a scale hitherto unseen in the Arab Middle East, at least not in unison and certainly not since the struggles for independence from colonial and imperial rule. We have also witnessed a strong affinity among these publics for learning from each other's experience, creating a domino effect across the Arab countries. This signals the persistent, even if amorphous, historical, cultural, and political dimensions that continue to bind many Arabs in a systemic way—though we should not overstate this affinity as it remains at the level of triggers and signaling, not cooperation and collaboration. Beyond that, the commonality dwindles, and in some cases, stops. It is more productive to focus instead on the significant differences among these polities, in terms of social structure, political-economic, ethnic, regional, social, and sectarian diversity.

In any case, we, at *Jadaliyya*, do hope that the forces of change win this battle, and understand that in some cases the situation might be less straightforward than others (for example, Syria and Libya), especially where foreign intervention plays a more prominent role. Moreover, calls for too much caution regarding change and fear of the chaos that might ensue henceforth—such as that currently taking place in Egypt—are not justified from any historical perspective. After all, replacing decades-old authoritarian political orders that have long destroyed most forms of popular political participation cannot take place peacefully, or overnight. The alternative is for the same popular struggles to occur in years to come, except that citizens of the respective countries would have to endure the wrath of unaccountable and often brutal regimes in the interim. The calculus is clear.

However, much of what is usually missed in the examination of societies happens beyond the corridors of power. Observers and participants alike now have an opportunity to examine, chronicle, and share narratives, processes, and a whole series of practices and events that did not always make it into the purview of interested onlookers and analysts—precluding direct field research, which often accesses abridged realities. We at *Jadaliyya* have tried to cover what has received short shrift elsewhere and prior to the uprisings, and we look forward to a much busier year in this regard.

Herein, we present a collection of already-published *Jadaliyya* articles on the uprisings as a slice of what transpired in the region and how *Jadaliyya* editors and contributors represented it. It is by no means exhaustive, and is not intended to be so. Rather, we deem these events too precious to not record in some manageable volume or archive, beyond the pages of an electronic publication that is constantly expanding. It is an act of arresting the representation of the uprising and presenting it to those who wish to reflect, share, educate, and/or remember. Most importantly, we intend to capture in this volume the first irretrievable moments of the uprisings, when the impossible became inevitable, and when the belief that the status quo cannot be sustained was new and captivating. These early moments capture feelings and thoughts that are already long forgotten: the disbelief, the hope, the relief, the moment of multiple possibilities, the solidarity. Most of these sentiments have become a thing of the past, sometimes distant past, not just in time, but also in space. The violence, bloodshed, and counter-revolution have relegated the initial euphoria less meaningful, which betrays the emergence of new tangible realities and possibilities. Thus, this book is a "reminder" of these early positive moments that signal the beginning of the unraveling of a rigid regional order. In retrospect, it may very well be that these series of events were simply the original minor tremor along the path of undoing decades of dictatorship and corruption, dependency, and subordination. Whatever the outcome of the more stubborn cases like Syria, or counter-revolution in Egypt, the effacing of the collective will is no longer an option for autocrats everywhere in the region.

We have divided the reader into sections that represent the most affected countries (Tunisia, Egypt, Libya, Bahrain, Yemen, and Syria), with a Foreword, Introduction, and Epilogue. Because revolutionary tremors were only felt, but did not impose themselves consistently in some quarters, we decided to group these in one section entitled "Regional Reverberations of the Arab Uprisings." Irrespective of this diversity in degree, the uprisings have also highlighted various issues related to how the Arab world is analyzed and represented, as well as the nature of US foreign policy in the face of changes many in the region believe in. One challenge was to decide when to stop considering articles for inclusion in this volume, given this is an ongoing development. We opted for being Spring 2011 heavy, and Summer 2011 light, in order to capture the first moments more fully. Even within such a strategy, it was difficult to make selections as we were also limited by space. Other *Jadaliyya* volumes will pick up where this one leaves off.

Section I

Opening Articles

1
Impromptu: A Word

Sinan Antoon[2]

28 January 2011

We were told, time and again, that "revolution" and "the people" were obsolete terms, irrelevant in a post-revolutionary world, especially in the Arab world. This, after all, was a place where the burden of the past weighed so heavily and the cultural DNA somehow preconditioned those who carried it to feel more at home with tyrants and terror. Too many trees were killed theorizing about the region's inhospitability to democracy. "Reform" was the most one could hope for. Revolution? No way! That was the stuff of outmoded leftists and dreamers left behind as history marched forward. The referent for "revolution" resided in the past (or in the West), but never in the present, or near future. The latter, was eternally deferred. Revolutions were dormant in archives, dictionaries, and documentary footage. Revolutions were celebrated and imagined in songs and poems fading from collective memory and oral history.

Even those of us who did not buy into this narrative for obvious reasons fell prey to despair and pessimism. It was not just hereditary dictatorships mushrooming left and right, but neocolonialism, military occupations, sectarianism, and civil wars. It was even difficult, at times, to be a pessoptimist à la Habibi.

Then there was Tunisia. The people forced "fate to respond" to their will to live (to echo the great Tunisian poet al-Shabbi [1909–1934]) and restored meaning to a crucial signifier. Men and women consigned a dictator and his brutal reign to the past tense and are still demonstrating, because they will not settle for cosmetic change. The dictator's friends in the "civilized world," who sustained him just as they sustain his species elsewhere, were shocked and disoriented. Now, the people are trying to summon revolution back to the material world in Yemen. And in Egypt, with creativity and courage, anger and suffering are transformed into colossal human waves.

The tide is turning. Something has changed for good. Dictatorial regimes are not invincible. A modern-day pharaoh and his corrupt family are about to be consigned to the past tense. But he will cling to his throne with bloody hands. As I write this, news reports confirm that army units are being deployed in anticipation of Friday's "Day of Anger." In addition to killing several demonstrators, massive arrests, brutality, blocking Facebook, Twitter, YouTube, and Blackberry, the regime, with the collusion of multinationals, has disabled internet services in Cairo and other cities to disrupt mobilization and disable the revolution. An electronic siege.

Friday promises to be a monumental day. The various groups have called for demonstrations after Friday prayers. Our hearts are with the Egyptian people as they teach the world a valuable lesson, but we should express our solidarity with them and demand that the siege be lifted immediately so their voices can be heard, loud and clear.

Since the United States is the main $ponsor of Husni Mubarak's brutal and corrupt regime and American politicians have shamelessly reiterated their support, American citizens should speak up and tell the media and these politicians where they stand: with the Egyptian people and their revolution (in the present tense), or with dictatorship? You cannot have it both ways.

2
Preliminary Historical Observations on the Arab Revolutions of 2011

Rashid Khalidi[3]

21 March 2011

Toward the end of his long, eventful life, in 1402, the renowned Arab historian Ibn Khaldun was in Damascus. He left us a description of Taymur's siege of the city and of his meeting with the world conqueror. None of us is Ibn Khaldun, but any Arab historian today watching the Arab Revolutions of 2011 has the sense of awe that our forbear must have had as we witness a great turning in world affairs.

This juncture may be unprecedented in modern Arab history. Suddenly, despotic regimes that have been entrenched for forty years and more seem vulnerable. Two of them—in Tunis and then in Cairo—crumbled before our eyes in a few weeks. Others in Tripoli and Sanaa are fighting to survive. The old men who dominate the rest suddenly look their age, and the distance between them and most of their populations, born decades after them, has never been greater. An apparently frozen political situation has melted overnight in the heat of the popular upsurge that began in Tunisia and Egypt, and now is spreading. We are all privileged to be experiencing a world-historical moment, when fixed verities vanish and new potentials and forces emerge. Perhaps one day some of us can say, as Wordsworth said of the French Revolution, "Bliss it was in that dawn to be alive, but to be young was very heaven."

These have so far mainly been revolutions fashioned by ordinary people peacefully demanding freedom, dignity, democracy, social justice, accountability, transparency, and the rule of law. Arab youth at the end of the day have been shown to have hopes and ideals no different from the young people who helped bring about democratic transitions in Eastern Europe, Latin America and South, South-East and East Asia. These voices have been a revelation only to those deluded by the propaganda of the Arab regimes themselves, or by

9

the Western media's obsessive focus on Islamic fundamentalism and terrorism whenever it deals with the Middle East. This is thus a supremely important moment not only in the Arab world, but also for how Arabs are perceived by others. A people that has been systematically maligned in the West for decades is for the first time being shown in a positive light.

Nothing has yet been decided in these Arab Revolutions. And the most complex tasks are yet to come. It was difficult for the people to overthrow an out-of-touch tyrant and his greedy family, whether in Tunis or Cairo. Thoroughly changing the regime and building a functioning democratic system will be much harder. It will be harder still to ensure that a democratic system, if one can be established, is not dominated by entrenched, powerful interests. Finally, it will be a daunting task for any new popular democratic regime to achieve the social justice and rapid economic growth that will be necessary to provide equal opportunity, quality education, good jobs, decent housing, and desperately needed infrastructure. The old regimes failed to provide these very things: those in Egypt living on less than two dollars a day grew from thirty-nine to forty-three percent of the population during Husni Mubarak's last decade in power. Failure at any of these daunting tasks could well lead to a comeback for the lurking forces of reaction and repression, and indeed the Arab counter-revolution is active in Libya, Bahrain, and elsewhere. Failure in these tasks could also favor violent tendencies that prosper in circumstances of chaos and disorder, such as were unleashed by the American occupation of Iraq. And we must never forget that this is the Middle East, the most coveted region of the world and the most penetrated by foreign interests. It is vulnerable, as it has been throughout history, to external intervention that could easily distort outcomes.

Nevertheless, what has started in Tunisia and Egypt has opened up horizons that have long been closed. The energy, dynamism, and intelligence of the younger generation in the Arab world has been unleashed, after being dammed up by a system which treated them with contempt, and which concentrated power in the hands of a much older generation. Seemingly out of nowhere, young people in the Arab world have gained a confidence, an assurance, and a courage that have made fearsome police state regimes that once looked invincible tremble.

Is this revolutionary upsurge truly unprecedented? The Arab world has been a scene of uprisings and revolts for its entire modern history. During the French occupation the people of Cairo revolted repeatedly, briefly liberating the city from the French in 1800. Egypt revolted again against foreign rule in the years up to 1882; it revolted again against the British in the great revolution of 1919, and once again in 1952. During the Syrian revolt of 1925–26, the French were driven out of most of Damascus, and bombarded the city savagely. Similar examples abound elsewhere. The Libyan resistance against the Italians that started in 1911 and went on for over twenty years, the great Iraqi Revolution of 1920, that of Morocco in 1925–26, the Palestinian Revolt of 1936–39, all provoked ferocious colonial campaigns. These episodes marked the beginning of a somber chapter in human history: the first use of aerial bombardment against civilians in Libya in 1911; and the first use of poison gas against civilians in Iraq in 1920.

What so far distinguishes the revolutionary upsurge that we have been watching across the Arab world from its many predecessors? One of the apparent distinctions is that in Tunisia, Egypt, Bahrain, and in several other countries, it has so far been largely peaceful: "*Silmiyya, silmiyya*" the crowds in Tahrir Square chanted. But so were many of the great Arab uprisings of the past. These included many episodes in Egypt and Iraq's long struggles to end British military occupation, and those of Syria, Lebanon, Morocco, and Tunisia to end that of France, not to speak of the first Palestinian Intifada against Israeli occupation from 1987–1991. While tactics of non-violence were broadly employed in the recent uprisings in Egypt and elsewhere, this is by no means the first time that Arab uprisings have been largely non-violent, or at least unarmed.

Commentators have also said that what distinguishes these revolutions from earlier ones in the Arab world and elsewhere in the Middle East is that they are focused on democracy and constitutional change. It is true that these have been among their most central demands. But this is not entirely unprecedented. There was sustained constitutional effervescence in Tunisia and Egypt in the late 1870s until the British and French occupations of those countries in 1881 and 1882. Similar debates led to the establishment of a constitution in the Ottoman Empire in 1876 that lasted with interruptions until 1918. All the successor states to the Ottoman Empire were deeply influenced by this checkered constitutional experiment. In 1906, Iran established a constitutional regime, albeit one that was repeatedly eclipsed. In the inter-war period and afterwards, the semi-independent and independent countries in the Middle East were mainly governed by constitutional regimes.

These were all flawed constitutional experiments, which faced massive obstacles in the form of entrenched interests, the autocratic proclivities of rulers, and massive illiteracy and poverty. In the end, they solved few of the problems faced by their societies. But the failures to establish sustained constitutional regimes were not solely due to these internal factors. They were also due to these governments being systematically undermined by the Western powers, whose ambitions were often obstructed by democratic parliaments and a nascent public opinion and press that insisted on national sovereignty and a fair share of their own resources. From the late nineteenth century onward, this was a pattern that was constantly repeated. Far from giving support to democratic rule in the Middle East, the Western powers generally undermined it, preferring to deal with pliable and weak autocrats who did their bidding, and conspired with anti-democratic local elites.

So it is not the democratic nature of the revolutionary uprisings of 2011 that makes them unprecedented. Rather, the revolutions that took place from 1800 until the 1950s were primarily directed at ending foreign occupation. These revolutions for national liberation ultimately succeeded in the expulsion of the old colonial powers and their hated military bases in most of the Arab world. These revolutions eventually produced nationalist regimes in most Arab countries. Those in Algeria, Libya, Sudan, Syria, and Yemen still cling to power. That in Iraq was removed by an invasion and occupation that have devastated the country. Only in Tunisia and Egypt have such regimes so far been removed by their peoples, an outcome that is by no means assured.

What distinguishes the revolutions of 2011 from their predecessors is that they mark the end of the old phase of national liberation from colonial rule, and are largely inwardly directed at the problems of Arab societies. Of course, with the Cold War the old colonialism eventually gave way to a more insidious form of external influence, first of the two superpowers, and for the last two decades of the United States alone. The entire Arab regional system was upheld by that hyperpower, whose support was crucial to the survival of most of the dictatorial regimes now trembling as their peoples challenge them. But while this important factor was always in the background, the focus of the 2011 revolutions has been on the internal problems of democracy, constitutions, and equality.

There was another demand in 2011, however. This was for dignity. And this has to be understood in two senses: the dignity of the individual; and the dignity of the collective, of the people, and of the nation. The demand for individual dignity is easily understandable. In the face of frightful police states that crushed the individual, such a demand was natural. The incessant infringements by these authoritarian states on the dignity of nearly every Arab citizen, and their rulers' constant affirmations of their worthlessness, were eventually internalized and produced a pervasive self-loathing and an ulcerous social malaise. This manifested itself among other things in sectarian tensions, frequent sexual harassment of women, criminality, drug use, corrosive incivility, and a lack of public spirit.

One of the worst things about the authoritarian Arab regimes, beyond their denial of the dignity of the individual, was the contempt the rulers showed for their peoples. In their view, the people were immature, dangerous, and unready for democracy. The patronizing, patriarchal tone of Mubarak in his final speeches perfectly characterized all of these regimes: we still hear such a tone from Muammar al-Qaddafi in his ramblings, and from the kings and presidents for life in the other Arab states. Only al-Qaddafi is saying openly what other rulers believe: that their peoples are easily deluded and misled, that in fact they have no dignity.

This brings us to the demand for collective dignity, which the revolutions of 2011 have also raised. The absence of a sense of Arab collective dignity relates to the situation of this region, one of the few to be unaffected by the democratic transitions which have swept other parts of the world in the late twentieth century. Suddenly, the Arabs have proven that they are no different than anyone else. These revolutions have created a sense of collective dignity that was best reflected in the pride of Tunisians and Egyptians after the fall of their respective tyrants. "Raise your head. You are an Egyptian!" the crowds chanted in Tahrir. This was the collective dignity of the Egyptian people, and with them that of the entire Arab people, that was being asserted.

This relates to the question of the role of the United States and of its spoiled protégé, client, and enforcer in the region, Israel. While there has been little mention of this huge elephant in the room in the popular ferment of the 2011 revolutions, it was always there in the background. So was the fact that the Arab police states benefited from top-of-the-line equipment, and extensive training in the best facilities the United States and Europe could provide. American tear gas canisters were used copiously against peaceful protesters in Tunis and Cairo, as they have been systematically used for years against Palestinians demonstrating at villages like Bil'in in the West Bank. The thugs of Ben Ali and Mubarak were on excellent terms with the intelligence services of the United States, and European countries. Western support for "stability" really meant support for repression, corruption, the frustration of popular demands, and the subversion of democracy. It also meant the subordination of the Arab countries to the dictates of US policy, and to the demands of Israel. The demand for collective dignity is a call to end this unnatural situation.

The Arab revolutions of 2011 raise many questions. After a night seemingly without end, a spirit of liberation has been released in the Arab world. It is impossible to say whether it can be sustained sufficiently to surmount the daunting structural problems of the Arab countries, and to overcome the forces of reaction that want to preserve the status quo. Although entrenched elites in Tunisia and Egypt have been shaken by the revolutionary wave, they will not easily cede their privileges. Moreover, other elites still in power will do everything they can to stop this wave throughout the region.

A related question is whether what started in Tunisia and Egypt has the potential to overthrow other Arab tyrants. For all the similarities between their regimes, each Arab country is different from the others. The populations of several of them, notably Jordan, Algeria, Yemen, Bahrain, and Iraq are less homogenous than Egypt or Tunisia, with significant ethnic, regional, or religious cleavages that rulers can exploit to divide and rule. And in some cases, notably Algeria, Iraq, and Jordan, there is memory of bloody civil strife that recently or not so recently rent these societies, and may make people hesitant about protesting. All of these factors have been marshaled by the forces of Arab reaction as they operate across borders to sustain undemocratic and discriminatory systems, whether in Bahrain or elsewhere.

Nevertheless, the new spirit abroad in the Arab world has been contagious, and demands for democracy and constitutional limits on the powers of the rulers that started in Tunisia and Egypt can now be heard in Morocco, Algeria, Sudan, Jordan, Syria, Yemen, Iraq, and the Gulf countries. The slogan raised first by the Tunisian and Egyptian revolutionaries is now everywhere from the Atlantic to the Gulf: "*Al-sha'b yurid isqat al-nizam*" ("The people want the fall of the regime").

Whatever the result, these events are a spectacular confirmation not only of the common aspirations for freedom and dignity of an entire generation of young Arabs, but of the existence of a common Arab public sphere. Although this owes much to modern media, it is a mistake to focus excessively on the specifics of the technology, whether Facebook, Twitter, cell phones, or satellite television. Such a common public sphere existed in the past, relying on earlier forms of technology, whether the printing press or radio. As with all revolutions, this one is the result not of technology but of a ceaseless struggle over many years, in this case by workers' unions, women's groups, human rights activists, Islamists, intellectuals, campaigners for democracy, and many others who have paid dearly for their efforts. If there is anything new, it is the non-hierarchical and networked forms of organization that developed among many of these groups.

The last question that the Arab revolutions raise is that of the role of the Western powers in upholding the Arab status quo. The United States has always been torn in its foreign policy between its principles, including support for democracy, and its interests, including upholding dictators who do what is wanted of them. When there is little public scrutiny, the latter impulse invariably predominates in US policy in the Middle East. Today, with the American media featuring stories of charismatic young Arabs bringing down hated dictators and calling for democracy in perfectly comprehensible English, the American public is watching, and Washington has responded by tepidly supporting a democratic transition, and weakly calling for restraint by its other Arab clients in repressing their peoples. The role of sordid interests has already reasserted itself in US policy on Bahrain and Libya, which are being treated differently from one another and from other Arab countries witnessing upheavals.

This new moment in the Middle East will make the old business-as-usual approach much harder in Washington, in Tel Aviv, and in the Arab capitals. The Mubarak regime was a central pillar of both American and Israeli regional domination, and it will be difficult if not impossible to replace. The other absolute Arab rulers, even if they manage to stay in power, can no longer ignore public opinion, as they have always done in the past. Whether this meant submissively following Washington's lead in its Cold War against Iran, or in protecting Israel from any pressure as it colonized Palestinian land and entrenched its occupation, these unpopular policies of most Arab governments are harder to sustain. The systematic input of public opinion into the making of the Arab states' foreign policies is still in the future. But one can reasonably hope that the day when Arab rulers could ignore Arab public opinion and cozy up to Israel while it brutalized the Palestinians is past.

No one in Washington can rely on the complaisance and submissiveness toward Israel and the United States that was one of the key features of the stagnant Arab order that is being challenged all over the region. What will replace it will be determined in the streets, as well as in the internet cafés, the union halls, newspaper offices, women's groups, and private homes of millions of young Arabs. They have announced that they will no longer tolerate being treated with the contempt their governments have shown them throughout their entire lives. They have put us all on notice: "The people want the fall of the regime." They mean by this the regimes in each and every Arab country which have robbed citizens of their dignity. They also mean a regional regime whose cornerstone was a humiliating submission to the dictates of the United States and Israel, and which robbed all the Arabs of their collective dignity.

3
Awakening, Cataclysm, or Just a Series of Events? Reflections on the Current Wave of Protest in the Arab World

Michael Hudson[4]

16 May 2011

Perhaps the best starting point for understanding the current remarkable wave of protest spreading across the Arab world, would be to examine the nomenclature used to describe or frame it. To some observers it is seen as a "cataclysm." Others speak of the "contagion effect." Still others might see it as simply a series of (fortunate or unfortunate) events not significantly related to each other. The terminology we use influences the conclusions we draw. We can see this if we juxtapose this Western branding—which invokes undesirable images—with the terms used by many commentators in the Arab world such as a "blossoming" or "renaissance." What are these movements: a "disease" or a "cure?" Are they monolithic or locally distinct? Is the outbreak of one protest related to, or caused by another? Finally, are the various Arab countries (and must they be only Arab?)* equally "susceptible" to the contagion?

WHAT'S IN A NAME?

As the aftershocks of regime change in Tunisia and Egypt reverberate throughout the Arab world and beyond, political analysts are struggling to define what is going on. They point to the varying degrees of popular protest in almost every Arab country, including Libya, Yemen, Bahrain, Syria, Oman, Mauritania, Morocco, Algeria, Jordan, Sudan, the Palestinian Authority, Iraq, and Saudi Arabia.

Surveying the flood of analysis, one notices that commentators from outside the region are frequently writing about what they

---

* "Jitters over jasmine in China; online calls for jasmine revolution lead officials to ban sale of the flower," *The Straits Times* (Singapore), 12 May 2011.

call the "contagion effect;" others are asking whether we are seeing an "epidemic" of popular protest and revolution. In the more Realpolitik policy circles some speak of "cataclysm" and forecast grim consequences for the regional and global status quo. With no disrespect intended to the Japanese who are suffering a human catastrophe, I have heard the Arab upheavals described as a "tsunami." But many commentators of liberal disposition in the Arab world and the West use very different nomenclature: they may speak of "a new dawn," "a blossoming," even a "renaissance" of democracy, freedom, and good governance.

The terminology we use often influences the conclusions we reach. The dictionary defines a "contagion" as "the spreading of a harmful idea or practice." An "epidemic" is "a sudden, widespread occurrence of a particular undesirable phenomenon." On the other hand, "blossoming" means "to mature or develop in a promising or healthy way" and "renaissance" in its broad sense refers to "a revival or a renewed interest in something," and their Arabic equivalents—*baath* and *nahda*—mean "awakening, renewal, reemergence, rebirth."

HISTORICAL PERSPECTIVE

In 1938 the Palestinian–British intellectual George Antonius published his famous book *The Arab Awakening*. It described the *nahda*—the Arab literary and cultural renaissance of the nineteenth century—and the development of organized groups in an emerging modern and civil society in the early twentieth century. While the term "awakening" to some[5] connotes a kind of benign Orientalism—it took Westernization to rouse these people from their long slumber—one might yet claim that this "awakening" was the emergence of a new national self-consciousness that would lay the groundwork for the populist Arab unity movement that rocked the Arab world in the 1950s and 1960s.

The original *nahda* was about constructing a collective identity and community. But what is the "awakening" of the present about? I do not yet have a clear answer. It does appear, however, that the thrust of today's wave of protest is less about identity than it is about authority. In every case the discourse is challenging the legitimacy of the rulers and/or the ruling elites and objecting their arbitrary, unaccountable, corrupt, and often-brutal behavior. And yet is there not something about the powerful "contagion effect" that suggests that some kind of latent identity politics—a tacit understanding that "we are all in the same boat"—is also in play?

The story of how the struggle for Arab national independence and unity was derailed into a system of segmented authoritarianisms is well known. Arab nationalist aspirations were cut short by the colonialist interventions after World War I. The map of the old, mostly Ottoman-dominated Arab world was redrawn. Instead of a unified Arab state constructed along liberal and constitutional lines, the pre-existing colonial creations became independent and took on an authoritarian character of their own. The "progressives," led most famously by Egypt's Gamal Abdel Nasser and the Baath Party pursued the dream of Arab unity, liberation, and socialism (*wahda, hurriyya,* and *ishtirakiyya*) through the modalities of a military-dominated, single-party "republicanism." The "conservatives," mainly traditional monarchies (some of them oil-rich), preferred paternalism, capitalism, and protection from the West. Their legitimacy rested on their claims to represent authentic cultural traditions and Islamic rectitude, but they were no less authoritarian than their "republican" counterparts.

This state of affairs has lasted for half a century. Political scientists specializing in the Middle East might be forgiven, then, for focusing on why authoritarianism has been so persistent. They came up with multiple explanations, among them the following:

- The *mukhabarat* state. Whether republican or patrimonial, Arab regimes were able to build up formidable bureaucracies of control: intelligence agencies, multiple police forces, paramilitary organizations, and of course the military establishment. People obeyed because they were afraid.
- "Deferential" Arab political culture. Although this argument is almost universally rejected by serious social scientists, it still enjoys wide currency in Western policy circles, public opinion, and even among many people in the Middle East. It holds that authoritarian rule "fits" the political culture because that culture privileges the elites over the masses (the *khassa* over the *'amma*) and because people are socialized from earliest childhood to defer to patriarchal authority. These commentators argue that Islam also counsels obedience even to a bad ruler over the worse alternative of *fitna* or chaos.
- Western domination. By this argument the colonial period put in place the structures and habits of authoritarianism that would outlast the colonial period itself. Moreover,

the post-colonial period itself was marked by significant manipulation of local politics by the new global hegemons—the Soviet Union, and then, solely, the United States. Through economic and military assistance, intelligence cooperation, and diplomatic support the United States propped up friendly authoritarian regimes for reasons of Realpolitik and especially because it feared the anti-American tendencies in Arab public opinion. That condition, of course, was due primarily to America's support for Israel and its occupation of Palestinian territory. To this very day American politicians and officials debate whether the United States should support friendly dictators or take its chances with emerging (but possibly unstable) democratic forces.

PROSPECTS FOR DEMOCRATIZATION

Not all social scientists were convinced that persistent authoritarianism would be a permanent condition for the Arab world. Some analysts (and I was one of them) were arguing as long ago as the late 1980s that democratization could occur and, indeed, that it would ease the tensions that the region is known for and advance its prosperity. And indeed there were some indications that the political arenas might be opening up. Scholars noted a significant proliferation of civil society organizations. In the late 1980s and early 1990s there were significant—but all too brief—movements for democratization (or at least liberalization) in Algeria, Jordan, Yemen, and Egypt, as well as for a return to a kind of democracy in Kuwait and Lebanon.

But these signs proved to be premature. More "realistic" scholars labeled those who thought democracy was coming to the Arab world as "demo-crazy."[*] And others observed that the structures supporting authoritarianism were not only deeply rooted but also capable of adaptation to modern conditions—thus keeping ahead of the developing societal forces. For example, commentators said that while civil society was benefiting from new information technologies, regimes could also turn these instruments to their own advantage to enhance their surveillance capabilities.

---

[*] Valbjorn, Morten and André Bank, "Examining the 'Post' in Post-Democratization: The Future of Middle Eastern Political Rule through Lenses of the Past," *Middle East Critique*, Vol. 19, No. 3 (2010), 183–200.

TODAY'S WAVE OF PROTEST

We now come to the events that began in December 2010. Nobody, to my knowledge, predicted that the self-immolation of Mohamed Bouazizi would set in motion the wave of upheavals that we are witnessing today. It is not that political scientists were unaware of the theoretically destabilizing effects of mediocre economic growth, increasing income inequality, the demographic "youth bulge," high unemployment, inadequate educational infrastructure, bureaucratic inefficiency, and—above all—corruption. But most of us assumed that the collective "mind-set" (if you will) of the public in the Arab countries was not attuned to these issues and was far from being mobilizable for action to deal with them. It seems we were wrong.

What Antonius and those analysts who came afterwards were describing was what Benedict Anderson would later theorize as an "imagined community."[6] What would today's social movement theorists[7] have to say about the Arab protest wave? They might seek to depict the collective "re-framing" of the Arab political landscape, prioritizing the values of dignity, participation, and democracy. What we are seeing is a collective change of mood—away from grudging and passive acceptance of the authoritarian political order and toward an active questioning of its legitimacy. They might help us understand how political opportunity structures made the impossible possible. They might help us conceptualize "movements" and their interactive relationship with repressive states.

THE STORY SO FAR

Let us summarize what has happened so far. We begin with Egypt and Tunisia, the only two cases so far in which the protests led to the deposing of the authoritarian head of state. In Tunisia, the self-immolation and death of Mohamed Bouazizi on 17–18 December led to things never before seen in the Tunisia of Zine El Abidine Ben Ali: nationwide protest and the occupation of public spaces, which led to the defection of the army, the erosion of Ben Ali's trusted security forces, and finally the departure of the leader himself. Death toll estimate: 147. In Egypt, after a series of massive protest gatherings in Tahrir Square in Cairo and in other Egyptian cities, President Mubarak, who had been defiant to the last minute, stepped down on 11 February, probably at the behest of the Armed Forces command, and Egypt has embarked on a process of constitutional and electoral reform. Over eight hundred people were killed and over six thousand wounded.

A second group of countries have and are continuing to experience significant protests and casualties; regimes, though challenged, are still very much in place. They include Libya, where protesters have been waging an inconclusive, see-saw war with the regime of Muammar al-Qaddafi since mid-February, with limited air support from the United States and NATO. So far there have been an estimated ten thousand deaths; the United Nations estimates that some 335,000 people have fled, including at least two hundred thousand non-Libyans. In Yemen a series of large mass protests starting on 18 January has continued, gaining momentum up to the present. The protests have turned bloody, and as of early May at least 290 demonstrators have been killed by government forces. A series of concessions offered by President Ali Abdullah Saleh and a mediation effort by the Gulf Cooperation Council seems not to have stemmed the unrest. In Bahrain, where I happened to be at the time of the crackdown, the government initially oscillated between conciliatory positions as articulated by the crown prince and a hard-line approach, which led to the death of seven protesters in the Lulu Roundabout on 14 February. But then the authorities decided on a policy of total repression. It invited armed forces from Saudi Arabia and the UAE (part of the Gulf Cooperation Council's "Peninsula Shield Force") to help it crush the ongoing protests, and they did so on 16 March. There have been some thirty-six deaths to date, amid a continuing wave of arrests. Bahrain today remains deeply divided. Much of the population, especially in the Shi'ite villages, remains sullen. And in Syria one of the bloodiest confrontations is still under way: a minor demonstration on 26 January was violently dispersed by the *mukhabarat*—one person was killed and a number of political activists were arrested. Some thought that nothing more would happen, as President Bashar al-Asad seemed to enjoy some popularity because of Syria's "nationalist" stands, but this proved not to be the case. Syria had been relatively untouched by protest, but on 18 March there began a series of large demonstrations in Deraa, which were met with deadly force; protests spread to several other cities including Baniyas and Homs. By early May there were an estimated eight hundred or more deaths.

Other Arab countries have also experienced unusual public protests, though not on the scale of the countries just mentioned. To the surprise of many observers, Oman has seen unrest on a limited scale. Starting on 17 January there was an unusual and significant labor protest in the industrial port of Sohar. In that and a subsequent demonstration two protesters were killed by government forces. Sultan Qaboos, although not the target of the demonstrations, moved quickly to dismiss half of his cabinet and offer economic concessions, but demonstrations continue. In Algeria, protests began on 28 December and have continued sporadically. In Jordan protests have been directed (thus far) to the government and not to the King, but the King has been sufficiently concerned to replace his prime minister and offer minor economic concessions. In Mauritania on 17 January there was a self-immolation and protests. In Sudan on 17 January there were demonstrations sufficiently strong to persuade President Omar al-Bashir not to seek another term in 2015. In Iraq there was an outburst of protest in late February against poor government services, though not against the regime itself; twenty-nine people died and three hundred were detained. Since then regular but smaller demonstrations have continued in several provinces, with particular force in the Kurdish region. One Iraqi commentator complained[8] that the news media have been ignoring the Iraqi protests compared to the attention given to other Arab countries. Prime Minister Nourai al-Maliki promised to crack down on corruption, firing provincial officials, and also said he would not run for another term. In Kuwait there have been demonstrations by and on behalf of the *bidoon*—people without citizenship.

In Morocco in February thousands of protesters took to the streets demanding constitutional changes but not attacking the monarchy. King Muhammad VI has promised "to continue to make structural reforms" and created an Economic and Social Council to advise him on economic recovery. In Lebanon, a perennially tense stand-off between the opposition "March 8" and "March 14" coalitions had led to demonstrations, focusing on the role of Hizbollah as an armed militia. These protests do not seem linked to the larger wave of protests in the region; however, there was a small demonstration protesting Lebanon's institutionalized confessionalism, which does seem linked. Similarly, in the Palestinian territories, like Lebanon, the particularities of the local political environment have largely diverted attention from the demands for good governance sweeping the Arab world. In the United Arab Emirates, while there have been no public protests, there has been a petition from intellectuals to President Shakyh Khalifa bin Zayed al-Nahyan for free and democratic elections, including a comprehensive reform of the Federal National Council (FNC), free elections with universal suffrage for all citizens, a reform of legislation governing the work of the FNC and necessary constitutional amendments. The UAE authorities have arrested at least one blogger and imposed certain curbs on media expression. Finally, we have the case of Saudi Arabia. While the monarchy seems not to be directly targeted, there has been a series of small but concentrated protest demonstrations in Qatif, and there have been calls on Facebook for further protests. Protesters' demands include the release of political prisoners. The government has responded harshly, forbidding public demonstrations, and King Abdullah bin Saud, instead of offering reforms, has announced an enlargement of the security forces and the release of billions of dollars for public assistance.

SOME TENTATIVE CONCLUSIONS

This survey, which has sought to place the recent events in historical and theoretical context, raises at least five questions about the apparent ripple effect we are seeing across the region.

First, is it like a "disease" or a "cure?" Obviously it depends on where you stand. But names do matter. To label a phenomenon in a subjective, let alone pejorative, way invites faulty analysis: one needs look no farther than "the war on terror" for a good example. If you are analyzing a "contagion" you are tempted not just to study what it is, but to find ways to eradicate it. At the same time it serves little purpose to romanticize the "awakening." But we are social scientists, not epidemiologists. For better or for worse, the wave suggests to me that political legitimacy has emerged as the fundamental issue—more important than economic grievances, foreign interference, religious agendas, or even Israel. This is not to say that these matters do not play an important contributory role in the current upheaval, but the main issue seems to me to be a questioning of the right of ruling establishments to govern. "Why should we obey you?" people are asking. "Because you always have," does not seem any longer to be a satisfactory answer.

Second, is it a coherent, monolithic "thing?" Is it singular or plural? Is it an organic region-wide movement or just a series of incidents that happened to occur roughly at the same time? Here we have to be careful. Only a careful study of the message and the composition of the protesters can tell us, but we do see common threads in the message. It seems to be all about governance: a demand for meaningful popular participation, the condemnation of authoritarianism and corruption, the call for better governance, and a demand for social and economic development. There is also a "negative" similarity: we do not hear demands for an Islamic polity, nor, for that matter, for Arab unity. So while protesters focus on particular rulers, regimes, and local situations, there are these broad similar themes being expressed across the board.

Third, on the reasonable assumption that these protests are causally linked, how do we account for it? I would argue that the role of satellite television and social media as a "force multiplier" is crucial. There is plenty of anecdotal evidence that protesters are communicating and collaborating across borders. *Al Jazeera Arabic*, with an estimated forty million-plus viewers, has provided an unprecedented platform for viewing the protest drama. Even if it is beginning to pull its punches on coverage of arenas considered sensitive by the Gulf rulers, its effect should not be underestimated. On Facebook and Twitter protesters in Yemen, Bahrain, Libya, Syria, and no doubt in the salons of Saudi Arabia, are saying, "We celebrate and support the protesters of Tunis and Egypt; they have broken 'the wall of fear' and we would like to see something similar (but not necessarily identical) happen in our countries."

Fourth, are the various Arab countries equally "susceptible" to "infection" by the "virus?" Here the answer is "probably not." As Gretchen Head has pointed out in the case of Morocco,[9] protesters there are not targeting the king and do not necessarily want a complete change of political system. Ziad Abu-Rish has made a similar point about Jordan,[10] where the monarch (so far) seems insulated from the anger of the "street." And, incidentally, we should be careful in assuming that "the Arab street" is a homogenous entity, which is similar across the Arab world. Again, with due apology for the pejorative metaphor, we might observe that so far the two most effective "vaccines" for the "democratic contagion" are (1) riches (the rentier effect) and (2) legitimacy of the political system as a whole. But with respect to the rentier effect, one must note that it has not completely immunized the ruling establishments of the GCC (namely, Bahrain, Oman, and Saudi Arabia). In terms of the legitimacy factor, leaders who enjoy some moral or political authority, based on their perceived heritage or their policies (namely, Morocco and Jordan) may ride out the current epidemic of protest. But for the others, they may not be sleeping so well. They may be reminded of the autobiography of one of the more successful Arab rulers, King Hussein of Jordan: *Uneasy Lies the Head.*

Fifth, what happens to the "wave" when the protesters meet the tanks? It will soon be a half-year since the first protests broke out. The speedy and decisive outcomes in Tunisia and Egypt have not been replicated elsewhere. Now we have to consider that protests may follow different trajectories and different places. Waves washing up on beaches may quickly erode sand castles, but what of waves crashing against rocks? In Bahrain a swift and relentless crackdown broke the protests, although the story is far from over. In Libya, Yemen, and Syria the outcome may ultimately depend on which side has the greater endurance. Mass protests probably cannot be sustained indefinitely without developing mobilization structures and resources. To what extent is this happening in these countries? On the regime side, how long can the ruling elites afford to maintain thousands of security forces and equipment in combat mode? And how long can they maintain their moral cohesion as innocent citizens die? In some cases the outcome is win or lose. In others, where the momentum of protest is less intense and the regime response more flexible perhaps one can expect a "no victor–no vanquished" trajectory. But rulers who are paranoid about mass political action and followers who are utterly unconvinced that "reform from above" is anything more than a charade will make negotiations very difficult. In such cases, perhaps we should expect the enormous popular energy first manifested in mass peaceful protests to be transformed into armed attacks and low-level guerrilla warfare. Simultaneously the initial democracy discourse might be transformed into more radical ideological formulas. The besieged rulers of Libya, Yemen, Syria, and Bahrain unconvincingly claim that they are a bulwark against religious or sectarian extremists, but as time goes on and conflict smolders it would be alarming if these claims turned into a self-confirming prophecy.

THE CHALLENGE TO MIDDLE EAST ANALYSTS

The surprising demise of authoritarian rulers in Tunisia and Egypt and the sustained wave of popular protest that has shaken regimes in Libya, Yemen, Bahrain, and Syria (not to mention the tremors that have occurred in Morocco, Jordan, and Oman) requires political scientists and other analysts to re-examine some of the conventional wisdom about Arab and Middle East politics. (1) The "durability of authoritarianism." How valid now is the argument that *mukhabarat* states can keep several steps ahead of societal opposition through better access to and use of new technologies of information and repression? (2) Democratization is an inappropriate goal and impossible to achieve in the Arab world. Were the so-called "demo-crazy" analysts really so blinded by their presumed liberal preferences? (3); Populations are passive—anaesthetized by the opium of the rentier state or bowed down by the burdens of daily life or cowed by fear of the *mukhabarat*. How then to explain the extraordinary massive popular protests? (4) Arab nationalism is dead; people are reverting to their primordial affiliations. But how then to explain the so-called "contagion effect" of the Tunisian and Egyptian upheavals? Facebook alone did not cause them. And (5) the Middle East regional system is essentially stable; states still are the prime units; the regional balance of power is stable; and the system is still encased in American hegemony. But how then to explain the strategic setback suffered by the United States and Washington's apparent inability to manipulate the new situation.

Quite a lot of analytical attention has been devoted to the instruments of state authoritarianism, but not enough has been paid to the strength and durability of the protest movements. It would seem that a combination of factors—group-think, theoretical tunnel vision, ideological agendas, insufficient attention to the work of Arab intellectuals, and a lack of multidisciplinary approaches—all help account for the difficulties. Is it not time for a rethinking of categories such as state (failed or otherwise), regime (rogue or otherwise), nation, society (civil or otherwise) and leadership? And must we not emphasize the importance of new media and information technologies in clarifying (and energizing) the Arab "imagined community?"

Yes, it does matter what we call it—contagion, epidemic, awakening, blossoming, dawning, commencement, renaissance and the like. But what matters even more is what it is. Shakespeare put it most famously: "What's in a name? That which we call a rose by any other name would smell as sweet." To my mind the fragrance of jasmine, lotus, and—yes—roses is wafting across the Arab world.

4
Paradoxes of Arab Refo-lutions

Asef Bayat[11]

3 March 2011

Many in the revolutionary and pro-democracy circles in Egypt and Tunisia have expressed serious concerns about the sabotage of the defeated elites, and speak of a creeping counter-revolution. This is not surprising. If revolutions are about intense struggle for a profound change, then any revolution should expect a counter-revolution of subtle or blatant forms. The French, Russian, Chinese, Iranian, and Nicaraguan revolutions all faced protracted civil or international wars. The question is not whether the threat of counter-revolution is to be expected; the question rather is whether the "revolutions" are revolutionary enough to offset the perils of restoration. It seems that the Arab revolutions remain particularly vulnerable precisely because of their distinct peculiarity—their structural anomaly is expressed in the paradoxical trajectory of political change.

Historically, three types of bottom-up regime/political change stand out. The first is the "reformist change." Here, social and political movements usually mobilize in a sustained campaign to exert concerted pressure on the incumbent regimes to undertake reforms through the institutions of the existing states. Resting on their social power—the mobilization of the grassroots—the opposition movements compel the political elites to reform themselves, their laws and institutions often through some of kind of social pacts. So, change happens within the framework of the existing political arrangements. The transition to democracy in countries like Mexico and Brazil in the 1980s was of this nature. The leadership of Iran's Green Movement currently pursues a similar reformist trajectory. In this trajectory, the depth and extent of reforms varies. Change may remain superficial, but it can also be profound if it materializes cumulatively by legal, institutional, and politico-cultural reforms.

The second mode of political change is the "insurrectionary model," where a revolutionary movement builds up over a fairly extended span of time during which a recognized leadership and organization emerge along with some blueprint of future political structure. At the same time that the incumbent regime continues to resist through police or military apparatus, a gradual erosion and defection begins to crack the governing body. The revolutionary camp pushes forward, attracts defectors, forms a shadow government, and builds some organs of alternative power. In the meantime, the regime's governmentality gets paralyzed, leading to a state of "dual power" between the incumbent and the opposition. The state of "dual power" ends by an insurrectionary battle in which the revolutionary camp takes over the state power via force; it dislodges the old organs of authority and establishes new ones. Here we have a comprehensive overhaul of the state, with new functionaries, a new ideology, and a new mode of governance. The Iranian Revolution of 1979, the Sandinista Revolution in Nicaragua, or the Cuban Revolution of 1959 all exemplify such insurrectionary courses.

The third possibility pertains to "regime implosion," when the revolutionary movement builds up through general strikes and broad practices of civil disobedience, or through a revolutionary warfare progressively encircling the regime, so that in the end the regime implodes. It collapses in disruption, defection, and total disorder. In its place come the alternative elites and institutions. Ceausescu's regime in Romania imploded in a dramatic political chaos and violence in 1989, but gave rise eventually to very different political and economic systems under the newly established political structure, the National Salvation Front. Muammar al-Qaddafi's Libya may experience such an implosion if the revolutionary insurgency continues to strangle Tripoli. In both "insurrection" and "implosion," and unlike the reformist mode, attempts to reform the political structure take place not through the existing institutions of the state, but overwhelmingly outside of them.

Now, Egypt's revolution, just like that of Tunisia, does not resemble any of these experiences. In Egypt and Tunisia, the powerful political uprisings augmented into the fastest revolutions of our time. Tunisians in the course of one month and Egyptians in just eighteen days succeeded in dislodging long-serving authoritarian rulers, dismantling a number of institutions associated with them, including the ruling parties, the legislative bodies, and a number of ministries, in the meantime establishing a promise of constitutional and political reform. And all these have been achieved in manners that were remarkably civil, peaceful, and fast. But these astonishing rapid triumphs did not leave much opportunity for the opposition to build parallel organs of authority capable of taking control of the new state. Instead, the opposition wants the institutions of the incumbent regimes, for instance the military in Egypt, to carry out substantial reforms on behalf of the revolution—that is, to modify the constitution, to ensure free elections, to guarantee free political parties, and in the long run to institutionalize democratic governance. Here again lies a key anomaly of these revolutions— they enjoy enormous social power, but lack administrative authority; they garner remarkable hegemony, but do not actually rule. Thus, the incumbent regimes continue to stand; there are no new states or governing bodies, nor novel means and modes of governance that altogether embody the will of the revolution.

It is true that, like their Arab counterparts, the Eastern European revolutions of the late 1990s were also non-violent, civil, and remarkably rapid—East Germany's revolution took only ten days—but they managed, unlike in Tunisia and Egypt, to completely transform the political and economic systems. This was possible because the imploded East German communist state could simply dissipate and dissolve into the already existing West German governing body. And broadly, since the difference between what East European people had (one party, communist state) and what they wanted (liberal democracy and market economy) was so distinctly radical, the trajectory of change had to be revolutionary. Half-way, superficial, and reformist change would have been easily detected and resisted, which is something quite different from the Arab revolutions in which the demands of "change, freedom, and social justice" are broad enough to be claimed even by the counter-revolution. Consequently, the Arab revolutions resemble perhaps more Georgia's Rose Revolution of 2003 and Ukraine's Orange Revolution of November 2004–January 2005 where in both cases a massive and sustained popular protest brought down incumbent fraudulent rulers. In these instances, the trajectory of change looks more reformist than revolutionary, strictly speaking.

But there is a more promising side to the Arab political upheavals. One cannot deny the operation of a powerful revolutionary mode in these political episodes, which make them more profound than those in Georgia or Ukraine. In Tunisia and Egypt, the departure of despotic rulers and their apparatus of coercion have opened up an unprecedented free space for citizens, notably the subaltern subjects, to reclaim their societies. As is the case in most revolutionary turning points, an enormous energy has been released in the society's body politics. Banned political parties have come to surface and new ones are getting established. Societal organizations have become more vocal and extraordinary grassroots initiatives are under way. In Egypt, working people, free from fear of persecution, aggressively follow their violated claims. Laborers are pushing for new independent unions; some of them have already formed the "Coalition of the 25 January Revolution Workers" to assert the revolutionary principles of "change, freedom, and social justice." Small farmers (with less than ten *feddans*) in rural areas are organizing themselves in independent syndicates; others continue fighting for better wages and conditions. The first Organization of the Residents of Cairo's *ashwa'iyyat* (slums), established recently, has called for the removal of corrupt governors, and for the abolition of regime-sponsored "local councils." Youth groups organize to clean up slum areas, engage in civil works and reclaim their civil pride. Students pour into the streets to demand that the Ministry of Education revises the curricula. The stories of Coptic and Muslim cooperation to fight sectarian rumors and provocations are already known and need not be repeated here. And of course the Tahrir Revolutionary Front continues to exert pressure on the military to speed up reforms. These all represent popular engagement of exceptional times. But the extraordinary sense of liberation, the urge for self-realization, the dream of a new and just order—in short the desire for "all that is new" are what define the very spirit of these revolutions. At these turning points, these societies have moved far ahead of their political elites, exposing albeit the major anomaly of these revolutions: the discrepancy between a revolutionary desire for the "new," and a reformist trajectory that may lead to harboring the "old."

How do we then make sense of the Arab revolutions? These may be characterized neither as "revolutions" per se nor simply as "reform" measures. Instead we may speak of "refo-lutions"— revolutions that want to push for reforms in, and through the institutions of the incumbent states. As such, refo-lutions express paradoxical processes—something to be cherished and yet vulnerable. Refo-lutions do possess the advantage of ensuring orderly transitions, avoiding violence, destruction, and chaos—the evils that dramatically raise the cost of change. In addition, revolutionary excess, the "reign of terror," exclusion, revenge, summary trials and guillotines can be avoided. And there are the possibilities of genuine transformation through social pacts, but only if the society—the grassroots, civil society associations, labor unions, and social movements—continue to remain vigilant, mobilized, and exert pressure. Otherwise refo-lutions carry with them the perils of counter-revolutionary restoration precisely because the revolution has not made it into the key institutions of the state power. One can readily imagine powerful stakeholders, wounded by the ferocity of popular upheavals, would desperately seek regrouping, initiate sabotage, and instigate counter-propaganda. Ex-high state officials, old party apparatchiks, key editors-in-chief, big businesses, members of aggrieved intelligence services and not to mention military men could penetrate the apparatus of power and propaganda to turn things into their advantage. The danger can be especially more pronounced when the revolutionary fervor subsides, normal life resumes, the hard realities of reconstruction seep in, and the populace gets disenchanted. There is little recourse for realizing a meaningful change without turning refo-lutions into revolutions.

5
The Year of the Citizen

Mouin Rabbani[12]

30 May 2011

During the spring of the so-called Arab Spring, the euphoria that characterized the winter of 2010/2011 has increasingly given way to more somber attitudes associated with winter. For those who were expecting a linear progression toward freedom, in which vain autocrats and sclerotic regimes would fall with growing ease and rapidity, despondency is an appropriate response to the increasing ferocity with which ruling elites seek to remain in power. Yet in the life of peoples, as in life itself, linear does not exist. There are no victories without defeats, hope is constantly shadowed by despair, the future consistently threatened by the combined weight of the present and the past. This is not to say that further Arab uprisings will necessarily triumph, but merely to point out that it would be rather naive to expect the ouster of one tyrant per month.

Regardless of the ultimate outcome of the Arab revolt, it has already transformed the region. Even if Zine El Abidine Ben Ali spends his remaining days in Jeddah playing solitaire, and Husni Mubarak is the last of his colleagues to go the way of Mubarak, 2011 will go down in Arab history as the Year of the Citizen. The year in which Arabs from Marrakesh to Muscat initiated the process of transforming the contemporary Arab state from private fiefdom to public property, thereby changing their status from subject to participant.

The assertion that Arabs are at long last beginning to exercise ownership of the state is very different than the ridiculous proposition that Arabs are overcoming a historical-cultural legacy that has produced congenital docility. The latter half of the twentieth century alone is littered with examples in which, individually as well as collectively, Arabs have been active agents of transformative change. The Algerian struggle for independence and the 1987–1993 Palestinian uprising are but two cases in point.

Nevertheless there are vital differences between then and now. In previous eras, the people were organized and mobilized by a clearly-defined leadership that sought to seize control of the state, or alternatively struggled autonomously to redress a specific (often local) grievance. The masses, in effect, served to catapult an elite into power—often willingly because such leaders were seen (at times correctly) as capable of successfully confronting existential challenges such as colonial or feudal servitude. Yet once they had served this purpose, "citizens" tended to be excluded from meaningful participation in public life, were re-assembled only irregularly, and then primarily to bolster the legitimacy of leaders in times of crisis, or that of one leadership faction in the context of its conflicts with others.

As the Arab state and post-independence Arab order gradually stabilized during the 1970s and 1980s, their populations were systematically neutralized through a combination of carrots and sticks—electricity for example being both a carrot and a stick. Given the increasingly narrow base of most regimes, their survival in fact depended upon the effective exclusion of the vast majority from political and civic life. The political party, military establishment, and civil service that had previously—however incompetently—served as instruments of national integration and personal advancement was replaced by the primacy of the security establishment. Assigned the role of keeping the population lobotomized, it additionally privileged (and encouraged) sub-national identities and loyalties. The end result was a state that saw every act of citizenship as a threat to be destroyed. Given that increasingly absolutist and rapacious rulers had simultaneously developed a habit of dealing with the state as a possession to be consumed by them and their cronies, the threat perception was entirely correct.

There is an argument to be made that it was the very success of this phenomenon that proved its undoing. As we have seen time and again since the martyrdom of Mohamed Bouazizi, this collection of ageing autocrats has had it so good for so long that they have become simply incapable of recognizing danger and proactively implementing basic reforms to save themselves. Time and again, relatively modest demands that could have easily been addressed without affecting the existence or structure of the regime have instead been met with brutality and contempt, thus producing popular revolts calling for the ouster of the regime. One after the other, Arab rulers and their security forces are producing dynamics which rapidly eliminate any middle ground and leave victory or destruction as the only possible outcomes. So effective have these regimes been in eradicating (through murder, imprisonment, and exile) not only organized opposition but activists of national stature, that they have left themselves no credible interlocutors with the millions of ordinary citizens assembling every week in squares and streets demanding their ouster.

The result has been a struggle about the nature and purpose of the Arab state. Will it continue to exist as a mechanism to enforce the docility of its subjects on behalf of corrupt rulers servile only to Washington and the International Monetary Fund (IMF), or will it be transformed into an institution through which citizens participate in the formulation of policy, select their leaders, and hold them accountable? Will state and citizen continue to be subject to lawless security forces enjoying blanket impunity to do as they please, or will the security sector become subordinate to the state and subject to its laws? Will power continue to be concentrated in the executive—with the judiciary and legislature serving as mere window-dressing—or will Abd al-Rahman Siwar al-Dahab lose his status as the only Arab leader living in voluntary retirement?

These are not issues that can be resolved by elections alone. In point of fact, elections—even free and fair ones—can serve to obscure the more fundamental and existential issue, which is the establishment of states based on the rule of law, enshrined in enforceable constitutions that limit the role of the security establishment rather than eliminate that of the citizen.

None of these issues will be resolved speedily or easily, and as we have seen in Egypt and Tunisia the *ancien régime* will fight tooth and nail to preserve its powers, and succumbs only to overwhelming pressure.

While the outcome remains uncertain and the regional and international efforts to prevent further change gather pace, there is nevertheless considerable ground for optimism. Most importantly, change has occurred in Cairo, the very epicenter of the Arab world. Secondly, the West ultimately proved incapable of preventing change in either Egypt or Tunisia, and in the end could deploy no more than Gene Sharp to seize control of two countries experiencing revolutionary upheaval. But perhaps most importantly, people across the region have seen that regime change can be achieved, and that the power which flows from the barrel of a gun is not without limits.

Throughout the region, rulers seem determined to push their subjects over the edge, past the point of no return, toward the struggle for citizenship. In Egypt, for example, the 2010 parliamentary elections were so blatantly and visibly fraudulent that the explanation that they were fixed incompetently by the regime defies belief. Rather, Mubarak seemed determined to demonstrate to Egypt that he could stage a complete charade, in fact trample the entire country underfoot in full public view, and retain the complete support of Europe and the United States so long as he remained loyal to them and Israel. He was right, and the Egyptian people understood only too well that the parliamentary exercise was in fact a presidential one and had been won by Gamal. The good news is that these rulers appear incapable of learning from each other's mistakes, and cannot seem to stop themselves from adding fuel to the fire whenever it abates. The bad news is that they retain an enormous capacity for mayhem and destruction, particularly once they realize the curtain has begun to fall. The curtain may have stopped falling once a month, but it is difficult to imagine that many of those who remain on stage will retain their roles in the new script being drafted by the Arab citizen.

6
Three Powerfully Wrong—and Wrongfully Powerful—American Narratives about the Arab Spring

Jillian Schwedler, Joshua Stacher, and Stacey Philbrick Yadav[13]

10 June 2011

The "Arab Spring" that actually began in the dead of winter has spread from Tunisia to Egypt, Libya, Yemen, Bahrain, and Syria… and the year is only half over. As the media, policymakers, and global audiences struggle to make sense of changes that have inspired hundreds of millions to "just say no" to decades of dictatorship, a number of narratives have taken hold in the United States—evident in remarks on cable news talk shows, at academic and policy symposia, and on Twitter—about precisely what is happening and what these massive crowds want. While elements of these narratives have some foundation in truth, they also present such a simplified view as to obscure the crucial dimensions of the power struggles across the region. Below we unpack three of the most common narratives whose "truth" has become almost conventional wisdom, tossed about at cocktail parties and across coffee shops and metros. We aim to highlight what kinds of politics are made possible (and what kinds of challenges to power are foreclosed) as these narratives become part of the "common sense" that shapes our understanding of these extraordinary events.

NARRATIVE NO. 1: THE OBAMA ADMINISTRATION HAS BEEN BEHIND THE CURVE

"The US government spent months watching from the sidelines until Barack Obama crafted a vision with his May speech."
Since January, the President and his National Security Council have gone to great pains to reassure all who are listening that US

policy is rightly calibrated concerning the changes introduced by the popular uprisings against incumbent autocrats in the Middle East. The Administration, they argue, has advocated a case-by-case set of policies that sees the protests as opportunities to improve relationships in the region.

Critics, by contrast, have charged the Administration with being "behind the curve" and reacting in an ad hoc manner, fumbling around because it does not have a policy toward the region's simultaneous eruptions (which in some cases have disrupted strong alliances). Such criticisms undoubtedly motivated Obama to take the short trip to the State Department on 19 May to deliver his latest policy speech toward the region.[14] The President tried to assuage concerns and signal the various interested constituencies that do business in the region, run the US government's aid industry, or oversee delicate diplomatic missions that America remains relevant and prepared for the new era that many brave protesters are trying to press on their political establishments.

But those who have seen the Administration's policies as being ad hoc or behind the curve are missing the ways in which Obama's policy constitutes a doubling-down on the failed neoliberal economic policies that have wrecked the region's infrastructure and drastically impoverished its citizens. While the regional and international media have focused on the more seductive theme of political freedom—after all, who could be opposed to more political freedom—this constitutes only one side of what inspired the uprisings against autocratic rulers. Neoliberalism in the region—which exceeds the particularities of the Mubarak or Ben Ali regimes, or even the Middle East as a region—has featured policies that have resulted in social dislocation, dramatically expanded income gaps, and widespread poverty.

In this regard, appearing to be "behind the curve" is an illusion that obscures a long-standing and deliberate strategy of privileging stability and profits over democratic political regimes and economic equity in the Middle East. Obama's administration has been given an opportunity to side with popular sovereignty and economic empowerment, but has chosen stability up until that choice has become utterly unviable, at least in the short-run. And even where US policy has ultimately aligned with demands for political reform, calls for greater economic empowerment have been marginalized. The Obama administration may have, for now, sided with popular sovereignty, but will not abide with calls for widespread economic empowerment.

Egypt is exemplary of this posture. Part of the Obama strategy is to call on the World Bank and the International Monetary Fund (IMF) to help with an economic stabilization package as the United States forgives a billion in debt and provides another billion in loans. These loans, however, will only compound the problem[15] and influence the transitional figures in Egypt to lean toward a continuation of a neoliberal economic regime. Yet, without serious guarantees that alter how economic aid will be distributed in Egypt (through policies that will benefit workers and others who have seen their social protections shrink as prices and unemployment rise), this strategy is tantamount to restarting a process that even the American Ambassador in Cairo acknowledged has left thirty-five to forty percent of the population living in poverty.[16] In other words, neoliberalism, as part of the problem of inequality and social dislocation, cannot logically be the solution.

So rather than a new start, the Administration's plan offers a familiar story. At best, these policies will create a new class of comprador capitalists, and at worst they will continue to benefit the existing elites while throwing only crumbs of "entrepreneurial opportunity" to the vast majority of the population. These policies will undoubtedly promote "growth" (that is, GDP), but just as surely they will intensify spiraling inequality, as they have in every country to which the policies have been applied. Insisting on the implementation of neoliberal economic policies will back US policymakers into a familiar corner in which they find refuge in authoritarian elites who can "insulate" technocratic decision-makers while waiting for the economic reforms to work their magic...a magic which never seems to come.

Many[17] have argued that this current moment in the Arab world is analogous to the Eastern European states[18] that emerged from the Soviet Union after 1989.[19] The contagion effect is undeniably a factor, but the comparisons may end there. First, the uprisings have not yet been successful in producing fundamental change to the existing regimes, either economically or politically. More militarization and securitization may actually be on the horizon for the region's citizens, rather than transitions to democracy, particularly if the armed forces continue to play a central role in establishing the "new" rules of the game. Entirely off the table, if the Administration has its way, is a fundamental challenge to the entrenched imperial hegemony.

This represents another key difference from 1989: the United States will tolerate no challenge to its dominant role in the region.

During that earlier wave of popular mobilization, authoritarian elites in the Kremlin accepted—or at least were divided—on the question of letting the USSR's satellite states go. Today, Washington's elites are undivided on the prioritization of the project of American Empire; they differ only on the question of how to get it "right."

So it is not 1989 in the Arab world; it is 1971. The United States has no appetite for letting the people of the region have autonomy in determining the direction of their futures, particularly if participatory elections mean upsetting the economic cart or messing with the balance of diplomatic relations. Besides the preservation of the neoliberal economic status quo, this also means safeguarding Egypt's peace treaty with Israel. Of course Administration officials affirm, quite rightly, that they cannot dictate to these new ruling coalitions what they should or should not do. But it is perfectly clear that this "hands-off" approach would rapidly dissolve if relations with Israel were put into question.

The alarm clock has sounded, but Washington has elected to hit the snooze.

NARRATIVE NO. 2: THESE REVOLUTIONS ARE ABOUT DEMOCRACY, NOT THE ECONOMY

"After decades of political repression, Arab peoples throughout the Middle East are rising in unprecedented numbers and demanding democratic political systems."

True. And the Arab Spring has been as extraordinary as all the rhetoric implies. But if we know anything about revolutions, it is that: (1) mass mobilizations of citizens are extremely difficult to accomplish, particularly in highly repressive police states; and (2) mobilizations happen when diverse individuals and groups, often with incompatible agendas, can agree on a focused outcome: the end of the current regime. The next step, as we know and are now seeing, is the inevitable struggle between competing groups over the direction of "what comes next." Often, new authoritarian regimes emerge in place of old regimes; almost never do we see every institution of the former regime entirely demolished. After all, the new regimes will have to do what the old regimes did: secure their rule, provide order in the streets, and get the economy running as quickly as possible—and find ways of silencing those citizens who disagree with their choices.

In practice, then, transitions are often examined and hailed as political transitions—the change of one regime for another. In the Arab Spring, unsurprisingly, the questions that have come to dominate are whether "real" transitions are taking place—Is it really a "revolution?"—and what sorts of processes are guiding that trajectory. Here elections become absolutely central: not only are they key to both substantive as well as façade democracy, but they are a highly effective means of demobilizing the population by involving them in debates about electoral systems and the practical challenges of creating new political parties.

Enter the foreign democracy experts from stage left. Need to know how to restructure the parliament? Whether the Muslim Brotherhood is likely to win more seats under a plurality system (winner take all) or under proportional representation? What about hybrid systems? What have other countries done?

The democracy expert is a special breed: They are deeply committed to promoting political freedoms worldwide. But while they are quick to point out that they do not offer a tool kit of one-size-fits-all reforms, they nevertheless believe that something in their tool kit will work. At consulting fees of hundreds of dollars a day (plus expenses), they would not be doing their job if they did not offer some sort of advice to the youthful revolutionaries who, many of them seem to believe, are not equipped to understand the more technical aspects of democratic transitions.

But the "youth"—another narrative category[20] that masks more than it reveals in terms of class relations,[21] as well as the aspirations and frustrations of a large swath of the population—do know what they want and they do have the technical know-how to intervene intelligently in debates about transitions. Labor organization was decisive in the success of Egypt's revolution, even as Western audiences were preoccupied with the "Facebook youth" who, they were relieved to discover, looked, and dressed very much like American youths. Indeed, the narrative of a "youth revolution" is orthogonal to class grievances, feeding arguments that these youths are desperately in need of assistance or else they might "lose" their revolution.

In Tunisia, they do not want the aid that the National Endowment for Democracy and the International Republican Institute are desperate to distribute to democracy-promotion projects because they already understand how to restructure the system; their uncertainty is only nervousness about whether they will be given a real opportunity to achieve that vision. In Egypt, they do not want the process rushed because they know that it takes time to establish viable and representative political parties capable of competing.

And they do not want to "go home" while the military and the transitional council made up of established elites "lead" the country, all while military trials are multiplying and torture has resumed in police stations. Perhaps what is most often overlooked in the dominant narrative is that they want their economic grievances to be remembered amid the disproportionate focus on electoral institutions and outcomes.

And yet despite the aspirations of many who helped to force the retreat of Zine El Abidine Ben Ali and Husni Mubarak, the dominant narrative that has emerged in both Tunisia and Egypt—the two countries that are currently negotiating and reimagining their futures—has become one of the technical challenges of restructuring the electoral system and amending the constitution.

It is not that these questions are the wrong questions, but they are not the only questions. And more importantly, many of the demands of the protesters throughout the region have not been focused exclusively (or at all) on questions of political process and representation. Many protesters have been from the beginning (and still are) demanding economic reforms, from the immediate and personal ("When am I going to get paid?"; "When will my working conditions improve?") to the broad and systemic ("Reject IMF Structural Adjustment").

For decades, buttressed by political scientists' skepticism about the "survivability" of new democracies under conditions of poverty (a skepticism that has long reduced success stories like India to statistical "outliers" unworthy of serious consideration), political reforms have been held at bay while economic reforms were advanced by authoritarian regimes. Apologists promised that this "sequencing" of reforms was in the long-term interest of democracy.[22] Increased political participation, the argument went, needs to wait until economic reforms work their magic, bringing a level of prosperity that will create a healthy, productive citizenry capable of informed political engagement. Few had the courage to point out against this scholarly and policy mainstream that waiting for the "good czar" might be like waiting for Godot. Even scholars were vague about how much economic development would be "enough," but the question was effectively tabled because the economy never improved in ways that benefited any but the rich. Client states developed dependent relationships on international financial institutions and hegemonic states; the people were compelled to wait.

Now that the people are unwilling to wait any longer, their remarkable accomplishments are being hijacked and they are being told to focus on political reforms...and to wait while the adults make the decisions that are best. In the meantime, Egyptians and Tunisians—and not only the youth and labor movements—are continuing to take to the street to demand a wide range of reforms, many of which are economic, but many more are local and specific. As the policymakers, journalists, democracy experts, and even many academics advance the narrative that the focus is (and should be) on the technical details of political transition, what is foreclosed are the truly democratic possibilities of realizing the demands of a diverse citizenry for a future that looks substantially different from their past. For the vast majority of people in the region, that future is impossible to realize as long as the question of substantive economic reform is off the table.

And as Obama made clear in his speech on the future of the region, the Administration will fully support political reforms, but only as long as the dominant neoliberal economic system remains intact. In this regard, the Administration finds no shortage of domestic comprador elites eager to decouple economic and political reforms before too many take notice. These local elites—who stand to profit mightily—are ready allies for the United States in "de-economizing" the so-called transitions and trying to promote a blind deference to electoral processes and political reforms while concealing the likely failure of these processes to resolve the socioeconomic imbalances that led to the uprisings in the first place.

NARRATIVE NO. 3: INCONSISTENCIES IN US POLICY REGARDING THE ARAB UPRISINGS ARE DRIVEN BY STRATEGIC INTERESTS (AND THAT'S OKAY)

"We really want to promote democracy and everything, but our first obligation has to be to our own vital interests."

First, the low-hanging fruit: the United States has never been consistently interested in the promotion of political freedom in the Middle East (or anywhere). This part of the narrative is met with a wink and a nod by all but the most deluded ideologues, like those who think that Iraq has been a successful example of democracy promotion. The existence of policy inconsistencies is less the issue than the arguments used to justify those inconsistencies. To be clear, we are not suggesting any one-size-fits-all policy, but a consistent approach does not require identical tactics. It requires unwavering support for the idea that people are entitled to accountable government and a say in their future, and even on this minimal front, US policy has been equivocal. To be sure, many individuals who work in the Administration or in other US government agencies are unquestionably committed to advancing political freedoms on a global scale. But when it comes to crafting actual policies, promoting political freedoms on a global scale slips quickly down the list in favor of "vital" (read: military and economic) interests.

Second: Implicit in this narrative that the United States must prioritize its own interests is the assumption that democracy is threatening because it holds the potential to produce the "wrong" winners. Not everyone is ready for the responsibilities of democracy, the argument goes, and unprepared electorates will probably choose wrongly. Aside from its utterly paternalistic and neocolonial logic, this approach reduces practice to outcome. The measure of democracy, according to this narrative, is the substantive outcome it produces, not the exercise of choice. Most people currently enjoying such choices elsewhere in the world would probably not agree that this is what is important about democracy, if it were put to them so starkly. Why do we herald choice when it comes to market practices, but evaluate outcomes when it comes to (other people's) politics?

The answer is the Islamists. The most commonly cited "wrong choice" stemming from a free election is undoubtedly the 2006 election of a Hamas majority in the Palestinian Authority. To be sure, this election and the US and Israeli economic sanctions that were applied to the PA in response, heralded a Palestinian civil war, the complete paralysis of the peace process, the 2009 war against Gaza, and the siege that has followed. The Palestinian electorate has collectively paid dearly for its choice. Indeed, one might expect this chain of events to have discredited democratic mechanisms among Palestinians. And yet the recent reconciliation between Hamas and Fatah was accompanied by a call for new elections— an affirmation of the centrality of political choice to an array of Palestinian political factions.

Islamist organizations throughout the region are eager to participate in meaningful elections, but each has a set of experiences and a set of demands that is unique to its local context. In Yemen, for example, the Islamist Islah party is central to a fully-legal opposition coalition (including Marxists and other leftists) that has been challenging Ali Abdullah Saleh through legal and peaceful channels for nearly a decade. In Jordan, the Islamic Action Front has been at the forefront of pushing for substantive democratic reforms, including a more fair electoral law that distributes seats evenly among the population, rather than locating a disproportionately small number of seats in areas where the majority Palestinian population is concentrated. For more than eighteen years, Jordan's Islamists have worked steadfastly with other oppositional political parties (including liberals and leftists) to achieve these reforms. In Egypt, though the Muslim Brothers were instrumental to Mubarak's downfall, they did not dominate the uprising itself, nor have they taken exclusive credit for the success of the 25 January revolution. Yet after years of US policy that abetted or encouraged incumbent autocrats to institutionally and physically suppress Islamists in all three countries, the closest the Administration has come to recognizing that Islamists may have legitimate aspirations for political voice is to commit to a policy of engaging those who "speak uncomfortable truths."

Indeed, one uncomfortable truth is that the United States has had little difficulty accepting the electoral participation of the Supreme Council for the Islamic Revolution in Iraq (renamed in 2007 the Supreme Islamic Council of Iraq) when the Administration desperately wanted to promote the vision of a pluralist and united Iraq in the aftermath of the 2003 invasion. The United States has been a close ally of one of the most repressive Islamic states in the world—Saudi Arabia—and has had little difficulties with Turkey's Islamic government. The "fear of Islamists" component of this narrative is clearly a red herring, brought into the conversation to distract from more durably uncomfortable discussions.

We can expect that Islamists are likely to point out the inconsistencies in our policies, most acutely (but not exclusively) with regard to Israel. It is, of course, perfectly reasonable to question the casual way in which US and Israeli interests have for so long been conflated. Governments accountable to emboldened electorates—regardless of the role played by Islamists—are likely to push that conversation along. But the justification of US policy inconsistencies rests on a more foundational myth about the very nature of interests as enduring and self-evident. The truth?? There are no US interests.

It is impossible to speak of interests in the absence of collective identities. One can describe the interests of a group, or identify one's interest as a member of a collective, but the idea that individuals (let alone states) have interests that exist outside of these categories of belonging just does not hold up. Speaking of "US interests" masks this fact with what sounds like a commonsensical idea: we have to look after our interests first. But in whose interest—precisely—does the government of the United States pursue a given policy? The "average" citizen (as if there is such a thing)? Congressional lobbyists? The contractors who directly profit from our relations with foreign regimes? Rather than viewing this as a polemical *bête noir*, this is a question that we should be asking regularly, as part of the practice of engaged citizenship.

If we view the United States as a democracy, then we ought to see the origin of US policy as the collective will of the demos that US institutions reflect, and we can work to change that collective will or at least represent it more accurately. If, by contrast, we view the United States as a plutocracy, we might find the answer in a particular constellation of specific industries, stakeholders, etc., and pursue a strategy of lobbying, targeted boycott, etc. Either approach requires that we ask how interests come to be articulated by people who see themselves as sharing something essential in common.

When people accept the argument that inconsistencies in US policies regarding the Arab uprisings are an unavoidable consequence of "our vital national interests," they are ceding serious ground. They are suggesting that we understand ourselves to be bound first and foremost along the dimension of national identity, and that we share an understanding of what precisely our interests are. They are also flattening what might be a robust understanding of ourselves and our interests into a nationalistic and/or plutocratic materialism. None of these assumptions match reality.

What this narrative forecloses is the possibility of alternative ways of imagining ourselves as being bound to others (whether along dimensions of class or gender solidarity, or a cosmopolitan commitment to global citizenship). In short, when we are cajoled into accepting a policy that supports Libyan rebels and renegotiates debt in Egypt but leaves Bahrainis to the wolves and shrugs its shoulders at that incomprehensible Yemen, it is because we have tacitly accepted a narrow definition of "ourselves" —as Americans principally interested in the projection of US power and the cultivation of regimes that we can influence, irrespective of how they are constituted.

Each of us—individually, through a myriad of institutional and communicative channels—can help to rework the forms of solidarity that will enable a more (consistently) progressive policy toward the popular uprisings in the Middle East. After all, we may not all be Khalid Said or Manal al-Sharif, but we can do more to show our support for what they have come to represent.

Section II
Tunisia

After approximately two weeks of mass demonstrations in which more than sixty-six protesters were killed, the Tunisian regime suddenly unraveled. On 13 January 2011, Zine El Abidine Ben Ali addressed the Tunisian people and said: *"fahimtukum"* (I understood you). During that same speech, Ben Ali promised policy reforms that would allegedly address the protesters' demands. These included calls for employment, reducing food prices, ending corruption, and providing basic freedoms. He also announced he would not run in the 2014 presidential elections. Despite these promises, protesters pushed forth with their demands, rejected Ben Ali's overtures, and called for his immediate resignation and the holding of elections at all levels. The next day, Ben Ali and his family boarded a plane and fled Tunisia to Saudi Arabia, where he continued to reside. The twenty-four year-old regime of Ben Ali had come to its end.

The Tunisian uprising contained within it several elements upon which many of the other uprisings pivoted. First among these was the cry for *karama* (dignity), most exemplified by Mohamed Bouazizi's self-immolation and manifested in the slogans and conduct of many of those that took the streets, including those Tunisians that waged hunger strikes at the doorsteps of various government buildings. Second was the explicit public articulation of the extent to which the Tunisian regime had defrauded the people of its national wealth. The post-uprising exposure of the vastness of Ben Ali's wealth (both abroad and at home) as well as the protesters' raiding of his houses in Tunisia symbolized a discursive and material practice of reclaiming the nation from the regime.

However, recalling the days leading up to 14 January 2011, one is struck by the reality whereby most observers were debating the timing of and conditions under which protesters would evacuate the streets, return to their homes, and business/politics as usual would resume in Tunisia. However, it was Ben Ali who left, after less than two weeks of protest, and without any conditions. Thus the barrier of fear was broken and the imaginative possibilities for both Tunisians and the rest of the Arab world's inhabitants were opened. "The revolution" was no longer a signifier of a bygone era. It was a lived experience, a reality, and the present.

7
The Tunisian Revolution:
Initial Reflections

Mohammed Bamyeh[23]

17 January 2011

At the moment, it is abundantly easy to sense elation everywhere in the Arab world at what appears to be one of the greatest events in modern Arab history. A genuine popular revolution, spontaneous and apparently leaderless, yet sustained and remarkably determined, overthrew a system that by all accounts had been the most entrenched and secure in the whole region. The wider implications beyond Tunisia are hard to miss. Just as in the case of the Iranian Revolution more than three decades ago, what is now happening in Tunisia is watched by all in the Arab world—as either a likely model of the transformation to come in their respective countries, or at least as a badly needed source of revolutionary inspiration.

The Iranian Revolution, too, had unexpectedly toppled what then seemed to be the most entrenched and secure regime in the region. Now the Tunisian Revolution appears to be part of a more immediate pattern; mass demonstrations had been taking place in Algeria and Jordan,[24] and virtually all commentators are drawing parallels to their own countries. Since the popular uprising in Sudan that toppled Jafar Numeiry in 1985, there has been no genuine (and equally peaceful) popular revolt against an Arab regime. And the outcome, thus far, of the Tunisian Revolution of 2011 seems more promising than that of Sudan in 1985, where the military took over and diffused the revolutionary moment. In the case of Tunisia, the army has remained on the sidelines, and the transition is thus far perfectly constitutional—although more radical voices of the revolution are calling for immediately drafting a completely new constitution. Time and future research will of course tell us more about the exact dynamics of this historic moment, which is continuing to unfold, as well as its regional ramifications. At this point, only some preliminary reflections are possible.

First, Tunisia had seemed for long to be an unlikely candidate for revolution due to its apparent stability, comparatively healthy economy, relatively good educational system, and strength of state apparatus. Stability and longevity were characteristic of the regime. In fifty-four years of independence, the country had known only two presidents. The idea of "president for life," which now is more or less the rule in the republican parts of the Arab world, was in fact pioneered as an official term by the first Tunisian president Habib Bourguiba in 1975. From today's perspective it is hard not to feel somewhat nostalgic to the bygone innocence of that moment: where else would a president now openly acknowledge the pointlessness of the cynicism and formality associated with being repeatedly re-elected, without opposition and always with practical unanimity?

Even among Arab governments distinguished in the arts of authoritarianism, the regime that had just been toppled stood out. The regime of Zine El Abidine Ben Ali allowed no opposition of any kind, no criticism of the president, hardly any civil society, banned much of the foreign and Arab press, and whatever part of the internet it deemed even remotely dangerous—including Facebook and similar social media. In 2009, the Committee to Protect Journalists placed Tunisia third among the most dangerous countries in the world from which to blog. At the same time the OpenNet Initiative, which traces the number of blocked sites and categories, found the former Tunisian regime to be the most hostile Arab regime to internet freedom. During the reign of Ben Ali, the security apparatus had a virtually free hand in arresting and torturing suspects everywhere, including in mosques.

In spite of this climate of total control, the revolution found ways to spread images and stories that proved crucial for its further growth and ultimate success. Mobile phones became uniquely valuable for taking images of confrontation and sending them around the country, and whatever communication or internet resources were available captivated the full attention of what appears to have been an enormous number of disaffected people, who without any prior plan staged a revolution. What is significant here is the factor of creativity. The revolution appears to have taken place not because it had resources—a model already familiar from the completely resourceless first Palestinian Intifada in 1987. The events in Tunisia suggest that when there is enough reason for it, a revolution invents the resources that are appropriate for it. That was the case in Tunisia in 2011, just as it was in Palestine in 1987 and in Iran in 1979.

In Tunisia, the opposition parties were clearly caught off-guard by the events, and remained unable to direct the revolution that maintained a character of spontaneity to this point, when the revolution appears to have already attained the basic demands on which all participants agreed—the departure of Ben Ali, the promise of free elections, free association, free media, and the release of political prisoners. By contrast, in the case of the first Palestinian Intifada and the Iranian Revolution, both of which lasted much longer than the Tunisian Revolution before they could reach any goals at all, leaderships and coordinating committees emerged after an initial period of spontaneity, and they served to introduce an element of planning into those uprisings. All those revolts were characterized by organizational or networking creativity, necessitated by the fact that the authorities had been highly vigilant in collecting knowledge about and then making inaccessible all revolutionary resources, including means of communication as well as potential leadership at all levels.

Second, the Tunisian Revolution seems to have been born out of a condition of closed possibilities and not simply out of economic grievances. The revolution began in marginal and neglected parts of the country, and the trigger appears to have been connected with economic grievances. Yet if revolutions were to be explained by economics alone, it would be hard to explain this revolution. For by any meaningful comparison (to the Maghreb countries, the southern Mediterranean, or the Arab world more generally), Tunisia did not seem to be doing exceptionally badly.

The worst economic news was unemployment figures, which officially remained high at fourteen percent and much higher among young people. But such rates are not unusual in the region, and several Arab countries have officially much higher rates of unemployment. Poverty rates have remained steady for years at a little over seven percent, but that was nearly half of what it had been in 2000, and it was a vast improvement over the twenty-two percent it had been when Ben Ali assumed power in 1987. In other countries nearby, poverty rates remained steady for years at much higher rates: twenty percent in Egypt, fifteen percent in Morocco, and nearly one-quarter of the population in Algeria. In 2009 per capita income in Tunisia worsened slightly and stood at 7,200 dollars, close to the level it had been at in 2005. But overall the decline was not drastic, and that amount was still higher than any neighboring country, except oil-producing Libya, but higher than neighboring oil-producing Algeria (6,600 dollars), as well as

Morocco (3,800 dollars), or Egypt (4,900 dollars). Tunisia's life expectancy compared very well with other Arab countries, as did its literacy rates. One may even question the gravity attached to one of the main grievances against Ben Ali's development policies, namely that they exacerbated class differences by benefiting some more than others. As measured by the Gini index (at 40), Tunisia's income distribution appears in fact to be more equal than that of Malaysia or China, for example, or as well as most Third World countries. It appears equivalent to that of Turkey and Israel, neither of which expect a revolution (at least not from those they regard to be their citizens).

It would therefore appear—again if economics were to explain things—that we should see a revolution in Egypt, for example, where relevant economic indicators are miserable. But as Amr al-Shobaki suggested, the saving grace of the Egyptian regime is that it has put into use a ventilation safety valve, meaning that grievances and criticisms of the government and even the president are allowed; that civil society is tolerated; that the opposition can publish its newspapers; and so on. At the same time, the ruling party in Egypt exercises a complete monopoly on power; openly engineers election fraud; and tolerates no real threat to its political hegemony. More interestingly—as seen in the bizarre parliamentary elections[25] in November 2010, the ruling party even allows, in fact seemed to encourage, competition within itself. Thus for the first time it nominated in that election several candidates who would compete against each other in several districts. In doing so it appeased several new power players as well as a variety of local leaders (traditional or otherwise), who demanded an official certification of their leading role in their communities, in exchange for offering support to the ruling party.

The equation in Egypt, therefore, has diffused revolutionary potentials in spite of the gravity of the situation, by allowing criticism but prohibiting change, and by inviting all ambitious politicians to join the party and compete against each other within it, even in public. This cynical game is still more sophisticated than what one sees in most other Arab countries, where authoritarian regimes play a schizophrenic game: on the one hand they see the point of allowing some safety ventilation valve to remain open, while on the other they exhibit paranoia when more than six people meet in a public place to discuss anything resembling politics. Jordan,[26] which is sometimes lauded in the West for its largely bogus democratic experiment,[27] is a good example of this deadly schizophrenia. There is a parliament, the election of which last October was manipulated more than usual to produce a completely pliable body. In comparison to Egypt, no criticism of the king is possible, and in fact every time his name appears in the press, the expected practice is that it should be followed by praise, even if it is mentioned in the context of reporting a fully innocuous event.

Since the Iranian Revolution (and some might argue that as of the late 1960s, in gradual response to the Arab disaster of 1967), Arab regimes have become completely obsessed with the question of regime survival, the obsession with which seemed to trump all other issues, including development, liberalization, and national liberation—as evidenced in their abandonment of the Palestinians and the Iraqis to their fate. Following the Nasser era, the priority assigned to the task of regime survival was coupled almost everywhere in the Arab world with an incoherent sense of grand mission. The post-Nasser era witnessed the gradual abandonment of important post-colonial claims that had been invested in the new states, thus justifying them and affording them legitimacy for a while. The idea then was that post-colonial governments embodied a grand liberationist and developmentalist mission. That claim was, gradually since 1970, paved over with more clientelist thinking, so that government was increasingly regarded, by its elites and constituents alike, as simply a source of situational favors. That idea became only more established with the commitment of almost all Arab governments to neoliberal economics,[28] which did not produce the intended results. It failed—for various possible reasons, but a definite factor is the pervasive corruption against which the Tunisians revolted. Throughout the Arab world the ruling elites have lived off and also encouraged corruption, since it corresponded to their understanding of the clientelist character of the state. Here, the Tunisian regime was no exception but in fact a perfectly typical example.

Political culture thus suffered a transformation that reflected the increasing clientelist character of the state and the lost hopes in the grand post-colonial aspirations that had been invested in it earlier. State ideology itself became more personalistic, infinitely magnifying a single element that under Nasser had been only one of the elements of his charisma. For the past three or four decades, the Arab region saw an unusual investment in the personality cult of the leader. However, unlike the case of Nasser, who in spite of all his faults and the subsequent critiques of his regime remained genuinely popular, all subsequent attempts at personality cults were purely state-engineered. The displays seemed only intended to impress by having the images, statues, and banal statements of largely ineloquent leaders occupy so much public space. This was most evidently the case in republican environments as Syria, Iraq, Libya, and Tunisia, but lesser pompous attempts at personality cults were evident everywhere in the Arab world. They indicate nothing other than the ideological emptiness of government on the one hand, and its (so far evidently unpersuasive) attempt to substitute symbolic populism for genuine democratization.

Here then we have states that lacked a sense of themselves as anything other than being sources of situational favor; that, furthermore, lacked and resisted democratic accountability; that had therefore no mechanisms (other than accident) by which they might produce visionary leaders. The states substituted all of these shortcomings by attempting to aggrandize the personality cult of the leader, whose cult became the only ideology of the government. And personality cults entailed, as a consequence, the gradual transformation of all Arab republics into quasi-kingdoms, with sons following fathers as presidents. The dynastic transition which has already happened in Syria, is apparently planned in Yemen, Egypt,[29] and Libya, and was the plan in Iraq and, until now, in Tunisia. The termination of the Iraqi experiment could not very well be inspiring, since the agent of change there was illegitimate and external, and was viewed by most Iraqis and Arabs as a manifestation of arrogant imperialism. That lesson has now been corrected in Tunisia, and from this the feeling that the personality cult of the leader, of which they were never persuaded anyway, could be undone by their own efforts has been disseminated to all Arabs.

The revolution in Tunisia was a response to a sense of closed possibilities. Nowhere do we see any identifiable "structure of opportunities" that could have made it possible. Everywhere we see the opposite—the absence of any opportunities whatsoever. The pre-revolutionary climate displays a scene of extreme desperation and exasperation. And it is precisely that scene that was so poignantly allegorized in the protest-suicide of a young man after the police took away from him the last meager resource he had for leading a decent life.

Revolution here is triggered in a closed political cosmos. Obviously, a regime's insistence on substituting the leader cult (or official populism) for democracy or civil society can at the end of the road only produce a revolution, regardless of how strong the regime's repressive apparatus might be. The weaknesses of this model of governing may now be apparent to Arab leaders, but their demonstrated short-sightedness, pervasive corruption, and entrenched ethic of self-service make it questionable as to whether they may be shaken into learning the right lesson, even though it might be in their own interest. But regime leaders could be just as suicidal as their opposition could be, especially if the political scene which they have spent decades creating and honing cannot accommodate any reform without it crumbling completely. This is perhaps the conundrum that we are facing now, and there are two likely reasons for it.

First, the fanatic priority attached to regime survival has entailed the elimination of all sustained voices of reform within existing regimes. This was manifested in the removal of all possible competition to the leader, although competition for prestige, positions, and resources at lower rungs of the system was not prohibited and in fact was to be expected. But what became increasingly apparent in the politics of republican, and in some cases even royal, Arab states over the last few decades, is the absence of a clear successor to the leader of the state. Over the years, such early collective leadership structures as the oft-called "revolution's leadership council," usually characteristic of regimes formed through military coups, were dismantled or weakened. In many countries the office of the vice-president was eliminated or replaced by a number of vice-presidents so as to dilute the ability of a single person to act as a magnet for an inner-regime reform movement. At the same time, we saw an investment in personality cults, which was meant to elevate the leader far above all other possible competitors; the investment in sons or other family members as likely successors; the frequent removal of all potential contenders within ruling parties; and the toleration, if not encouragement, of corruption among state elites, which had the effect of producing in them an attachment and loyalty to a system that worked so well for them. Often those tended to be new elites, meaning that they had no traditional power or wealth base in society to fall back upon were they to lose their state connection.

Thus over time it became less and less expected that reform would come from within existing regimes. No "free officers" were to be produced, and even military coups that had been so frequent and that served as channels of reform as well as for expressing popular resentments in the 1950s and 1960s, became unusual as of 1970. Within a decade thereafter, even power struggles over policy directions within existing regimes became rare, and especially the top leaders tended to rule more or less for life. One of their tools of longevity consisted of producing uncertainty about likely succession and fear about the consequences of any succession while they were alive.

This meant, essentially, that the end of regimes became associated with the end of their leaders. And it also meant that all public frustration and resentment would converge on the leader as a person. That reality rigidified the political scene. Any show of weakness meant the end. Thus when Ben Ali, having already ruled for twenty-three years and who is now seventy-four years old, sought to calm the revolutionary crowds by promising not to run for office again (in 2014!), he found himself forced to flee the country the following day. Following his speech, but before his departure, all commentators noted the single most exceptional fact about what he said: it was his first expression of weakness. The logic of the regime he had built meant that any first expression of weakness would be your last.

The revolution, by contrast, represents exactly the opposite qualities—weakness and martyrdom are its ideological fuel, absence of leadership is what keeps it together, weak organization is what makes it hard to capture. One of the most striking facts about this revolution is that even after a month of constant activism, it has remained leaderless and has seemed to be capable of going on as such. Furthermore, its relatively peaceful quality has been absolutely impressive—all deaths and injuries have been result of state violence. Surprisingly, these two qualities—sustained leaderless movement and sustained absence of violence—seem related. For the revolution would have been easily defeated by the state had it turned to violence, given the state's vastly superior repressive apparatus and the likely withdrawal from the streets of all those segments that had been drawn to the movement out of a sense of moral outrage but who were not prepared to be part of a violent crowd. In fact, it seems that the unusual longevity and sustained energy of the revolution has been dependent on a collective moral outrage alone, but not organization, leadership, or a detailed political program. And the absence of revolutionary violence in the face of state violence only deepened that sense of moral outrage, giving it the quality of messianic commitment.

This messianic commitment, another striking quality of this revolution, bears no resemblance to religion, and it may indeed appear as a mystery as to why religion did not play a greater part in this revolt, even though organized religious forces had been part of the Tunisian opposition for three decades. But religious opposition, which since 1979 has been the main internal obsession of Arab regimes, appears in the context of the Tunisian Revolution, so far largely secular, to have all along been part of a larger social consensus that transcends religiosity. The common demands to this point seem to be more basic, even intuitive: the right to be respected as a citizen, to enjoy a decent life and to participate in the creation of the system which rules over the person. These very old demands are not uniquely religious, nor uniquely communist, nor uniquely nationalist, even though these discourses have served as different vehicles for expressing them. Instead of addressing them, Arab governments have always preferred to fixate on the identity of what they regarded to be their internal enemy, assuming that the trouble (and the demand) would go away with the repression of a particular enemy. For the last three decades this enemy has been called "Islamists," before that it was known as "Communists."

But what makes any resourceless revolution into a relentless machine is not its name, nor its ideology. It is the persistence of the very old, basic expectation of citizenship and participation, an expectation whose intuitive nature and pure form is discovered again after having been mystified in the idiom of one discourse or another. Thus when Mohamed Bouazizi set himself and subsequently the whole country on fire, he certainly did not realize what he was about to symbolize, which was the grievances coming back to earth and expressed in the most earthly manner possible: not as mystification, not as re-enacting an ancient struggle between good and evil, not as an expression of a party ideology. He gave a human expression to suffering and protest that negated all need to engage in controversies about ideas, ideologies, political systems, proper course of action, and so on. He rejected his fate, and ended his life in public and in the most horrible manner. But before doing so he had followed all the usual recipes for survival—got an education, lived by the rules, belonged to no parties, bothered no one, was diligent, and was still content with the bare minimum existence, until that was taken away from him. Bouazizi's story was narrated time and again, and its ethic was very simple: resistance was not his first choice; he had sought all other options first. All doors and possibilities then appeared closed, just as the system itself in which he had languished all his life. That he expressed a highly tragic form of a collective feeling is evident in the immense emotional energy that quickly engulfed the entire country and made it impossible for anyone to feel that life could continue as it was before. The revolution begins at the point when an act of someone burning himself appears as an act that anyone can identify with, rather than as an expression of personal pathology or insanity. Bouazizi may not have intended to stir up a revolution, and clearly he was unaware of any opportunities or resources for such a revolution. Neither was apparently anyone who initially rose up to protest his fate, and against a system that had long believed that it had left no room for error and no opportunity for a revolution.

8
Tunisia's Glorious Revolution and its Implications

Noureddine Jebnoun[30]

26 January 2011

On 17 December 2010 disturbances erupted in Tunisia after Mohamed Bouazizi, a young unemployed high school graduate, who sold fruit and vegetables on a street stall for a living, immolated himself in protest after authorities had beaten him and impeded him from exercising his unlicensed activity. His act crystallized and incarnated the Tunisians' feelings of humiliation and the lack of justice to which they had been subjected by one of the most brutal Arab authoritarian regimes that thrived on its infamous corruption and nepotism. A spontaneous nationwide uprising ensued, resulting in the downfall of President Zine El Abidine Ben Ali, who was serving his fifth consecutive five-year term and who was poised to maintain himself or his family in power eternally. His authoritarian regime was disguised in an institutional façade of democracy which was mainly concerned with its own survival rather than enhancing the emergence of a vibrant society engaged in the defense and permanent creation of new liberties that allows societies to renew themselves. During his first decade in power Tunisia enjoyed a notable economic development backed by progressive social policies that saw the reinforcement of its middle class. While entertaining fear internally, and scaring the West with a "horrific Islamic" alternative if it failed to back it up, the regime was able to stifle civil society in exchange for a relative economic well-being. However, with the onset of the second millennium the adverse effects of globalization had started to make themselves felt. The pauperization of the fragile middle class ensued. Indeed, slowing exports were barely offset by output of other sectors; higher growth levels have been difficult to attain to create sufficient employment opportunities for an already large number of unemployed as well as the growing number of university graduates. The challenges ahead include: privatizing industry, liberalizing the investment code to increase foreign investment, improving government efficiency, reducing the trade deficit, and reducing the socioeconomic disparities in the impoverished south and west. A better balance between growth and development remains to be achieved. Still, the main reasons that led to the present unbearable accumulation of dissatisfaction and the destructuring of civil society can only be imputed to the corruption and nepotism practiced by Ben Ali's uncultured family under the umbrella of a well-lubricated repressive system. In fact, a mafia-like regime paying scant respect to the human rights and dignity of Tunisia's citizens was instituted, ultimately contributing to discouraging entrepreneurship and the freezing of local private investment. The result is attested to, among other things, by the unemployment figures, the uneven distribution of wealth, the rise of insecurity and violence, the degradation of education, the pursuit of unethical and immoral practices, the lack of solidarity, political repression, humiliation, and most of all the absence of a sentiment of justice. The latter was with time amplified by the traditional "word of mouth" system as well as the internet, despite all forms of censorship. Indeed, Facebook and Twitter proved critical to breaking the total blackout of information sought by the regime, while the international media coverage was very slow in covering the unfolding events with the notable exception of the *Al Jazeera* television network.

The immediate consequences of the unprecedented protests may be summarized as follows:

- The failure of a twenty-three-year-old police regime to totally stifle civil society and prevent it from communicating and expressing its craving for social and economic justice in the absence of organized structures.
- The breakdown of the psychological wall of fear that subdued the people while depriving them of their dignity and basic freedoms.
- The unsustainability of economic and social development in a centrally-controlled, one-man state solely preoccupied in promoting the illegal financial pursuits of his family clan.

The fall of the "sweet little rogue regime"—to paraphrase Clement M. Henry—has sparked the hope of seeing a genuine liberalization of political life and the instauration of the first democratic system in the Arab world. Yet, this hopefulness now faces the challenge of having to create a framework within which the dialogue between the various components of Tunisian society can take place freely and openly in such a way as to bring about, from the inside, a genuine process of reform. In this regard, advances in political and economic liberalization and progress on human rights and in the social and educational fields are the only way to ensure the country's stability.

The unfolding events in Tunisia have underlined, inter alia, the following important facts:

- Popular grievances at the lack of political governance are common to Tunisia and the rest of the Arab world. Pervasive popular economic misery compounded with a corrupt autocratic rule relying exclusively on security apparatuses make the region vulnerable to political turmoil. The grievances that Tunisians expressed during their revolution are indeed widely shared by the overwhelming majority of Arabs. These concern corruption, lack of political and financial accountability, non-legitimate electoral and political systems, absence of peaceful alternation of power, abuse of power, and excessive reliance on security forces. In the case of Tunisia, Ben Ali may have provided the stability wished for by his foreign supporters—a high-cost stability that generated suicide either by fire or by fatal attempts to cross the Mediterranean Sea in search of the European *el dorado*.

- The widespread peaceful demonstrations in Tunisia seem to have set a new pattern for political change by citizens who dare to challenge an undesirable status quo by braving the bullets of security forces.

- Arab regimes are dysfunctional, sclerotic, corrupt, and ruthless. Ben Ali depicted Tunisian protesters as "terrorists" a few days before his fall, and was totally incapable of any political or social change. The main goal of the Arab "Pinochets" is to subdue their people through oppression, and to serve Western interests. In this context, Tunisia is a main ally in the fight against Islamist networks. It is therefore no surprise that the United States did not react vigorously to the brutality of Ben Ali's police against the demonstrators. Authoritarian regimes have thus benefited from an ambiguous American discourse on democracy. This encourages furthering political suppression and the postponement *sine die* of genuine reform, particularly in the aftermath of 11 September, which has been used as a pretext for the fight against terrorism. Tunisia perfectly illustrates this situation, in which securitization/police-itization have weakened the possibility for real democratization. This ultimately compromises the security objectives the United States is seeking to achieve in the region. Democracy promotion is thus rife with its own contradictions, such as the perceived threat of Islamism as a potential to fill the political vacuum. In this sense, democracy and security have become bound together; for security to be achieved, genuine political reform must occur. It is important to point out that the strategic interests of the United States, the European Union, and NATO in North Africa, such as fighting terrorism, have generated support for "friendly tyrants," rather than for democratization across the region. Instead, a clear US message in democracy promotion should be the foundation of a comprehensive American strategy toward the area. It should feature a multifaceted, realistic, and workable soft security approach that is based on supporting robust representative institutions, nurturing civil society and integrating Islamist parties and movements into politics. This new approach should look for the root causes of instability rather than fighting the symptoms such as radicalism and Anti-Americanism. In this context, the United States should be ready to accept criticism coming from forces that draw their legitimacy from the ballot box.

- Political elites in Tunisia and in the Arab world lack a political vision for the future and play more the role of bureaucratic administrators than political players. Rather than promoting genuine democracy, a reinvention of authoritarianism disguised in democratic dressing has emerged, succeeding in manipulating and co-opting civil society. The genuine fracture in the Arab world today is between the society and the regime as power is misused and abused without any political perspective or real will to change the situation. The Arab dictators view democratic reforms as harmful to their security while the radicalization of the population is closely related to their increased reliance on authoritarian methods of government—whence the vicious circle of radicalization and repression derives. From the outside, these regimes appear coherent and strong, but in reality they are made up of multiple factions, including intelligence and security apparatuses, business oligarchies, and robust executive power, which are constantly vying for power and renegotiating the legitimacy of the head of state.

- The general underlying feeling of impotence and discontent can be overcome; Arab societies are, indeed, now making their desire for emancipation increasingly felt and are demanding a political role tailored to their needs.
- Arab identity and Islamism are by no means incompatible with the notion of modernity nor with the initiation of serious reforms. Islamism in North Africa is a highly diversified and complex ideology. Islamism in Tunisia does not always mean radicalism and radicalization is not necessarily identical to terrorism. The Islamist movement is a general concept including a broad range of Islamic thought from Erdogan to the Taliban including Shaykh Rachid al-Ghannouchi, Abbassi Madani, Shaykh Abdessalam Yassine, and others. During the colonial period, this region overdosed on traumatic Westernization, and as a result Islamism manifested itself as a direct reaction to this phenomenon. The democratic roadmap for Tunisia should not exclude the Islamists, who should be considered as one of the major players within the Tunisian political landscape. Of course, the religious discourse can be used to justify violence, although it in no way defines the cause. As François Burgat has pointed out, "the Qur'an cannot explain Osama bin Laden any more than the Bible can explain the IRA." Arab regimes, which made the Islamists' political agenda appear more ideological, created a great deal of political violence in order to discredit Islamist movements, and used Islamist rhetoric to stigmatize Islamism in general. This is a process that could be labeled the *"bin-Ladenization"* of the Islamists in the Arab world.
- The notions of democracy, human rights, rule of law, independent courts, free media, workers' rights, and an educational system adapted to today's economic needs are fundamental and universal values indispensable for political stability. The pseudo-stability under Ben Ali was a ticking bomb that ended up exploding. Durable stability in Tunisia, as in any Arab country, will come only through genuine democracy that responds fairly to the needs and hopes of the people. This includes economic and social development, employment, proper public administration, the fight against corruption, the development and consideration of a strong and genuine civil society, the fight for gender equality, conservation of the global cultural heritage, inter-cultural dialogue, good governance, free and fair media, political participation and

the promotion of human rights and fundamental freedoms, freedom of expression and association, the rejection of torture and the abolition of the death penalty, and the rejection of intolerance and extremism.

Drawing on the lessons of the Tunisian revolution and looking at the Arab world, a few main policy guidelines may be highlighted:

- In spite of many reverses, the twentieth century brought the Arab world a number of benefits which enabled their societies to participate in the world market. This participation does not necessarily mean Westernization, but it does mean the acceptance of democratic values as a shared heritage of mankind. This is where cultural dialogue can be useful and fruitful.
- While it is true that reforms seek to give Arab societies ownership of their destiny, it is through a process of ownership that these reforms should be initiated. The aim here is to engender independent and indigenous dynamic processes in various sectors of society (justice, administration, education, and so on) in the context of cooperation programs.
- On both sides an effort is urgently needed to put an end to the ambiguities which encourage a culture-based process of confrontation, so as to develop normal relations between states and civil societies. While no concessions are possible on the *acquis* international in its various forms, it would be courageous and salutary for the West to strike a balance between its culture-based perceptions and political pragmatism. The West's relations with the Arab world will be all the more fruitful, credible, and legitimate if it takes a wide range of interlocutors, giving particular attention and visible political support to actors in civil society, associations, and religious life. Similarly it would help the quality of dialogue if a clearer distinction were to be drawn between intangible universal principles on the one hand and mechanisms for the devolution of power on the other. Respect for human rights and freedom of expression are universal and intangible principles, but changes in the mechanisms for the devolution of power are much more linked to history and local traditions.
- Oppression and violence generated by authoritarianism have brought Arab society to a dead end. Authoritarianism is dangerous in terms of lives lost and opportunities curbed.

If there is to be a meaningful engagement with Arabs, both *in situ* and in the West, more attention must be given to finding a democratic path that sails safely between the Scylla of the "Overseas Contingency Operation" (war on terror) and the Charybdis of entrenched authoritarianism and rising radicalism in the region.

- It would thus be advisable that the United States government rethink its strategic posture toward the Arab world by dissociating itself from policies of repression, social discrimination, and economic marginalization. It is important to note that the United States, unlike European countries, is unencumbered by colonial "baggage in the region." This comparative advantage could be promoted by US policymakers keen to implement genuine and constructive dialogue with different components of Arab civil society.

Ultimately, the objective of the Arab people is to enhance the emergence of vibrant societies engaged in the defense and permanent creation of fundamental liberties and rights that allow societies to regenerate themselves. In this context, the fall of the Brutus of Carthage has deconstructed the Western stereotypes which shape the image of Arab societies as incapable of moving toward democracy due to the absence of civic cultures and self-governance. Like Spain's and Portugal's transition, which began without any prior democratic experience, Tunisia is on its way to democracy building and learning. This might involve some fits and starts but Tunisians are mature and are resolved to assert their freedom.

9
Let's Not Forget about Tunisia

Nouri Gana[31]

30 January 2011

Now that world attention has irresistibly moved on to the next hotspot, Egypt, it is crucially important not to forget Tunisia. In the very same manner that revolutionary change in Tunisia has spread to Egypt and Yemen and, hopefully, will continue to travel to other parts of the Arab world, any setback in Tunisia may set in motion a reverse effect and may prove counter-productive in the long run. Failure is no less contagious than freedom. While our hearts and minds are with our brothers and sisters in Egypt, let us not forget Tunisia lest the new interim government should intimidate Tunisians into submission to more of the same old new police state. The latest cabinet reshuffle has left Tunisians divided between those who support the new government and the sit-in protesters in al-Qasbah who insist that all the symbols of the old regime must go.

While all eyes were set on Egypt's "Friday of Anger" on 28 January 2011, special security forces in Tunisia seized the opportunity to forcibly dislodge a five-day round-the-clock sit-in protest in the Qasbah Government Square in Tunis. The sit-in protestors are part of the "Freedom Caravan," which, in addition to the hundreds that joined from the capital, initially included a thousand participants who came all the way from Menzel Bouzayene, Regueb, and other villages and towns from the Governorate of Sidi Bouzid where the self-immolation of Mohamed Bouazizi sparked the "Dignity Revolution" that brought down Zine El Abidine Ben Ali on 14 January 2011.

The protesters ask for the resignation of the so-called interim government and the dismantlement of Ben Ali's party, the Constitutional Democratic Rally (RCD). Echoing Moncef Marzouki, the leader of the Congress for the Republic, the anti-government protesters believe that while they got rid of the dictator, Ben Ali, they still have to dismantle the system of dictatorship he kept in place after his unceremonious flight to Saudi Arabia. They demand that any former RCD members resign from the interim government, not exempting Prime Minister Mohamed al-Ghannouchi himself, and be replaced by other respectable technocrats from the Bourguiba era.

They fear that former RCD members in the interim government might tilt the playing field to their own advantage and use their roles to gather support for their own parties in the forthcoming elections. Their fears have been heightened by the fact that the interim government has not yet made it clear whether or not its current members will be eligible candidates in the much anticipated presidential elections.

On 27 January 2011, Prime Minister Mohamed al-Ghannouchi reshuffled his cabinet, replacing a dozen ministers in an attempt to appease the protesters and placate their anger at the Ben Ali-like style of the interim government ministers. Yet, while this move satisfied many labor unionists and shopkeepers in al-Qasbah, the sit-in protesters saw in it nothing but further proof of the suspect tactics of the interim government; for them this cabinet reshuffle, like the one that Mubarak announced in Egypt, is just another one of al-Ghannouchi's ruses to stay in power and continue doing business as usual. While many attest to al-Ghannouchi's innocence of the crimes committed by Ben Ali and his wife, Leïla Trabelsi, not all Tunisians, and certainly not the al-Qasbah protesters, are willing to forgive him for playing the role of a passive witness, a "dumb devil" (*shaytaan akhras*) of sorts. They think he is complicit in one way or another since he could have just resigned rather than tarried in power.

The sit-in protesters were therefore unequivocal in their demand for his resignation from the interim government. They now even fear that he would use his role to destroy all evidence, or whatever is left of it, that implicate him and others of his ilk in the crimes committed by Ben Ali, his regime, his wife, and their two extended families.

At any rate, the following day after the reshuffle of the government, the army, which had thenceforth protected the camps in the Qasbah Square, was ordered to withdraw and riot policemen were unleashed on the protestors. It is unclear why the army, whose firm support of peaceful demonstrators brought down Ben Ali, should have turned its back on them at a time when they needed it the most. One thing is clear, though: more and more Tunisians have grown bored with sights of protest and have given in to the apocalyptic rhetoric and politics of fear engineered by the interim government and which threaten, among other things, an economic catastrophe in the making, and a potential political vacuum that would leave the country at the mercy of the army, the Islamists, or foreign intervention if things do not go back to normal as soon as possible.

No wonder, then, that riot police were ordered to destroy the makeshift camp outside the prime minister's office. What happened in al-Qasbah on 28 January 2011 is unequivocal evidence of the unfinished project of the Tunisian Revolution. Nothing changed in terms of the dehumanizing manner in which policemen treat Tunisians. It is as if Tunisia were still under the rule of Ben Ali without Ben Ali. What is even worse is that the brutalities of the policemen were hardly covered by the media which was either absent or disallowed from entering the site. Only now and through eyewitness accounts have the atrocities of what happened begun to come to light.

The special forces of the police (known as the well-trained and merciless, *tigres noirs*) first besieged the camp and then unleashed a number of embedded gangs to provoke a clash with the sit-in protesters which was preparatory to intervening with full force to restore order. Nessma TV (The Television of the Grand Maghreb) ran a report in which eyewitnesses, including lawyers, all pointed out that the embedded gangs came from outside the camp and merged into the protesters and started pelting the policemen with rocks so as to provide them with an excuse to intervene. Under the umbrella of legitimate defense, the *tigres noirs* attacked the protestors with truncheons, dogs, and tear-gas canisters; they tore their tents and chased them away from al-Qasbah. They clubbed and injured dozens of them and, according to the Facebook page *al-haqaaiq al-qafiyya* (Hidden Facts), they killed seven: Mahran al-Behiri, Walid al-Bouni, Abdelrazzak al-Qasimi, Seif al-Akrmi, Isam al-Sadrawi, Imed al-Rouissi, and Jafar al-Misi.

No official statement has thus far been issued about the exact number of those who were injured or killed in the methodically premeditated and executed attack, but both local media and the interim government officials are still in denial of the excessive use of force witnessed and documented by many on the ground. The Tunisian national television network is still not free. Its team, which still receives orders from the government, has not come clean about the details of what happened, let alone about the number of the dead or injured. It has managed, however, to distort the story and tarnish the good reputation of the sit-in protesters who travelled from the interior of the country and who for five consecutive days and nights braved the cold weather, hunger, and even illness in order to make a principled statement to Prime Minister al-Ghannouchi: "Ghannouchi, out!"

It is therefore a treachery of the cruelest kind for the national television network and for the official discourse of the interim government to draw a negative portrait of these most courageous and foresighted Tunisians. I heard several stories swirling around the corruption and crookedness of the new interim government and the special police forces; the stories have a ring of truth about them, not least because they are reminiscent of the methods used in the days leading up to and following the departure of Ben Ali. Protesters speak about how they were approached by anonymous persons and were presented with bribes, whores, and drugs provided that they give up the fight and go back to Sidi Bouzid. Some even claim that government officials or their undeclared representatives made use of prison gangs in order to incite regional animosities between them and the inhabitants of al-Qasbah and in the process isolate them and break their will. These gangs are reminiscent of the ones that Ben Ali made use of in order to sow fear among his people and to convince his Euro-American allies that Islamist militias and terrorists—and not the Tunisian people—are behind the popular revolts that shook the country in the days leading up to 14 January 2011. The trick did not work then and it is not working now. What beggars the imagination, though, is the extent to which the new interim government is replicating the same methods of old in order to legitimatize its otherwise despicable tactics.

The sit-in protest was broken but the will of the protestors will not break easily. True, they experienced nothing less of a setback: they came under a brutal attack and were scattered and dispersed and now disallowed from re-entering al-Qasbah, which has been completely sealed off by barbed wire. Understandably, they are embittered and disappointed, even though they should boast of having sparked the revolution and forced the latest cabinet reshuffle. They surely wanted to go all the way and eradicate every remaining vestige of Ben Ali's regime and his party but felt as if the army and General Rachid Ammar failed them at the last minute. Or is it simply that the euphoria of success has lifted now and nothing more can be expected? This might be the feeling of some but some others will continue the non-violent demonstrations especially in the wake of al-Qasbah massacre. The new interim government has clearly proven untrustworthy and blind to the demands of the very people who made the revolution and whom it claims to serve. The massacre of sit-in protesters in al-Qasbah is a reminder that the project of the Tunisian Revolution is still unfinished. Tunisians have come this far and will not be satisfied with half-solutions, half-measures or any form of gradualisms. The blood of martyrs is not for bargain and nothing less than dismantlement of the RCD and the resignation of all its former members from the interim government will be worthy of celebration. Nothing less will be worthy of the Tunisian Revolution.

10
The Battle for Tunisia

Nouri Gana[32]

21 October 2011

Only days prior to the 23 October elections for a national constituent assembly, Tunisia continues to be an embattled and profoundly polarized terrain. Since the ouster of Zine El Abidine Ben Ali in January, peaceful and less than peaceful demonstrations and sit-ins have routinely taken place throughout the country, particularly in the capital, Tunis. The most memorable of these remains the second sit-in protest in the Qasbah Government Square (20 February–3 March), which led to the resignation of Prime Minister Mohamed al-Ghannouchi and his replacement by appointment of Béji Caïd Essebsi on 27 February 2011.

It may go down as one of the bitter ironies of Tunisian history that a revolutionary uprising accomplished primarily by youth resulted in an interim government headed by an eighty-five-year-old veteran who served in various posts under both Habib Bourguiba and Ben Ali. Indeed, in an interview on the eve of his recent visit to Washington, D.C., Essebsi alluded to the possibility that he might still be in function after the much anticipated elections this coming Sunday. Not unlike Bourguiba, his idol and former president whom in 1974 proclaimed himself president for life, Essebsi appears to be entertaining ambitions of eternal premiership.

Ever since Essebsi came to power, there have not been any successful demonstrations or sit-ins, despite many attempts made to organize a third sit-in in the Qasbah Government Square. With Ben Ali protégé Habib Sid as his interior minister, Essebsi has been able to pre-empt or repress any form of protest against his government, which has been consistently accused of complicity with the remnants of the *ancien régime* and the dissolved ruling party, the Constitutional Democratic Rally (RCD).

Essebsi has also been accused of drowning the country further in debt and failing to secure the return of funds looted by Ben Ali and his cronies. The trials of Ben Ali, his wife, Leïla Trabelsi, and their families have been regularly perceived by most Tunisians as nothing more than cheap reality TV shows. Essebsi's interim government has been quite reluctant to address and redress the grievances of the families of martyrs, and has routinely denied the existence of snipers that are believed to have killed more than three hundred Tunisians during and after the Tunisian Revolution.

With election day around the corner, many segments of Tunisian society have little faith that the interim government will conduct democratic elections. Essebsi has, after all, admitted on *Al Jazeera* to having rigged elections under Bourguiba. Moreover, Tunisian media has lately been acting very irresponsibly, and—reportedly at the direct instigation of French ambassador Boris Boillon—has on various occasions attempted to tilt the playing field in favor of certain parties with francophone agendas.

The battle for the future of post-revolutionary Tunisia has been and continues to be played out in the realm of culture. A number of leading public figures, party leaders and intellectuals have cautioned against the impertinence of debates around Tunisian identity at this particular historical juncture. Yet others, mostly francophone elites, media and financial gurus, fearing the resurgence of Islamism after decades of repression, have insisted that Tunisia's future hinges on the continuation of the secularist project initiated by Bourguiba and exhausted by Ben Ali.

The latest round in this battle occurred several weeks ago when Nessma TV, a self-proclaimed independent television station, infamous among Tunisians for its extremely secularist and francophone agendas, dubbed into Tunisian dialect, adapted and aired Marjane Satrapi's animated film, *Persepolis*. Like the Danish cartoons, which were deemed sacrilegious for representing (and lampooning) the figure of the Prophet Muhammad, the film also represented what Muslim tradition deems beyond representation, in this case the figure of God. Tunisians who remember the days of Ben Ali when a walk to the mosque might get them imprisoned, have grown impatient with incessant and virulent attacks on Islam, masquerading as attacks on Salafism or, more regularly, the Islamist Ennahda (Renaissance) Party. Those who under Ben Ali were comfortable calling for the reduction of the volume of the call to prayer, have however been experiencing nothing short of panic at what they perceive as an overnight return to Islam. All the more so given the repeal of the ban on the hijab has led to its revival and spread.

Some have dubbed the return to Islam as the return of the repressed. It would be more accurate to term it the redressing of the unaddressed. Secularist (actually pseudo-secularist) media icons, intellectuals, critics, and academics have for decades remained silent on the prohibition of hijab, and the profiling of Islamists and mosque-goers under Bourguiba and Ben Ali. They did so in the name of women's rights, secularism and modernity, which in actuality masked, condoned and licensed the brutal hold of Bourguiba and Ben Ali's regimes on Islamists and everyday Muslims. With the ouster of Ben Ali, the crimes of their so-called secularist creed have been exposed; rather than seizing the moment to elaborate a critique of Bourguiba's and Ben Ali's brands of *laïcité* and distance themselves from their vicissitudes, they hastened to perpetuate their profoundly flawed projects. No wonder, then, that most pseudo-secularists are currently members of the parties that have come into existence after the dissolution of Ben Ali's party, RCD (Constitutional Democratic Rally). Their inaugural gesture is reactionary and their search for credibility has consistently translated into an all-out campaign against the parties that have historical and oppositional credibility to both Bourguiba and Ben Ali, and which include particularly the Renaissance Party (Ennahda), the Tunisian Workers' Communist Party (PCOT) and the Congress for the Republic (CPR).

CPR and PCOT can be expected to do very well in these upcoming elections on account of the indisputable activist dissidence of Moncef Marzouki and Hamma Hammami, respectively. Yet there is no gainsaying the fact that Ennahda is a major player in the current political scene in Tunisia, and is expected to carry a good number of the 217 seats that will form the national constituent assembly whose task is, among others, to write a new constitution for the country and oversee the transition toward democracy. The Democratic Modernist Pole (El-Qutb), along with the Democratic Forum for Labour and Liberties (El-Takattul) as well as the Progressive Democratic Party (PDP), the Homeland Party (El-Watan), and variations on them, have more or less found in their outright opposition to Ennahda their very *raison d'être*. Few people know what the economic plans of these parties might be, but most Tunisians know that their claim to fame is their unbending opposition to Ennahda, an opposition that has regularly been voiced under the banner of *laïcité* (whose main pillar is the separation between religion and politics).

Clearly, though, if Ennahda were not a political party, it would not have been given a license by the Ministry of the Interior. This has been the case, for instance, with the Salafist party, Hizb

Ettahrir (Liberation Party), whose application for a license was turned down. The insistence of pseudo-secularists that Ennahda is a purely religious party that will end up instituting Sharia law in Tunisia is nothing but a red herring, part and parcel of the fear-mongering campaign against a formidable opponent whose history of struggle against dictatorship speaks for itself. One might wonder whether the venomous attacks on Ennahda (and at times on CPR whose leader, Moncef Marzouki, rightly pointed out that his party does not suffer from an "Ennahda complex") do not stem from a fear that Islam and democracy are coextensive. Undoubtedly, the compatibility of Islam and democracy threatens to undo the authority of *laïcité*, not to mention the entire tradition of secularist-authoritarian thought in Tunisia.

Perhaps the trouble with the electoral campaign in the end is that it has allowed questions of cultural identity, religion and *laïcité* to override other important and thorny issues that have to do with the economy, unemployment, justice, political reconciliation, and so on. On the one hand, Islamists have focused very much on their past histories of struggle and have insisted on their progressive civic agenda as well as on their preference for parliamentary democracy. On the other, pseudo-secularists have been fixated on the critique of Ennahda, all the while remaining reticent about or oblivious to the ideological underpinning of *laïcité*. By presenting their ideology as a form of critique, Tunisian pseudo-secularists have steadily, even dogmatically, constructed themselves beyond critique. A critique of Tunisian *laïcité*, however, is never more to be desired than at a time when its complicity with the old regime of Ben Ali and French cultural imperialism has become an everyday Tunisian reality. Tunisians who will go to the polls this Sunday cannot be expected to deliver such a critique—they will deliver their long overdue judgment.

Section III
Egypt

On 25 January 2011, Egyptians took to the streets and began their eighteen-day uprising that toppled Husni Mubarak. At first, many analysts were quick to argue that Egypt would not be like Tunisia. Some, however, stressed the caveat that should protesters overcome the constraints on sustained collective action, Mubarak could very well be forced to step down. Thus as Egyptian protesters held their ground in the face of multi-pronged attempts by the regime to clear the streets, they, along with the rest of the world, agonized over Mubarak's speeches, hoping that each one would be his last. The day the Supreme Council of the Armed Forces (SCAF) deployed troops onto the streets of Cairo, there were fears of either pro-Mubarak violent retaliations or a military coup against him. To the dismay of many around the world, Mubarak's 10 February speech asserted that he would continue to be the head of state, while the deployed military units continued to hold their standby position. A resignation was so expected that night that one popular leftist café in Beirut had announced free beer and chicken sandwiches in celebration of the Egyptian uprising. Nevertheless, as if to spite the relentlessly skeptical analysts, protests swelled even more the following day, 11 February, in what became known as the "Day of Departure." As people stared at their television screens in anticipation of another scheduled speech by Mubarak, viewers were shocked this time to see Vice-President Omar Suleiman and not President Husni Mubarak step up to the podium. Mubarak had resigned and "transferred" his powers to SCAF.

The implications of Mubarak's resignation were grand for Egypt and beyond. But the jubilation of the moment was reserved, as it should have been, for Egyptians who had struggled for decades under the weight of his regime's tyranny. They had, after all, brought the symbol of the Egyptian regime down in eighteen days of around-the-clock and country-wide protests. As the resignation was announced, all reactionary forces inside and outside of Egypt were put on notice. It was one thing for the Tunisian regime to unravel; it was another for Husni Mubarak to resign, given Egypt's centrality in regional politics. Thus the struggle quickly shifted to defining the nature of change in a post-Mubarak Egypt.

The combination of events in Tunisia and Egypt forced a shift in Arab political discourse, as well as in the strategies of regimes and opposition groups alike across the region. The eternal aura of Arab authoritarianism was finally collapsing. In Egypt, neighborhood committees, Muslim–Christian solidarity, and various efforts at coalition-building challenged the false choice between authoritarianism and chaos (a dichotomy that Arab regimes and their supporters always allude to). Nonetheless, the challenges ahead were immense, and by the summer of 2011 there were new dynamics at play. Central to them was the debate about whether formal politics or contentious politics provided the best means by which to ensure that Mubarak's toppling was the beginning of change rather than its limit. That debate is ongoing as voters head to the polls (whether parliamentary or presidential) while protesters continue to organize in the streets.

11
The Poetry of Revolt

Elliott Colla[33]

31 January 2011

It is truly inspiring to see the bravery of Egyptians as they rise up to end the criminal rule of Husni Mubarak. It is especially inspiring to remember that what is happening is the culmination of years of work by activists from a spectrum of pro-democracy movements, human rights groups, labor unions, and civil society organizations. In 2004, when Kefaya began their first public demonstrations, the protesters were usually outnumbered thirty to one by Central Security Forces. Now the number has reversed—and multiplied.

No less astonishing is the poetry of this moment. I do not mean "poetry" as a metaphor, but the actual poetry that has played a prominent role since the outset of the events. The slogans the protesters are chanting are couplets—and they are as loud as they are sharp. The diwan of this revolt began to be written as soon as Zine El Abidine Ben Ali fled Tunis, in pithy lines like "*Yā Mubārak! Yā Mubārak! As-Sa'ūdiyya fi-ntizārak!*" ("O Mubarak, O Mubarak, Saudi Arabia awaits!"). In the streets themselves, there are scores of other verses, ranging from the caustic "*Shurtat Masr, yā shurtat Masr, intū baaytū kilāb al-'asr,*" ("Egypt's Police, O Egypt's Police, You've become nothing but dogs of the Palace"), to the defiant "*Idrab idrab yā Habīb, mahma tadrab mish hansīb!*" ("Hit us, beat us, O Habib [Habib al-Adly, now former Minister of the Interior], hit all you want—we're not going to leave!"). This last couplet is particularly clever, since it plays on the old Egyptian colloquial saying, "*Darb al-habīb zayy akl al-zabib*" ("The beloved's fist is as sweet as raisins"). This poetry is not an ornament to the uprising—it is its soundtrack and also composes a significant part of the action itself.

A HISTORY OF REVOLUTIONS, A HISTORY OF POETS

There is nothing unusual about poetry playing a galvanizing role in a revolutionary moment. And in this context, we might

77

remind ourselves that making revolution is not something new for Egyptians—having had no less than three "official" revolutions in the modern era: the 1881 Urabi Revolution, which overthrew a corrupt and comprador royalty; the 1919 Revolution, which nearly brought down British military rule; and the 1952 Revolution, which inaugurated sixty years of military dictatorships under Gamal Abdel Nasser, Anwar Sadat, and Husni Mubarak. The first revolution succeeded in establishing the second parliamentary government on the African continent before it was crushed by foreign military intervention. In the aftermath of defeat, the British established a rapacious colonial rule over Egypt for more than seventy years. The second revolution was a sustained, popular uprising led by a range of pro-democracy activists from a range of civil institutions. Though savagely repressed, it did force the British to grant some concessions. The third revolution officially celebrated in Egypt stands apart from the first two in that it was a *coup d'état* that went out of its way to circumscribe popular participation. In any case, it was accepted in the moment since it finally ended the rule of the royal family first overthrown in 1881 and initiated a process of British withdrawal from Egypt.

Besides these three state-commemorated events, Egyptians have revolted against the corruption, greed, and cruelty of their rulers many more times in the last sixty years. On 26 January 1952, Egyptians emerged onto the streets to protest an array of issues—including the corruption of the monarchy, the decadence, power and privilege of foreign business elites, and the open-ended British occupation. The revolt was quickly suppressed, though the damage to property was massive, and it set in motion an exodus of foreign elites—and the military coup months later. In 1968, Egyptian students launched huge and daring protests against the repressive policies of Nasser's police state. In the early 1970s, Egyptian students engaged in sustained mass protests against the radical political reorientations of the new Sadat regime—and eventually forced the state to re-engage in military confrontation with Israel. On 18–19 January 1977, Egyptians rose up en masse to protest against IMF austerity measures imposed on the country by the corrupt, inept, and ruthless regime of Anwar Sadat. The Egyptian president was already on his jet ride into exile before the Central Security Forces and Army finally gained the upper hand. In Egypt it is the Central Security Forces rather than the military who deals with civil unrest and popular protest. Yet, even this "solution" to the problem of recurring popular revolt has proven uncertain at times. As in the military, the CSF has been the site of mutinies, one of which, in late February 1986, involved twenty thousand low-paid conscripts who were put down only when the army entered the fray. During the early 1990s, Islamist protests against the authoritarian rule of Mubarak escalated into armed conflict, both in the slums of the cities and in Upper Egypt. Hundreds of militants, soldiers, and innocent civilians were killed before the revolt was finally suppressed. This list leaves out other significant moments of mass civil protest and contestation—like the massive protests against the First Gulf War, the US invasion of Iraq and Israel's attacks on Lebanon and Gaza—but even so, the tally is impressive: no less than ten major revolts and revolutions in one hundred and thirty years. In other words, despite what commentators might say, modern Egyptians have never passively accepted the failed colonial or post-colonial states that fate has dealt them.

Many of these revolts have had their own poets. 1881 had the neo-classical *qasidas* of Mahmoud Sami al-Baroudi. 1919 had the colloquial *zajals* of Bayram al-Tunsi. Salah Jahin became one of the leading colloquial poets of the 1952 Revolution, and his patriotic verse became core material for Abdel Halim Hafez, who pinned his career to Nasser. From the same period, Fu'ad Haddad's *mawwals* also stand out—and are still sung today. Since the 1970s, it has been Ahmed Fouad Negm who has played the leading role as lyricist of militant opposition to the regimes of Egypt. For forty years, Negm's colloquial poems—many set to music by Sheikh Imam—have electrified student, labor and dissident movements from the Egyptian underclass. Negm's poetry ranges from praise (*madh*) for the courage of ordinary Egyptians, to invective (*hija'*) for Egypt's overlords—and it is no accident that you could hear his songs being sung by the leftist activists who spearheaded the first day of revolt on 25 January. Besides these poets, we could add many others—Naguib Surur, Abd al-Rahman al-Abnoudi, Tamim Barghouti—who have added to this literary–political tradition in their own ways.

But beyond these recognized names are thousands of other poets—activists all—who would never dare to protest publicly without an arsenal of clever couplet-slogans. The end result is a unique literary tradition whose power is now on full display across Egypt. Chroniclers of the current Egyptian revolt, like As'ad AbuKhalil, have already compiled lists of these couplets—and hundreds more are sure to come. For the most part, these poems are composed in a colloquial, not classical, register and they are extremely catchy and easy to sing. The genre also has real potential for humor and play—and remind us of the fact that revolution is also a time for celebration and laughter.

HOW TO DO THINGS WITH POETRY

The poetry of this revolt is not reducible to a text that can be read and translated in words, for it is also an act in and of itself. That is, the couplet-slogans being sung and chanted by protesters do more than reiterate complaints and aspirations that have been communicated in other media. This poetry has the power to express messages that could not be articulated in other forms, as well as to sharpen demands with ever keener edges.

Consider the most prominent slogan being chanted today by thousands of people in Tahrir Square: "*Ish-sha'b/yu-rīd/is-qāt/in-ni-zām.*" Rendered into English, it might read, "The People want the regime to fall"—but that would not begin to translate the power this simple and complex couplet-slogan has in its context. There are real poetic reasons why this has emerged as a central slogan. For instance, unlike the more ironic—humorous or bitter—slogans, this one is sincere and states it all perfectly clearly. Likewise, the register of this couplet straddles colloquial Egyptian and standard media Arabic—and it is thus readily understandable to the massive Arab audiences who are watching and listening. And finally, like all the other couplet-slogans being shouted, this has a regular metrical and stress pattern (in this case: short-LONG, short-LONG, short-LONG, short-short-LONG). While unlike most others, this particular couplet is not rhyming; it can be sung and shouted by thousands of people in a unified, clear cadence—and that seems to be a key factor in why it works so well.

The prosody of the revolt suggests that there is more at stake in these couplet-slogans than the creation and distillation of a purely semantic meaning. For one thing, the act of singing and shouting with large groups of fellow citizens has created a certain and palpable sense of community that had not existed before. And the knowledge that one belongs to a movement bound by a positive collective ethos is powerful in its own right—especially in the face of a regime that has always sought to morally denigrate all political opposition. Likewise, the act of singing invective that satirizes feared public figures has an immediate impact that cannot be explained in terms of language, for learning to laugh at one's oppressor is a key part of unlearning fear. Indeed, witnesses to the revolt have consistently commented that in the early hours of the revolt—when invective was most ascendant—protesters began to lose their fear.

And having lost that fear, Egyptians are showing no signs of wanting to go back. As the Mubarak regime has continued to unleash more violence, and as it steps up its campaign to sow chaos and confusion, the recitation of these couplet-slogans has continued, as if the act of repeating them helps the protesters concentrate on their core principles and demands. Only hours ago, as jets and helicopters attempted to intimidate protesters in Tahrir Square, it seemed as if the crowd understood something of this—for with each sortie, their singing grew louder and more focused. It was difficult to determine whether the crowd sustained the words, or the words the crowd.

POETRY AND CONTINGENCY

Anyone who has ever chanted slogans in a public demonstration has also probably asked herself at some point: Why am I doing this? What does shouting accomplish? The question provokes a feeling of embarrassment, the suspicion that the gesture might be rote and thus empty and powerless. Arguably, this nervousness is a form of performance anxiety that, if taken seriously, might remind us that the ritual of singing slogans was invented precisely because it has the power to accomplish things. When philosophers speak of "doing things with words," they also remind us that the success of the locutionary act is tied to the conditions in which it is performed. This is another way to say that any speech act is highly contingent—its success only occurs in particular circumstances, and even then, its success is never a given. Success, if it is to occur, happens only in the doing of it.

Since 25 January, Egyptians have been leaping into the uncertainty of this revolutionary performance. They have now crossed multiple thresholds—and each time, they have acted with no guarantee of success. This is, I think, the core of their astonishing courage: at each point it has been impossible to say that victory is already theirs. Even now, six days into the revolt, we still cannot say how things will eventually turn out. Nor are there rules of history and previous examples that can definitively tell us. Certainly, revolutions follow patterns—and those who rise up tend to be the most diligent students of past uprisings. Activists in Cairo ask comrades in Tunis about tactics, while others try to glean Iran's Green Revolution for lessons that might be applied now. Yet, in the end, each revolution is its own moment.

Those who decide to make their own history are, in the end, not only required to write their own script and build their own stage, they are also compelled to then play the new roles with enough force and conviction to make it cohere, even in the face of overwhelming violence. We have already seen one example of this re-scripting in the extraordinary, original pamphlet from Egypt entitled, "How to Revolt Intelligently." The poetry of the streets is another form of writing, of redrafting the script of history in the here and now—with no assurances of victory, and everything in the balance.

12
Why Mubarak is Out

Paul Amar[34]

1 February 2011

The "March of Millions" in Cairo marks the spectacular emergence of a new political society in Egypt. This uprising brings together a new coalition of forces, uniting reconfigured elements of the security state with prominent business people, internationalist leaders, and relatively new (or newly-reconfigured) mass movements of youth, labor, women's, and religious groups. President Husni Mubarak lost his political power on Friday, 28 January. On that night the Egyptian military let Mubarak's ruling party headquarters burn down and ordered the police brigades attacking protesters to return to their barracks. When the evening call to prayer rang out and no one heeded Mubarak's curfew order, it was clear that the old president had been reduced to a phantom authority. In order to understand where Egypt is going, and what shape democracy might take there, we need to set the extraordinarily successful popular mobilizations into their military, economic, and social context. What other forces were behind this sudden fall of Mubarak from power? And how will this transitional military-centered government get along with this millions-strong protest movement?

Many international media commentators—and some academic and political analysts—are having a hard time understanding the complexity of the forces driving and responding to these momentous events. This confusion is driven by the binary "good guys versus bad guys" lenses most use to view this uprising. Such perspectives obscure more than they illuminate. There are three prominent binary models out there and each one carries its own baggage: (1) People versus Dictatorship: This perspective leads to liberal *naïveté* and confusion about the active role of military and elites in this uprising; (2) Seculars versus Islamists: This model leads to a 1980s-style call for "stability" and Islamophobic fears about the containment of the supposedly extremist "Arab street;" or (3) Old Guard versus

83

Frustrated Youth: This lens imposes a 1960s-style romance on the protests but cannot begin to explain the structural and institutional dynamics driving the uprising, nor account for the key roles played by many seventy-year-old Nasser-era figures.

To map out a more comprehensive view, it may be helpful to identify the moving parts within the military and police institutions of the security state and how clashes within and between these coercive institutions relate to shifting class hierarchies and capital formations. I will also weigh these factors in relation to the breadth of new non-religious social movements and the internationalist or humanitarian identity of certain figures emerging at the center of the new opposition coalition.

Western commentators, whether liberal, left, or conservative, tend to see all forces of coercion in non-democratic states as the hammers of "dictatorship" or as expressions of the will of an authoritarian leader. But each police, military, and security institution has its own history, culture, class-allegiances, and, often its own autonomous sources of revenue and support as well. It would take many books to lay this all out in detail, but let me make a brief attempt here. In Egypt the police forces (*al-shurta*) are run by the Interior Ministry, which was very close to Mubarak and the presidency and had become politically co-dependent on him. But police stations gained relative autonomy during the past decades. In certain police stations this autonomy took the form of the adoption of a militant ideology or moral mission: some Vice-Police stations have taken up drug running; some ran protection rackets that squeezed local small businesses. The political dependability of the police, from a bottom-up perspective, is not high. Police grew to be quite self-interested and entrepreneurial on a station-by-station level. In the 1980s, the police faced the growth of "gangs," referred to in Egyptian Arabic as *baltagiya*. These street organizations had asserted self-rule over Cairo's many informal settlements and slums. Foreigners and the Egyptian bourgeoisie assumed the *baltagiya* to be Islamists but they were mostly utterly unideological. In the early 1990s the Interior Ministry decided: "if you can't beat them, hire them." So the Interior Ministry and the Central Security Services started outsourcing coercion to these *baltagiya*, paying them well and training them to use sexualized brutality (from groping to rape) in order to punish and deter female protesters and male detainees, alike. During this period the Interior Ministry also turned the State Security Investigations (SSI) (*mabahith amn al-dawla*) into a monstrous threat, detaining and torturing masses of domestic political dissidents.

Autonomous from the Interior Ministry we have the Central Security Services (Amn al-Markazi). These are the black uniformed, helmeted men that the media refer to as "the police." Central Security was supposed to act as the private army of Mubarak. These are not revolutionary guards or morality brigades like the Basiji, who repressed the Green Movement protesters in Iran. By contrast, the Amn al-Markazi are low-paid and non-ideological. Moreover, at crucial times, these Central Security brigades have risen up en masse against Mubarak, himself, to demand better wages and working conditions. Perhaps if it were not for the sinister assistance of the brutal *baltagiya*, they would not be a very intimidating force. The look of unenthusiastic resignation in the eyes of Amn al-Markazi soldiers as they were kissed and lovingly disarmed by protesters has become one of the most iconic images, so far, of this revolution. The dispelling of Mubarak's authority could be marked precisely to that moment when protesters kissed the cheeks of Markazi officers, who promptly vanished into puffs of tear gas, never to return.

The Armed Forces of the Arab Republic of Egypt are quite unrelated to the Markazi or the police and see themselves as a distinct kind of state altogether. One could say that Egypt is still a "military dictatorship" (if one must use that term) since this is still the same regime that the Free Officers' Revolution installed in the 1950s. But the military has been marginalized since Egyptian President Anwar Sadat signed the Camp David Accords with Israel and the United States. Since 1977, the military has not been allowed to fight anyone. Instead, the generals have been given huge aid pay-offs by the United States. They have been granted concessions to run shopping malls in Egypt, develop gated cities in the desert, and beach resorts on the coasts. And they are encouraged to sit around in cheap social clubs.

These buy-offs have shaped them into an incredibly organized interest group of nationalist businessmen. They are attracted to foreign investment, but their loyalties are economically and symbolically embedded in national territory. As we can see when examining any other case in the region (Pakistan, Iraq, the Gulf), US military-aid money does not buy loyalty to America; it just buys resentment. In recent years, the Egyptian military has felt collectively a growing sense of national duty, and has developed a sense of embittered shame for what it considers its "neutered masculinity," that is, its sense that it was not standing up for the nation's people. The nationalistic Armed Forces want to restore their honor and they are disgusted by police corruption and *baltagiya* brutality. And it seems that the military, now as "national capitalists," have seen themselves as the blood rivals of the neoliberal "crony capitalists" associated with Husni Mubarak's son Gamal, who have privatized anything they can get their hands on and sold the country's assets off to China, the US, and Persian Gulf capital.

Thus we can see why in the first stage of this revolution, on Friday 28 January, there was a very quick "coup" of the military against the police and Central Security, and the disappearance of Gamal Mubarak (the son) and of the detested Interior Minister Habib al-Adly. However, the military is also split by some internal contradictions. Within the Armed Forces there are two elite sub-branches: the Presidential Guard and the Air Force. These remained closer to Mubarak while the broader military turned against him. This explains the contradictory display of the General Chief of the Armed Forces, Muhammad al-Tantawi, wading in among the protesters to show support on 30 January, while at the same time the chief of the Air Force was named Mubarak's new Prime Minister and sent planes to strafe these same protesters. This also explains why the Presidential Guard protected the Radio/Television Building and fought against protesters on 28 January rather than siding with them.

The Vice-President, Omar Suleiman, named on 29 January, was formerly the head of the Intelligence Services (*mukhabarat*). This is also a branch of the military (and not of the police). Intelligence is in charge of externally oriented secret operations, detentions, and interrogations (and, thus, torture and renditions of non-Egyptians). Since Suleiman's *mukhabarat* did not detain and torture as many Egyptian dissidents in the domestic context, they are less hated than the *mabahith*. The Intelligence Services (*mukhabarat*) are in a particularly decisive position as a "swing vote." As I understand it, the Intelligence Services loathed Gamal Mubarak and the "crony capitalist" faction, but are obsessed with stability and have long, intimate relationships with the CIA and the American military. The rise of the military, and within it, the Intelligence Services, explains why all of Gamal Mubarak's business cronies were thrown out of the cabinet on Friday 28 January, and why Suleiman was made interim vice-president (and functions in fact as acting president). This revolution or regime change would be complete at the moment when anti-Mubarak tendencies in the military consolidate their position and reassure the Intelligence Services and the Air Force that they can confidently open up to the new popular movements and those parties coalesced around opposition leader Elbaradei. This is what an optimistic reader might judge to be what Obama and Clinton describe as an "orderly transition."

On Monday, 31 January, we saw Naguib Sawiris, perhaps Egypt's richest businessman and the iconic leader of the developmentalist "nationalist capital" faction in Egypt, joining the protesters and demanding the exit of Mubarak. During the past decade, Sawiris and his allies had become threatened by Mubarak-and-son's extreme neoliberalism and their favoring of Western, European, and Chinese investors over national businessmen. Because their investments overlap with those of the military, these prominent Egyptian businessmen have interests literally embedded in the land, resources, and development projects of the nation. They have become exasperated by the corruption of Mubarak's inner circle.

Paralleling the return of organized national(ist) capital associated with the military and ranged against the police (a process that also occurred during the struggle with British colonialism in the 1930s–1950s) there has been a return of very powerful and vastly organized labor movements, principally among youth. 2009 and 2010 were marked by mass national strikes, nationwide sit-ins, and visible labor protests often in the same locations that spawned this 2011 uprising. And the rural areas have been rising up against the government's efforts to evict small farmers from their lands, opposing the regime's attempts to re-create the vast landowner fiefdoms that defined the countryside during the Ottoman and British colonial periods. In 2008 we saw the one hundred thousand strong April 6 Youth Movement emerge, leading a national general strike. And in 2008 and just in December 2010 we saw the first independent public sector unions emerge. Then just on 30 January 2011 clusters of unions from most of the major industrial towns gathered to form an Independent Trade Union Federation. These movements are organized by new leftist political parties that have no relation to the Muslim Brotherhood, nor are they connected to the past generation of Nasserism. They do not identify against Islam, of course, and do not make an issue of policing the secular–religious divide. Their interest in protecting national manufacturing and agricultural smallholdings, and in demanding public investment in national economic development dovetails with some of the interests of the new nationalist capital alliance.

Thus behind the scenes of the non-governmental organizations (NGOs) and Facebook-driven protest waves, there are huge structural and economic forces and institutional realignments at work. Egypt's population is officially recorded at eighty-one million, but in reality goes well beyond one hundred million since some parents do not register all their children to shield them from serving in the Amn Al-Markazi or army. With the burgeoning youth population now becoming well organized, these social and internet-coordinated movements are becoming very important. They can be grouped into three trends. One group of new movements is organized by and around international norms and organizations, and so may tend toward a secular, globalizing set of perspectives and discourses. A second group is organized through the very active and assertive legal culture and independent judicial institutions in Egypt. This strong legal culture is certainly not a "Western human rights" import. Lawyers, judges, and millions of litigants—men and women, working-class, farmers, and elite—have kept alive the judicial system and have a long unbroken history of resisting authoritarianism and staking rights claims of all sorts. A third group of new social movements represents the intersection of internationalist NGOs, judicial-rights groups, and the new leftist, feminist, rural, and worker social movements. The latter group critiques the universalism of UN and NGO secular discourses, and draws upon the power of Egypt's legal and labor activism, but also has its own innovative strategies and solutions—many of which have been on prominent display on the streets this week.

One final element to examine here is the critical, and often overlooked role that Egypt has played in United Nations and humanitarian organizations, and how this history is coming back to enliven domestic politics and offer legitimacy and leadership at this time. Mohamed ElBaradei, the former director of the United Nations International Atomic Energy Agency has emerged as the consensus choice of the United Democratic Front in Egypt, which is asking him to serve as interim president, and to preside over a national process of consensus building and constitution drafting. In the 2000s, ElBaradei bravely led the IAEA and was credited with confirming that there were no weapons of mass destruction in Iraq, and that Iran was not developing a nuclear weapons program. He won the Nobel Prize for upholding international law against a new wave of wars of aggression and for essentially stopping the momentum for war against Iran. He is no radical and not Egypt's Gandhi; but he is no pushover or puppet of the United States either. For much of the week, standing at his side at the protests has been Egyptian actor Khaled Abou Naga, who has appeared in several Egyptian and US films and who serves as Goodwill Ambassador for UNICEF. This may be much more a UN-humanitarian led revolution than a Muslim Brotherhood uprising. This is a very twenty-first century regime change—utterly local and international simultaneously.

It is a good time to remind ourselves that the first-ever United Nations military-humanitarian peacekeeping intervention, the UN Emergency Force, was created with the joint support of Egypt's Gamal Abdel Nasser and US President Dwight D. Eisenhower (both military men, of course) in 1960 to keep the peace in Gaza and to stop the former colonial powers and Israel from invading Egypt in order to retake the Suez Canal and resubordinate Egypt. Then in the 1990s, Egypt's Boutros Boutros-Ghali served as the Secretary-General of the United Nations. Boutros-Ghali articulated new UN doctrines of state-building and militarized humanitarian intervention. But he got fired for making the mistake of insisting that international human rights and humanitarian law needed to be applied neutrally and universally, rather than only at the convenience of the Security Council powers. Yet Egypt's relationship to the UN continues. Notably, Aida Seif Ad-Dawla, one of the most articulate, brave, and creative leaders of the new generation of Egyptian social movements and feminist NGOs, is a candidate for the high office of UN Rapporteur on Torture. Egyptians have a long history for investing in and supporting international law, humanitarian norms, and human rights. Egyptian internationalism insists on the equal application of human rights principles and humanitarian laws of war even in the face of superpower pressure. In this context, ElBaradei's emergence as a leader makes perfect sense. Although this internationalist dimension of Egypt's "local" uprising is utterly ignored by most self-conscious liberal commentators who assume that international means "the West" and that Egypt's protesters are driven by the politics of the belly rather than matters of principle.

Mubarak is already out of power. The new cabinet is composed of chiefs of Intelligence, Air Force and the prison authority, as well as one International Labor Organization official. This group embodies a hard-core "stability coalition" that will work to bring together the interests of new military, national capital, and labor, all the while reassuring the United States. Yes, this is a reshuffling of the cabinet, but one which reflects a very significant change in political direction. However, none of it will count as a democratic transition until the vast new coalition of local social movements and internationalist Egyptians break into this circle and insist on setting the terms and agenda for transition.

I would bet that even the hard-line leaders of the new cabinet will be unable to resist plugging into the willpower of these popular uprisings, one-hundred million Egyptians strong.

13
Egypt's Revolution 2.0: The Facebook Factor

Linda Herrera[35]

12 February 2011

The call for a Day of Rage on 25 January 2011 that ignited the Egyptian revolution originated from a Facebook page. Many have since asked: Is this a "Facebook Revolution?" It is high time to put this question to rest and insist that political and social movements belong to people and not to communication tools and technologies. Facebook, like cell phones, the internet, and Twitter, do not have agency, a moral universe, and are not predisposed to any particular ideological or political orientation. They are what people make of them. Facebook is no more responsible for Egypt's revolution than Gutenberg's printing press with movable type was responsible for the Protestant Reformation in the fifteenth century. But is it valid to say that neither the Reformation nor the pro-democracy rights' movements sweeping Tunisia, Egypt, Iran, and much of the region would have come about at this juncture without these new tools? Digital communications media have revolutionized learning, cognition, and sociability, and facilitated the development of a new generational behavior and consciousness. And the old guard simply does not get it.

Around the globe, far beyond Egypt and Tunisia, we are witnessing a monumental generational rupture taking place around digital literacy, and the coming of age of Generation 2.0. They take for granted interaction, collaboration, and community-building online. The digital "non-literate" or "semi-literate" tend to be either the very poor lacking the means, access to, or time for digital media, or the older generation, the pre-digitals, who do not see the value in changing their communication habits. Many from the pre-digital generation are quick to deride innovations such as Facebook and Twitter as being tools that indulge the egoistic tendencies of the young or which are colossal time-wasters. While these critiques hold some validity, they capture only one side, and a small side at that, of a complex and epic generational sea change that is underway and that is being facilitated—not driven in some inevitable process—by the availability of new communication technologies and social tools.

A youthful global digital generation is growing in leaps and bounds, and social media, of which Facebook is just one platform, is a decisively important factor in it. Youth use social media for a range of social, academic, political, leisure, personal, creative, sexual, cultural, commercial, and other activities. Some characteristics of this global generation are excessive communication, involving many people in decision-making, multi-tasking, group work, blurring the public and the private, sharing, individual expression, and collective identification. Another important distinction between the generations is that the digital generation takes what media theorist Clay Shirky calls "symmetrical participation" for granted. In other words, they are not passive recipients of media and messages, as in the days when television and print media ruled, but take for granted that they can play a role in the simultaneous production, consumption, interaction with, and dissemination of online content. Youth in the Middle East and North Africa share the features of their global generational counterparts but with some important additions and differences.

In politically authoritarian states like Egypt, Tunisia, and Iran, youth have been fashioning Facebook into a vibrant and inclusive public square. They also use it to maintain their psychological well-being as a space to metaphorically breathe when the controls and constrains of the social world become too stifling. A twenty-two-year-old blogger and avid Facebook user explains, "It's such a release to go on Facebook. I feel so liberated knowing there's a place I can send my thoughts."

THE RISE OF THE "EL-FACE" GENERATION

In October and November 2010 I was in Egypt conducting research with university students in Alexandria and Cairo from diverse social class backgrounds on their media use. Many of them were using a new colloquial term, "El-Face" ("The Face") when talking about Facebook. These Facebook users carry traits of being politically savvy, bold, creative, outward looking, group regulating, and ethical. And their numbers are fast growing. In March 2008 there were some 822,560 users. After the Arabic version of Facebook was launched in March of 2009 usership jumped. By 1 July 2010 there were some 3,581,460 Facebook members,[36] making for an increase of 357.2 percent over a two-year period. The site has become increasingly Arabized, though many users show dexterity in using both English and Arabic.

In the months running up to the parliamentary elections in November 2010 there was much speculation about a possible shutdown of Facebook. Adult pundits in the more mainstream media (semi-governmental newspapers, and popular Arabic television talk shows) took up the cause of Facebook. They expressed their paternalistic concern about the potentially corrupting force of Facebook on the youth in a familiar moral panic mode. On her popular television talk show, for instance, Hala Sarhan lamented the lawlessness of Facebook, asserting it to be a dangerously free zone in need of restrictions. Others argued that without adult supervision, youth could be lured and tricked by dangerous elements into sedition (*fitna*). They worried that Facebook was fueling sectarian tensions between Christians and Muslims that could lead to violence.

These public Facebook experts are mainly sexagenarian and septuagenarian educators, policymakers, government officials, and academics of a pre-digital age. They are using a pre-digital political cognition and institutional understanding to discuss new media today, and they are direly off the mark. Drawing on older understandings of the media, they view Facebook as the new space for ideological control, the place to capture the minds and hearts of the citizens—like state television but accessible through the internet. Some of them are sincere in their worry that dangerous elements, like radicals and criminals, will try to befriend youth on Facebook and lure them in subversive activities. Others are clearly more interested in maintaining raw power and want to find effective ways to keep youth in their fold and under their thumbs. The ones vying to maintain control of the youth reason that if youth are spending time on Facebook, then all the government needs to do is go in and set up its propaganda machinery there, capture and control the hearts and minds of youth on Facebook; it is that simple. The government has established a presence on Facebook, though a somewhat pitiful one, setting up pages for the National Democratic Party (158 people "like" it), Gamal Mubarak (the page has been removed since the uprising), Husni Mubarak, and other government figures and causes. But these are not picking up traction. The youth are not buying it, and the more the regime people interlope into Facebook, the more they lose legitimacy.

The community of "El-Face" is developing a cultural, political, and ethical universe of its own. It has its own codes and is a regulated space to some degree. There are certain red lines, as Hoda and Amir, both twenty-one-year-old university students at Alexandria University say should not be crossed: you should not use the space to insult each other's religion, for pornography or sexual harassment, for advertising or selling things, for spreading false rumors, or for spying. When a Facebook friend crosses these lines, others intervene by way of posting a corrective comment on their wall, starting a conversation on the post in question, or by defriending them.

Last October many youths were worried that the government would close down Facebook. In discussions with a group of students from the Political Science department at Cairo University, they explained that the government feared the flurry of critical political activity that would invariably precede an election. Though many expressed that turning off Facebook would be akin to suffocating them, as one young man put it, it would be like "blocking the air to my lungs," they insisted they would not ease up on their pre-election Facebook activities. These included mocking the president, his son, the system, and the whole electoral process. They stood defiant. A twenty-one-year-old female student proclaimed, "We don't care! We're not afraid of them. What are they going to do, arrest millions of us?"

Their Facebook activities also included a commitment to demanding justice for the brutal killing of one of their own, Khaled Said. It was striking last October how every youth I encountered in and out of the university was talking about Khaled Said. His story, which came out of Facebook, not *Al Jazeera*, the newspaper, or any other media, has by now received much international coverage. The events leading to Khaled's killing originated when he supposedly posted a video of two police officers allegedly dividing the spoils of a drug bust. This manner of citizen journalism has become commonplace and youth is getting more emboldened to expose the festering corruption of a police force that acts with impunity. On 6 June 2010, as Khaled Said was sitting in an internet café in Alexandria, two police officers entered and asked him for his ID. He refused to produce it and they proceeded to drag him away and allegedly sadistically beat him to his death as he pleaded for his life in the view of witnesses. The officers claimed that Khaled died of suffocation after swallowing a packet of drugs. His family released a photograph to an activist of the broken, bloodied, and disfigured face from Khaled's corpse. This photo, and a portrait of the gentle, soft-skinned face of the living Khaled, went viral. The power of photographic evidence combined with eyewitness accounts and popular knowledge of police brutality left no doubt in anyone's mind that he was senselessly and brutally murdered by police officers, the very people who are supposed to act in the interest of public safety.

A Facebook page, "We are all Khaled Said" was set up and we now know that activists from the group 6 of April Youth Movement, and Google executive Wael Ghoneim who is becoming a national hero as instigator of the Day of Rage (see below), were involved in this. The page led to a movement, first for justice to bring the killers to court to pay for their crime, and then, something much bigger. On the heels of the Tunisian revolution and fleeing of the dictator Zine El Abidine Ben Ali, the "We are all Khaled Said" group called for a Day of Rage, a march against "Torture, Corruption, Poverty and Unemployment" for 25 January 2011, the date the regime designated to "celebrate" the police. Scores of Facebook users changed their profile pages to show their support for this march.

The uprising took off in a way that no one had anticipated. On 27 January, Facebook, along with telephones and internet, went off. Nevertheless the revolution grew and persisted. When the internet came back up on 2 February there was a conspicuous fluttering of pro-Mubarak profile pictures scattered around college students' friends' lists that had the uncanny look of Iron Curtain style propaganda posters. Though this is pure speculation, it is highly likely that a committee from the Ministry of Information got together to try to decipher how to infiltrate and conquer Facebook. Operating on a pre-digital mindset, they designed and released a poster about 25 January to appropriate the Day of Rage and rewrite history. The poster reads: "Day of Allegiance to the Leader and Commander. We are all with you and our hearts are with you. The campaign for Mubarak, Security for Egypt."

Another profile photo, which showed up among university students after the blackout, was one that reads: "With all my heart I love you Egypt, and I love you oh President."

These posters lacked the spontaneity, show of emotion, creativity of the other profile posters, and smelled of infiltrators, something not well tolerated in the Facebook public square. This pitiable attempt to turn back history and try to capture the allegiance of youth through manipulating Facebook was a sign of how desperately out-of-touch the regime has become. It is also indicative that it has lost its grip on the ideological state apparatuses, and once that occurs there is nothing left at its disposal but the use of force—or surrender.

Within three days these images of 25 January as a day of loyalty to the President disappeared from Facebook. On 8 Feburary, a new profile photo among Egyptian youth began spreading spontaneously. It was the image of one of their own, Wael Ghoneim, on the day of his release after disappearing for twelve days (he was detained by police). The image is from a game-changing interview conducted with him on 7 February 2011 on a satellite channel. This interview, where he admits to organizing the initial protest, set to rest doubts that the revolution was the plot of enemy foreign agents. His display of emotion for the martyrs of the revolution touched the nation, and beyond. That may very well have been the nail in the coffin of the state's media wars.

What is happening in Egypt is not a Facebook revolution. But it could not have come about without the Facebook generation, Generation 2.0, who are taking it, and with their fellow citizens, making history.

14
Egypt's Three Revolutions: The Force of History Behind this Popular Uprising

Omnia El Shakry[37]

6 February 2011

When the Egyptian Uprising of 2011 began, we heard media pundits, friends, and colleagues milling about in search of apt metaphors to describe the mass protests and revolution in Egypt. In so far as "history" was mobilized in these discussions, it was generally as repetition or analogy. Hence: the Berlin Wall; Tiananmen Square; the first Palestinian Intifada; the Iranian Revolution; the Paris Commune; and the French Revolution, as well as Egypt's own 1919 and 1952 revolutions. But do these vivid comparisons conceal more than they reveal? Indeed, one could argue that one of the most striking aspects of the contemporary media discussions surrounding Mubarak's Egypt is the absence of any real sense of history. It is not enough to fill this void with rhetorical comparisons and poetic license.

While an understanding of the process of privatization, economic marginalization, consumerism, and structural adjustment that we refer to as "neoliberalism" is crucial to understanding the contemporary unfolding of events, particularly in terms of the existence of vast economic inequalities and the impoverishment of the demographic masses, a focus on neoliberalism alone fails to address the question of the historical relationship in Egypt between the ruler and the ruled. What would a longer-term historical perspective, a deeper structural view of the events in Egypt look like? Focusing on popular protest and mobilization in Egypt's 1919, 1952, and 2011 revolutions, I focus on the internal dynamics of, and discontinuities between, each of these revolutions, characterizing them as nationalist, passive, and popular, respectively.

A PRIMER IN EGYPTIAN HISTORY

1919 Revolution

Egypt, occupied by Great Britain in effect since 1882, achieved its independence from colonial rule only in the aftermath of sustained protests. In the wake of the 1919 revolution, and after two years of stalled negotiations, the British abolished martial law and granted Egypt unilateral nominal independence from colonial rule in February 1922. Despite this, the British continued to maintain control over the security of imperial communications, the defense of Egypt, the protection of foreign interests and minorities, and the Sudan. The 1919 revolution had two stages: the violent and short period of March 1919 that involved large-scale mobilizations by the peasantry in rural areas that were suppressed by British military action; and the protracted phase beginning in April 1919 that was less violent and more urban, with the large-scale participation of students, workers, lawyers, and other professionals.

The economic and political crises of World War I, experienced in Egypt as the expansion of the colonial–state bureaucracy, the forced conscription of Egyptians, the state appropriation of cotton production, and the forcible provision of supplies for British troops resulted in a crisis of political control. In the competition for political power that ensued between the *effendiyya* (middle-class nationalists) and the colonial regime, the Wafd or delegation Party (Egypt's major nationalist political party throughout much of the first half of the twentieth century) and the 1919 rebellion were born. But was 1919 a unified uprising in which peasants, workers, and politicians coalesced in support of a nascent nationalism when the British failed to give Egypt its promised independence?

In the urban context, 1919 represented the consolidation of a labor movement (trade unions, labor activism, nationwide strikes) that was forged at the intersection of national and class-consciousness. Such labor movements were enveloped within the anti-colonial nationalism of the time, while more radical leftist groups were unable to gain a foothold in the context of the Wafd's moderate nationalist platform of removing foreign economic and political exploitation. Further, the mobilization of the peasantry and momentary subversions of the rural order did not in fact materialize into a wide-scale peasant revolution; the Wafd (striving for political sovereignty and parliamentary democracy) continued to oscillate throughout its tenure between populism and social conservatism. Some have argued that the nationalist call for "independence, freedom, and justice" could not have held the same meaning for peasants, who sought to liberate themselves from the colonization of their economic life by landowning interests, as it might have had for the urban intelligentsia. Whatever perspective we adopt, it is clear that the 1919 revolution meant different things to different segments of the population. But, at least from the perspective of the emergent dominant national ruling elements, it did not aim at the radical transformation of the social structure or class relations, but rather at the assertion of territorial nationalism in the face of British colonialism. In other words, it was a nationalist revolution.

1952 Revolution

Prior to 1952, the Palace, the Wafd, and a multitude of oppositional groups ranging from Communists to Muslim Brothers characterized Egypt's political landscape. This intensely variegated ideological landscape was marked by a commitment to economic nationalism and a desire to rid Egypt completely of foreign control, in particular the presence of British troops on Egyptian soil. Further, the larger question of complete political independence was cross-hatched with the economic difficulties faced by the majority of the population. The years after 1929 were the years of the worldwide economic depression, and during this time agricultural wages fell by an estimated forty percent. The 1930s were characterized by wide-scale unrest with the increased activity of peasants, workers, and trade unions, student agitation, and demonstrations.

Egypt's 1952 military coup and revolution led by Gamal Abdel Nasser and the Free Officers ousted Egypt's decadent monarch, King Faruq, and put Muhammed Naguib as president of the new republic in his place. An understanding of this period of Egyptian history helps to clarify somewhat the ambivalent attitudes toward the military in Egypt, and the initial expectations of protestors that the military would help protect them from Egypt's violent security and police services.

Interpretations of Nasserism have centered on the state apparatus. Discussions have focused on the authoritarian-bureaucratic state structure, characterized by a highly state-centralized process of socioeconomic development, a corporatist patrimonial state bourgeoisie, a single-party system bolstered by a repressive state apparatus, and a populist nationalist ideology. This political formation, interpreters argue, proved incapable of radically restructuring the Egyptian state, society, and economy, as signaled by the failure to build a fully industrialized, capitalist or socialist, liberal democratic nation-state. This is the classic "authoritarian military dictatorship model" we have been reading about in the press. But such a monolithic model fails to adequately capture the complexity of Nasserism.

Nasserism was equally characterized by an ideology and practice of social welfare, premised upon the state apparatus as arbiter not only of economic development, but also of social welfare. Such a social welfare model was premised on an ethical covenant between the people and the state, a social contract in which the possibility of revolutionary or democratic political change was exchanged for piecemeal social reform and the amelioration of the conditions of the working classes. It was further based on a view of "the people" (al-sha'ab) as the generative motor of history and as resources of national wealth (the motor of its development, as it were), and an interventionist policy of social planning and engineering. Social welfare, of course, should not be understood as a benevolent process whereby the state shepherds citizens in their own welfare. Rather, it entails the social and political process of reproducing particular social relations, often based on violence and coercion, at least partly to minimize class antagonisms.

Such a model was predicated on a foundational violence which can be traced back to the spring of 1954 during which a united front of Wafdists, Communists, Muslim Brothers, and others demanded an end to the military dictatorship and a return to civilian rule and the constitutional system. Demonstrators, led largely by students, flooded the streets in March as they surrounded Abdin Palace and demanded political freedoms. After a series of negotiations and political maneuvers, Nasser consolidated his rule, becoming premier and president of the Revolutionary Command Council in April 1954. Politically, the regime sought to contain the possibility of any broad-based popular movement, hence the attempts at co-optation and the violence perpetrated against its two main ideological contenders, the Muslim Brothers and the Marxist-Communist Left, as well as the abolition of political parties and organizations. Similarly, the regime's policy toward labor activism and trade unionism was characterized by a two-pronged policy of co-optation of labor and union leaders through their incorporation into the state apparatus and extensive revisions of labor legislation (for example, legislating job security and improved material benefits). Autonomous labor action and the political independence of the trade unions were curtailed by a legislative ban on all strikes, laws on the arbitration and conciliation of labor disputes, and a new trade-union law. This provides an important larger context for understanding the historical significance of the newly emerging independent public sector trade unions active in the 2011 protests.

The Nasser regime concentrated its efforts on dismantling the old landed aristocracy through agrarian reform and co-opting the old industrial bourgeoisie to further its own aims of large-scale national industrialization. The new class that emerged and characterized the state public sector, however, was a "state bourgeoisie," made up of the new class of technocrats together with older elements of the industrial, financial, and commercial bourgeoisie who worked their way into the public sector.

Nasserism thus represented the formation of a state capitalist class, the liquidation of its main ideological rivals, and the suppression of popular mobilization from below even as it was coupled with a powerful social welfare ideology and a charismatic anti-imperialist rhetoric (immensely strengthened by Egypt's mobilization in the face of a tripartite foreign aggression and nationalization of the Suez Canal). This social welfare model can be seen as a Faustian bargain in which "the people" exchanged democratic political liberties and a more radical restructuring of the social order for social welfare programs that deflected attention away from the restructuring of class relations, by emphasizing the piecemeal and palliative reforms for the laboring classes. In other words, it was a passive revolution.

1974 Neoliberalism

The demise of Nasserism was a complex product of both internal ideological and class contradictions within the regime's pursuit of socialism, and of external political conflicts, namely, the 1967 war with Israel. The liberalization policies of Egypt's Infitah (opening) were inaugurated by Anwar Sadat's Presidential Working Paper of October 1974, in an attempt to create a transition to a free-market economy. Infitah paved the way for a different set of international and domestic relations, characterized by a general rapprochement with foreign capital and a strengthening of the private sector through a series of governmental concessions, that is to say, a dual internal and external process of liberalization.

Among the marked features of Infitah, enabled through a series of regulatory interventions as well as a shift in global conditions of capitalism, were the creation of a favorable environment for foreign investment projects (usually in the form of joint ventures), through a new investment law containing various privileges (such as tax exemptions for foreign ventures). Foreign trade was decentralized and liberalized, signaling the end of the public-sector monopoly on foreign trade and the opening up of the economy to foreign goods through the private sector. Egypt received an expansive influx of international aid, and the government liberalized its fiscal policy. Public holding companies previously in charge of planning, coordinating, and supervising the public sector were abolished, and there was a concomitant decentralization in state economic planning. The state's control over public enterprise was weakened through a liberalization of wage and employment regulations, facilitated in part by a redefinition of the public sector, thereby leaving private-sector management with more autonomy.

The predominant agents and architects of Infitah came from a combination of numerous different groups. One of these groups consisted of members of the old industrial bourgeoisie who had managed to insinuate themselves into the state apparatus after the 1952 revolution. A second broad group consisted of members of the state technocratic bourgeoisie that emerged under Nasser (the upper stratum of the bureaucratic and managerial elite, high-ranking civil servants, army officers and directors, managers of public-sector companies, and so on). A third category consisted of the emerging commercial bourgeoisie whose financial activities were opened up by Infitah—wholesale traders, contractors, and importer–exporters. This, in part, explains the complexity of the military apparatus divided between the elite echelon of the military (given their involvement in capital accumulation during Infitah) and rank and file soldiers, and the economic gap between them.

With the IMF-mandated structural adjustment policies of the 1990s, these processes were greatly intensified with the concentration of capital into ever fewer hands. Thus large business oligopolies, such as those of the Sawiris family—local agents of Hewlett Packard and Microsoft, founded Orascom in 1976, a family business that has prospered greatly under Husni Mubarak. Naguib Sawiris, one of the individuals put forth for the so-called "Committee of the Wise," built his fortune, it is worth recalling, at the intersection of government (both civilian and military) contracts and ties with private banks. This is the distinction currently being drawn by many business leaders in Egypt between nationalist and neoliberal capital, in an effort to bolster their legitimacy. Such an attempt at legitimacy, however, will not be easily digested in a post-Mubarak era by those who have suffered immensely under this neoliberal regime. With neoliberalism has come the retreat of the state sector and the elimination of many of the safety net social welfare benefits won by the working classes under Nasser. The immense polarization of wealth, drastically exacerbated since the 1990s, has left many Egyptians consumed by the search for food, shelter, and human dignity, with an estimated forty percent living below or near the poverty line. Crucially, these policies have not gone entirely uncontested as demonstrated by the Bread Riots in 1977 and the Central Security Services (*amn al-markazi*) riots in 1986.

2011

Rather than view the spontaneous eruption of protests on 25 January 2011 as signaling the absence of ideological or political cohesion, we can view it instead as the product of an unprecedented historical assemblage of complex forces and contradictions. As Mohammed Bamyeh noted in *The Egyptian Revolution: First Impressions from the Field*,[38] the revolt has been characterized by a large degree of spontaneity, marginality, a call for civic government, and an elevation of political grievances above economic ones. Thus, we have seen the participation of a wide range of groups with differing ideological orientations but nonetheless coherent and articulate in their demand for an end to the *ancien régime*. These have included strong elements of trade unions and other labor movements, inspired by the 2006 strike in Mahalla. But labor movements do not exhaust the types of players involved—including, of course, the new social movements (whether leftist, feminist, legal-judicial, NGO based, or social-media galvanized organizations) discussed in Paul Amar's "Why Mubarak is Out,"[39] as well as the Muslim Brotherhood, who have publicly declared their commitment to a civil and pluralist government.

Those on the ground in Egypt know what they want: an end to Mubarak, an end to the emergency laws that have strangled political expression in Egypt since 1981; a civil government with a new constitution guaranteeing elections and the curtailment of political power; and trials for those involved in the massacres of the protesters. Despite the machinations of the West, it is clear that what will simply not do is an insinuation of *ancien régime* forces of any kind into a post-Mubarak Egypt, whether neoliberal robber barons, counter-revolutionaries, or political opportunists. The voices from Tahrir, Alexandria, Mahalla, Suez, and Minya must be heard in their call for a "reversal of the relationship of forces." In other words, this is a people's revolution.

15
The Architects of the Egyptian Uprising and the Challenges Ahead

Saba Mahmood[40]

14 February 2011

On 11 February 2011, President Husni Mubarak finally resigned, less than twenty-four hours after he refused the protesters' demand "Go Mubarak Go!" that has been echoing across Egypt for the past two weeks. The euphoria that swept the protestors gathered in Tahrir Square cannot be described in words: all those tuned into *Al Jazeera* (Arabic or English) around the world witnessed one of the most moving events of our lifetime as Egyptian demonstrators roared in victory over what they had achieved. The reverberations of this historic turn of events are being felt all over the region as Algerians and Yemenis take defiantly to the streets chanting the same slogan that emanated from Egypt: "The People Want the Regime to Fall!" If the Tunisians inspired the Egyptians to rise and scream "Enough!" then the Egyptians might go down in history for giving a new meaning to Maya Angelou's prophetic cry at a time when no one expected it:

> You may write me down in history
> With your bitter, twisted lies,
> You may trod me in the very dirt
> But still, like dust, I rise...I rise. I rise. I rise.

The question that continues to occupy many observers of Middle East politics is: How could a people chided for their political apathy manage to achieve such an organized and seismic mobilization? How could a country that only a month ago was headed down an escalating path of inter-religious and sectarian strife, unite to create one of the most seismic events of our times in the Arab world? Alexandria, where only a month ago a well-executed car bomb killed twenty-three Christians, has been host to demonstrations in which Copts and Muslims have prayed together, and churches, along with mosques, have served as centers for the congregation of protestors. As millions have poured out on the streets, not one church has been attacked nor a sectarian incident reported. All this despite the fact that the Coptic Pope, Shenouda III, announced his unequivocal support for Mubarak on the first day of protest.

So what are the factors that have birthed this historic expression of synergy and resistance to burst onto the scene? There is no doubt that the Tunisian uprising served as a catalyst that inspired Egyptians to take to the streets. The Tunisian government, as everyone knew in the Arab world, was more repressive than the Egyptian government: if the Tunisians could oust their brutal dictator why not the Egyptians? However, even though Tunisia might have lit the fuse, there are a number of critical transformations in Egypt's social and political landscape that account for this massive uprising that has shaken the Middle East to its core. In recent years, Egyptians have increasingly made recourse to demonstrations and street politics to voice their demands and shake the cultivated torpor of their rulers. Since 2004, Egypt has witnessed a growing number of strikes and sit-ins staged by health and textile workers, pharmacists, doctors, lawyers, judges, transportation and postal workers, and even real estate tax collectors. Their demands? Better wages and working conditions against the grueling poverty while the rich got conspicuously richer, public institutions that once served ordinary Egyptian fell into disrepair, and jobs dwindled.

Despite these strikes that escalated over 2009 and 2010 there were few victories: most of them were either ignored by the government or brutally broken and suppressed. There were rare and slim victories largely due to the sheer tenacity of the protestors:[41] such as the government agreeing to raise the minimum wage to four hundred Egyptian pounds (about seventy US dollars)—nearly four times what it had been before but hardly enough to address the rising inflation costs. Or the formation of two independent trade unions and an independent trade federation, an unprecedented break from the suffocating hold the government has exercised over labor activism since 1957.

These partially successful strikes created a simultaneous sense of despair and possibility noted by those who cared to listen to the beat and rhythms of Egyptian street life. Among them was Hossam Hamalawy—a prominent Egyptian blogger and consummate ethnographer of the Egyptian street—who posted the following[42] as far back as 31 October 2010: "There is something in the air in

Egypt. It could be Mubarak's Autumn of Fury, as I and increasingly many people around me sense. Not a day passes without reading or hearing about a strike. No one knows when the explosion is going to happen, but it seems everyone I meet or bump into today feel it's inevitable."

The fact that this simmering anger was most potently felt by "the youth" who were the worst victims of the Mubarak regime was widely acknowledged by Egyptians of all ages. Once again, Hamalawy quotes an aging old man addressing two young women in the same post: "I think your time now is worse than the time of the war [referring to the 1967 war with Israel]...And who said the war is over? The real war only started. Look at the poverty, corruption and hunger. It's an internal war. It's worse than the war with Israelis. May God bless you and give you strength. Your generation is at war. It's a disaster, a bigger disaster than our generation faced."

As if this was not enough, the legendary brutality of the security police had become only more entrenched, violent, and impudent over the last several years. The victims of their torture were not simply political activists, but ordinary citizens picked up for one reason or another, tortured and humiliated for crimes they never committed. "*Amn ad-dawla*" was and is the most hated institution of the country—far more than the underpaid police force that was ubiquitous in Egyptian cities but which vanished into thin air in the first twenty-four hours of the protests. Khalid Said, the blogger and internet café operator, who was beaten to death publicly and subsequently became the icon of the pro-democracy movement is only one example of the legendary ferociousness of the security police. It is no wonder that the protestors have resoundingly rejected Vice-President Omar Suleiman as an honest arbiter for any transition to democracy—the Obama administration's insistence notwithstanding: he served not only as the former head of security police but also the chief collaborator in the CIA's rendition program in Egypt.

One might ask at this point, however horrible these conditions might have been, they are no different than many other Third World countries—such as Pakistan, India, and Indonesia—where people continue to suffer but do not topple the governments responsible for their misery. What made Mubarak's rule distinct, however, is that there was no aspect of the system that did not carry Mubarak's personal imprimatur. In India and Pakistan, for example, people might blame the corrupt political culture of their country or the institution of the military but there is no stable symbol of power that has persisted over the past three decades. In Egypt, Mubarak's personage symbolizes the repression of the system at large—not unlike Saddam Hussein in Iraq. Hence the insistence with which Egyptians cried in unison: "*Irhal Irhal, Ya Mubarak*" (Leave, Leave, O Mubarak!). The personal sense of rage ordinary Egyptians felt toward Mubarak is captured in these prescient remarks made by a cab driver to Hossam Hamalawy (posted 31 October 2010):

> This country is going on fire soon, very soon. We can't take it anymore… It's Husni Mubarak himself who is responsible for this situation we have reached… Mubarak is responsible… There will be another bread initfada [uprising], like that of 1977. And this time we will burn the country down. We will not burn the cars, buses or shops. These are ours. No, no. We will burn them. We will burn this government. We will burn down the police stations.

What made the Mubarak regime distinct from Saddam's Iraq, however, was the careful balance he maintained over the years between keeping his authoritarian and increasingly brutal control over power while granting limited freedoms to his restive populace in order to maintain Egypt's pride-of-place as America's number one ally in the Arab Middle East. Whenever the White House has made noises about "bringing democracy to the region," Mubarak has minimally loosened his leash to abide by such empty calls. One important effect of this has been the creation of space, however limited, for Egyptians to engage in civil and political rights activism through bursts of protests (nothing like the scope we are witnessing now) and through NGOs and legal aid organizations.

The most conspicuous and relatively new face of this activism in the last five years has been the blogosphere. The current Egyptian rebellion has been often dubbed as the "Facebook Revolution." There are countless articles and commentaries documenting how social networking websites have played a crucial role in mobilizing the sit-ins and demonstrations. Yet one needs to think beyond the techno-centric view that characterizes these commentaries. The technology after all is available worldwide but has seldom been mobilized to serve the ends it is currently serving in Egypt. Who exactly is "the Facebook generation" in Egypt? What work has it done to substantively transform the political culture of Egypt?

The Egyptian blogosphere first came into existence in Egypt around 2004 with the birth of the Kifaya! (Enough!) movement and its sizeable demonstrations which were brutally crushed and its leaders jailed by Mubarak. Many of the prominent young bloggers date the beginning of their online commentary and activism to these demonstrations. By 2005, the numbers of blogs had jumped from a handful to the hundreds and are now estimated in the thousands. Currently there are over three million Facebook members—still a relatively small percentage of the eighty million population. Despite their relatively small numbers in a country that is also overwhelmingly illiterate, these bloggers have put a face and a voice to the ubiquitous police brutality that most Egyptians have experienced but seldom saw reported or condemned in the news media. YouTube videos, shot with shaky cell phone cameras, of innocent Egyptians tortured and violated for crimes they never committed were a regular feature of these blogs and Facebook pages. By 2008 when I was living in Cairo, the blogs had become a surrogate form of journalism given the censorship laws in Egypt.

These activist blogs cut across the Egyptian political spectrum—Islamists, nationalists, secularists, liberals, and leftists. Their political demands have coalesced around a four-point agenda that has now become the beacon call of the current demonstrations: (1) an end to Mubarak's rule; (2) rejection of the "succession" of Mubarak's son, Gamal Mubarak, as president; (3) expansion of political freedoms and the creation of democratic institutions that would yield to free elections; (4) an immediate stop to, and persecution of perpetrators of, state violence. These were demands behind which the vast majority of Egyptians could unite—regardless of their religious and political affiliations. In a country where Muslim on Christian violence was increasing at an alarming rate, the activist blogs provided a rare space where a new ethics of political engagement could be forged. Why? As Charles Hirschkind notes,[43] this was partly due to the political platform outlined above that cut across customary political divides, and partly due to the form of address and protocol internal to the individualized medium of the blogosphere itself. The blog and Facebook format, with its personal profile page, allows for individual bloggers to fashion a political persona that transcends the Islamist-versus-secular divide, allowing young women and men to write critically about hot political issues. Once a topic would acquire a momentum in the blogosphere (such as sexual harassment or HIV-AIDS), participants who might "not have been inclined to address such an issue were led to engage the issue openly as a condition of sustaining the arena of discourse" they had collectively forged.

Initially, the vast numbers of activist bloggers were secular, but they were soon joined by those sympathetic to the Islamists. These Islamic-minded bloggers were, like their secular compatriots, equally disillusioned with the aged leadership of the political parties that purported to represent them. They too were tired of the inertia, fear, and the claustrophobia that characterized these older formations. Hence they broke with the geriatric wing of the groups they had traditionally belonged to and joined hands with those Egyptians who in the political language of the 1990s would have been deemed their enemy. For example, the young bloggers who wrote for the website Islamonline (initially a traditional Islamic website) were a part of this generation. As their contributions grew more critical, the funders of Islamonline from the Gulf states decide to shut down the website in 2010—convincing many of these Islamic bloggers that the only effective avenue of change would have to be nationally manufactured.

This transformed political consciousness that cuts across the old divide between Islamists and secularists was on ample display among the demonstrators who coalesced around issues most essential to their collective flourishing. A clear example of this was evident on 3 February 2011, when the Mubarak regime set loose its armed thugs on the crowds in Cairo and Alexandria. As Hossam Bahgat, one of the leading figures in the human rights movement in Egypt, reported in an interview[44] on the show *Democracy Now!*, members of the Muslim Brotherhood were at the forefront of protecting the protesters from these goons, standing guard against the attacks throughout the weekend as the attacks escalated. Asked if he would oppose an alliance with the Brotherhood, Bahgat responded that while he continues to disagree with their stance on a number of issues (including women and minority rights), as a civil rights activist he cannot in good conscience oppose their full participation in the political process. They are, just as much as he and his comrades, an integral part of the revolution unfolding in Egypt, committed to the same set of goals.

Much has been said about the absence of central leadership among the protesters, an absence that makes the task of forging a new government difficult if not impossible. Some commentators in the US State Department and the media have gone so far as to suggest that figures from the Mubarak regime must be retained in order to ensure order and stability. But this line of argument is wrong for two important reasons. One, it is precisely because there was no central and singular political authority that called or orchestrated this rebellion that it has been so effective. Indeed if it was the work of the coalition of the largely corrupt existing political parties, it would have been infested with the symptoms of the dying order. Two, many of the young men and women who have participated in this rebellion are not simply naive and idealistic individuals who do not know what they are doing or talking about.

As to how sophisticated and politically astute some of the architects of this revolution are may be ascertained by an early op-ed piece written for *The Washington Post* by Hossam Bahgat and Soha Abdelaty, both leading figures in the civil rights movement. In the early moments of the Egyptian uprising, they laid out the constitutional transformations that needed to be put into place before Mubarak resigned[45] in order to secure the conditions for free and fair elections—including an end to the thirty-year-old state of emergency and the annulment of a series of constitutional decrees passed by Mubarak that made elections a sham. Bahgat and Abdelaty are representative of young human rights activists who have cut their teeth on Egypt's compromised judicial and political system. Given the suffocating hold the government has exercised over the political process, Egypt's brightest minds concerned with improving the affairs of their country turned to non-governmental and legal aid organizations to pursue goals of economic and social justice over the past two decades. In the process, these young men and women learned the ins and outs of the maze of Egypt's legal and political structure—they are not extraneous to the business of the Realpolitik of the country but are an essential part of it. One needs to think of them as giving real direction to the country's future—rather than as bystanders who birthed the demonstrations and must now withdraw to their offices to let the politicians do their business.

With Mubarak's resignation, these architects of the Egyptian revolution face a series of daunting tasks—key among them is ensuring not only civil and political rights for the vast majority of Egyptians but also economic justice for the millions who exist on less than two dollars a day (over forty percent of Egyptians lived under the poverty line). While there is no doubt that the new order in Egypt must be based on civil and political liberties characteristic of a liberal democracy, what is equally at issue in a country like Egypt is an economic system that serves only the rich of the country at the expense of the poor and the lower and middle classes. The vast majority of public institutions and services in Egypt have been allowed to fall into a dismal state of disrepair since the time of Gamal Abdel Nasser when they were first established. Countless Egyptians die in public hospitals from lack of medical care and staff; Egyptian public universities are no longer capable of delivering the education they once boasted of. Lack of housing, jobs, and basic social services, while real wages decline and the inflation rate escalates, make everyday life impossible to bear for most Egyptians. It is these conditions that prompted the workers—from the industrial and service sector—to stage strikes and sit-ins over the past ten years mentioned earlier. These workers have been an integral part of the demonstrations over the past two weeks in Egypt, and various unions formally joined the protests in the days immediately preceding Mubarak's resignation—prompting some to suggest that this was a turning point in the evolution of the protest.

While a new liberal democratic regime might ensure civil and political rights (which itself would be a serious achievement in the months to come), it is unclear whether the reforms necessary for addressing economic injustice and inequality can be implemented within this framework. Since the 1970s, the Egyptian economy has been increasingly subject to neoliberal economic reforms by the World Bank, the IMF and USAID at the behest of the United States government. Egyptian elites have been beneficiaries of, and partners in, these American-driven reforms. Will this sector of Egyptian society accommodate the demands of the poor, the unemployed, and the workers who have so far been equal partners in their struggle against political corruption and autocracy? Will the protestors in Tahrir Square continue to fight for economic justice even as they gain political and civil rights in the months to come?

The role the US government plays in all of this will be enormously consequential. While the Obama administration has reluctantly yielded to the Egyptian people's demand for real democratic reform, it is highly doubtful that this administration will tolerate the restructuring of US economic interests in Egypt and in the region more generally. Even in his domestic policy, Obama has shown no signs whatsoever that he is willing to reign in the rapacious tendencies of neoliberal capital. There is no reason to believe that he would do otherwise when it comes to the suffering of non-Americans whose votes do not even count in his re-election. As a result, substantive economic reform in the lives of ordinary Egyptians would have to come at their own behest—despite the opposition they will likely face from the Egyptian elites and from the larger Euro-American neoliberal order. All this sounds immensely difficult however, based on what we have seen in the last few weeks, Egyptians have indeed achieved the impossible. At the very minimum, they have set into motion a new political calculus that cannot be ignored by the ruling classes of Egypt. All eyes are riveted on this momentous struggle of our time.

16
The Revolution Against Neoliberalism

Walter Armbrust[46]

23 February 2011

On 15 February 2011 at 9:45am a comment was posted on the wall of the *Kullina Khalid'id*[47] ["We Are All Khalid Said"] Facebook page, administered by the now very famous Wael Ghonim, referring to a news item reporting that European governments were under pressure to freeze bank accounts of recently deposed members of the Mubarak regime. The comment said: "Excellent news...we do not want to take revenge on anyone...it is the right of all of us to hold to account any person who has wronged this nation. By law we want the nation's money that has been stolen...because this is the money of Egyptians, forty percent of whom live below the poverty line." By the time I unpacked this thread of conversation twenty-one hours later, 5,999 people had clicked the "like" button, and about 5,500 had left comments. I have not attempted the herculean task of reading all five thousand odd comments (and no doubt more are being added as I write), but a fairly lengthy survey left no doubt that most of the comments were made by people who clicked the "like" icon on the Facebook page. There were also a few by regime supporters, and others by people who dislike the personality cult that has emerged around Wael Ghonim.

This Facebook thread is symptomatic of the moment. Now that the regime of Husni Mubarak has fallen, an urge to account for its crimes and to identify its accomplices has come to the fore. The chants, songs, and poetry performed in Midan al-Tahrir always contained an element of anger against *haramiyya* (thieves) who benefited from regime corruption. Now lists of regime supporters are circulating in the press and blogosphere. Mubarak and his closest relatives (sons Gamal and Alaa) are always at the head of these lists. Articles on their personal wealth[48] give figures as low as two to three billion dollars[49] to as high as seventy billion dollars (the higher number was repeated on many protesters' signs). Ahmad 'Izz, the General Secretary of the deposed National Democratic Party and the largest steel magnate in the Middle East, is supposed to be worth eighteen billion dollars; Zohayr Garana, former Minister of Tourism, thirteen billion dollars; Ahmad al-Maghrabi, former Minister of Housing, eleven billion dollars; former Minister of the Interior Habib al-Adly, much hated for his supervision of an incredibly abusive police state, also managed to amass eight billion dollars—not bad for a lifetime civil servant. Such figures may prove to be inaccurate. They may be too low, or maybe too high, and we may never know precisely because much of the money is outside of Egypt, and foreign governments will only investigate the financial dealings of Mubarak regime members if the Egyptian government makes a formal request for them to do so. Whatever the true numbers, the corruption of the Mubarak regime is not in doubt. The lowest figure quoted (in *The New York Times*) for Mubarak's personal wealth, of "only" two to three billion dollars, is damning enough for a man who entered the Air Force in 1950 at the age of twenty-two, embarking on a sixty-year career in "public service."

The hunt for the regime cronies' billions may be a natural inclination of the post-Mubarak era, but it could also lead efforts to reconstitute the political system astray. The generals who now rule Egypt are obviously happy to let the politicians take the heat. Their names were not included in the lists of the most egregiously corrupt individuals of the Mubarak era, though in fact the upper echelons of the military have long been beneficiaries of a system similar to (and sometimes overlapping with) the one that enriched civilian figures who were much more prominent in the public eye, such as Ahmad 'Izz and Habib al-Adly.

To describe the blatant exploitation of the political system for personal gain as corruption misses the forest for the trees. Such exploitation is surely an outrage against Egyptian citizens, but calling it corruption suggests that the problem amounts to aberrant behavior from a system that would otherwise function smoothly. If this were the case then the crimes of the Mubarak regime could be attributed simply to bad character: change the people and the problems go away. But the real problem with the regime was not necessarily that high-ranking members of the government were thieves in an ordinary sense. They did not necessarily steal directly from the treasury. Rather they were enriched through a conflation of politics and business under the guise of privatization. This was less a violation of the system than business as usual. Mubarak's Egypt, in a nutshell, was a quintessential neoliberal state.

Although neoliberalism is now a commonly used term, it is still worth pausing a moment and thinking about what it means. In his *A Brief History of Neoliberalism*, social geographer David Harvey outlined "a theory of political economic practices that proposes that human well-being can best be advanced by liberating individual entrepreneurial freedoms and skills within an institutional framework characterized by strong private property rights, free markets, and free trade." Neoliberal states guarantee, by force if necessary, the "proper functioning" of markets; where markets do not exist (for example, in the use of land, water, education, health care, social security, or environmental pollution), then the state should create them. Guaranteeing the sanctity of markets is supposed to be the limit of legitimate state functions, and state interventions should always be subordinate to markets. All human behavior, and not just the production of goods and services, can be reduced to market transactions. The market becomes an end in and of itself, and since the only legitimate function of states is to defend markets and expand them into new spheres, democracy is a potential problem insofar as people might vote for political and economic choices that impede the unfettered operation of markets, or that reserve spheres of human endeavor (education, for example, or health care) from the logic of markets. Hence a pure neoliberal state would philosophically be empowered to defend markets even from its own citizens. As an ideology neoliberalism is as utopian as communism. The application of utopian neoliberalism in the real world leads to deformed societies as surely as the application of utopian communism did.

Two observations about Egypt's history as a neoliberal state are in order. First, Mubarak's Egypt was considered to be at the forefront of instituting neoliberal policies in the Middle East (not un-coincidentally, so also was Ben Ali's Tunisia). Secondly, the reality of Egypt's political economy during the Mubarak era was very different than the rhetoric, as was the case in every other neoliberal state from Chile to Indonesia. Political scientist Timothy Mitchell published a revealing essay about Egypt's brand of neoliberalism in his *Rule of Experts: Egypt, Techno-Politics, Modernity*, in particular his chapter entitled "Dreamland"—named after a housing development built by Ahmad Bahgat, one of the Mubarak cronies now discredited by the fall of the regime—and a version of which was published in MERIP's *Middle East Report*.[50] The gist of Mitchell's portrait of Egyptian neoliberalism was that while Egypt was lauded by institutions such as the International Monetary Fund as a beacon of free-market success, the standard tools for measuring economies gave a grossly inadequate picture of the Egyptian economy. In reality the unfettering of markets and the agenda of privatization were applied unevenly at best. The only people for whom Egyptian neoliberalism worked "by the book" were the most vulnerable members of society, and their experience with neoliberalism was not a pretty picture. Organized labor was fiercely suppressed. The public education and the health care systems were gutted by a combination of neglect and privatization. Much of the population suffered stagnant or falling wages relative to inflation. Official unemployment was estimated at approximately 9.4 percent last year (and much higher for the youth who spearheaded the 25 January Revolution), and about twenty percent of the population is said to live below a poverty line, defined as two dollars per day per person.

For the wealthy, the rules were very different. Egypt did not so much shrink its public sector, as neoliberal doctrine would have it, as it reallocated public resources for the benefit of a small and already affluent elite. Privatization provided windfalls for politically well-connected individuals who could purchase state-owned assets for much less than their market value, or monopolize rents from such diverse sources as tourism and foreign aid. Huge proportions of the profits made by companies that supplied basic construction materials like steel and cement came from government contracts, a proportion of which in turn were related to aid from foreign governments. Most importantly, the very limited function for the state recommended by neoliberal doctrine in the abstract was turned on its head in reality. In Mubarak's Egypt business and government were so tightly intertwined that it was often difficult for an outside observer to tease them apart. Since political connections were the surest route to astronomical profits, businessmen had powerful incentives to buy political office in the phony elections run by the ruling National Democratic Party. Whatever competition there was for seats in the Peoples' Assembly and Consultative Council took place mainly within the NDP. Non-NDP representation in parliament by opposition parties was strictly a matter of the political calculations made for a given elections: let in a few independent candidates known to be affiliated with the Muslim Brotherhood in 2005 (and set off tremors of fear in Washington); dictate total NDP domination in 2010 (and clear the path for an expected new round of distributing public assets to "private" investors).

The political economy of the Mubarak regime was shaped by many currents in Egypt's own history, but its broad outlines were by no means unique. Similar stories can be told throughout the rest of the Middle East, Latin America, Asia, Europe, and Africa. Everywhere neoliberalism has been tried, the results are similar: living up to the utopian ideal is impossible; formal measures of economic activity mask huge disparities in the fortunes of the rich and poor; elites become "masters of the universe," using force to defend their prerogatives, and manipulating the economy to their advantage, but never living in anything resembling the heavily marketized worlds that are imposed on the poor.

The story should sound familiar to Americans as well. For example, the vast fortunes of the Bush era cabinet members Donald Rumsfeld and Dick Cheney, through their involvement with companies like Halliburton and Gilead Sciences, are the product of a political system that allows them—more or less legally—to have one foot planted in "business" and another in "government" to the point that the distinction between them becomes blurred. In the United States, politicians in office are supposed to divest their holdings in companies that would create conflicts of interest with their political positions, but this has become barely even a formality in recent decades. Politicians move from the office to the boardroom to the lobbying organization and back again. Cheney and Rumsfeld simply refused to cooperate with the conflict of interest rules, and both profited handsomely from companies that received privileged access to the government, including (in the case of Halliburton) contracts for privatized military services during the invasion and occupation of Iraq. As neoliberal dogma disallows any legitimate role for government other than guarding the sanctity of free markets, recent American history has been marked by the steady privatization of services and resources formerly supplied or controlled by the government. But it is inevitably those with closest access to the government who are best positioned to profit from government campaigns to sell off the functions it formerly performed. It is not just Republicans who are implicated in this systemic corruption. Clinton-era Secretary of Treasury Robert Rubin's involvement with Citigroup does not bear close scrutiny. Lawrence Summers gave crucial support for the deregulation of financial derivatives contracts while he was Secretary of Treasury under Clinton, and profited handsomely from companies involved in the same practices while he worked for Obama (and of course deregulated derivatives were a key element in the financial crisis that led to a massive Federal bailout of the entire banking industry).

So in Egyptian terms, when the General Secretary of the NDP Ahmad 'Izz cornered the market on steel and was given contracts to build public–private construction projects, or when former Minister of Parliament Tal'at Moustafa purchased vast tracts of land for the upscale Madinaty housing development without having to engage in a competitive bidding process (but with the benefit of state-provided road and utility infrastructure), they may have been practicing corruption logically and morally. But what they were doing was also as American as apple pie, at least within the scope of the past two decades.

However, in the current climate the most important thing is not the depredations of the deposed Mubarak regime cronies. It is rather the role of the military in the political system. It is the army that now rules the country, albeit as a transitional power, or so most Egyptians hope. No representatives from the upper echelons of the Egyptian military appear on the various lists of old-regime allies who need to be called to account. For example, the headline of the 17 February print edition of *Ahrar*, the press organ of the Liberal Socialist Party, was emblazoned with the headline "Financial Reserves of the Corrupt Total 700 Billion Pounds [about $118 billion] in 18 Countries." But the article did not say a single word about the place of the military in this epic theft. The military were nonetheless part of the crony capitalism during the Mubarak era. After relatively short careers in the military, high-ranking officers are rewarded with such perks as highly remunerative positions on the management boards of housing projects and shopping malls. Some of these are essentially public-sector companies transferred to the military sector when IMF-mandated structural adjustment programs required reductions in the civilian public sector. But the generals also receive plums from the private sector. Military spending itself was also lucrative because it included both a state budget and contracts with American companies that provided hardware and technical expertise. The United States provided much of the financing for this spending under rules that required a great deal of the money to be recycled to American corporations, but all such deals required middlemen. Who better to act as an intermediary for American foreign aid contracts than men from the very same military designated as the recipient of the services paid for by this aid? In this respect the Egyptian military-industrial complex was again stealing a page from the American playbook; indeed, to the extent that the Egyptian military benefited from American foreign aid, Egypt was part of the American military-industrial complex, which is famous for its revolving-door system of recycling retired military men as lobbyists and employees of defense contractors.

Consequently it is almost unthinkable that the generals of the Supreme Military Council will willingly allow more than cosmetic changes in the political economy of Egypt. But they could be compelled to do so unwillingly. The army is a blunt force, which is not well suited to controlling crowds of demonstrators. The latest statement of the Supreme Military Council reiterated both the legitimacy of the pro-democracy movement's demands, and the requirement that demonstrations cease so that the country can get back to work. If demonstrations continue to the point that the Supreme Military Council feels it can no longer tolerate them, then the soldiers who will be ordered to put them down (indeed, in some accounts[51] were already ordered to put them down early in the revolution and refused to do so) with deadly force, are not the generals who were part of the Mubarak-era corruption, but conscripts. Pro-democracy demonstrators and their sympathizers often repeated the slogans "the army and the people are one hand," and "the army is from us." They had the conscripts in mind, and many were unaware of how stark the differences were between the interests of the soldiers and those of the generals.

Between the conscripts and the generals there is a middle-level professional officer corps whose loyalties have been the subject of much speculation. The generals, for their part, want to maintain their privileges, but not to rule directly. Protracted direct rule leaves the officers of the Supreme Military Council vulnerable to challenges from other officers who were left on the outside. Also, direct rule would make it impossible to hide the fact that the elite officers are not actually a part of the "single hand" composed of the people and the (conscript) army. They are instead logically in the same camp as Ahmad 'Izz, Safwat al-Sharif, Gamal Mubarak, and Habib al-Adly—precisely the names on those lists making the rounds of regime members and cronies who should face judgment.

Ultimately the intense speculation about how much money the Mubarak regime stole, and how much the people can expect to pump back into the nation, is a red herring. If the figure turns out to be fifty billion dollars or five-hundred billion dollars, it will not matter if Egypt remains a neoliberal state dedicated (nominally) to free-market fundamentalism for the poor, while creating new privatized assets that can be recycled to political insiders for the rich. If one seeks clues to how deeply the 25 January Revolution will restructure Egypt, it would be better to look at such issues as what sort of advice the interim government of generals solicits in fulfilling its mandate to re-make the Egyptian government. The period of military government probably will be as short as advertised, followed, one hopes, by an interim civilian government for some specified period (at least two years) during which political parties are allowed to organize on the ground in preparation for free elections. But interim governments have a way of becoming permanent. One sometimes hears calls to set up a government of "technocrats" that would assume the practical matters of governance. "Technocrat" sounds neutral—a technical expert who would make decisions on "scientific" principle. The term was often applied to Youssef Boutros-Ghali, for example, the former Minister of the Treasury, who was one of the Gamal Mubarak boys brought into the cabinet in 2006—ostensibly to smooth the way for the President's son to assume power. Boutros-Ghali is now accused of having appropriated 450 million Egyptian pounds for the use of Ahmad 'Izz. I once sat next to Boutros Boutros-Ghali at a dinner during one of his trips abroad, and had the opportunity to ask him when the Egyptian government would be ready to have free elections. His response was to trot out the now discredited regime line that elections were impossible because actual democracy would result in the Muslim Brotherhood taking power. Conceivably Boutros-Ghali will beat the charge of specifically funneling the state's money to Ahmad 'Izz. But even if he proves innocent of the most blatant excesses of the Mubarak regime, as a key architect of Egypt's privatization programs he cannot possibly have been unaware that he was facilitating a system that enabled the 'Izz steel empire while simultaneously destroying Egypt's educational and health care systems.

The last time I encountered the word "technocrat" was in Naomi Klein's book *The Shock Doctrine*—a searing indictment of neoliberalism which argues that the free-market fundamentalism promoted by economist Milton Friedman (and immensely influential in the United States) is predicated on restructuring economies in the wake of catastrophic disruptions because normally functioning societies and political systems would never vote for it. Disruptions can be natural or man-made, such as...revolutions. The chapters in *The Shock Doctrine* on Poland, Russia, and South Africa make interesting reading in the context of Egypt's revolution. In each case when governments (communist or apartheid) collapsed, "technocrats" were brought in to help run countries that were suddenly without functional governments, and create the institutional infrastructure for their successors. The technocrats always seemed to have dispensed a form of what Klein calls "shock therapy"—the imposition of sweeping privatization programs before dazed populations could consider their options and potentially vote for less ideologically pure options that are in their own interests.

The last great wave of revolutions occurred in 1989. The governments that were collapsing then were communist, and the replacement in that "shock moment" of one extreme economic system with its opposite seemed predictable and to many even natural. One of the things that make the Egyptian and Tunisian Revolutions potentially important on a global scale is that they took place in states that were already neoliberalized. The complete failure of neoliberalism to deliver "human well-being" to a large majority of Egyptians was one of the prime causes of the Revolution, at least in the sense of helping to prime millions of people who were not connected to social media to enter the streets on the side of the pro-democracy activists. But the 25 January Revolution is still a "shock moment." Even from the activists who led the Revolution we hear calls to bring in the technocrats.[52] They presumably mean a caretaker government to keep the trains running and the bills being paid while a government can be formed. But we are told every day that the situation is fluid, and that there is a power vacuum in the wake of not just the disgraced NDP, but also in the largely discredited legal opposition parties, which played no role whatsoever in the 25 January Revolution. But in the context of a dazed population and a sputtering economy, calling for a government of technocrats is a bit like inviting the fox back into the hen house. The generals are probably happy with all the talk about reclaiming the money stolen by the regime, because the flip side of that coin is a related current of worry about the state of the economy. The notion that the economy is in ruins—tourists staying away, investor confidence shattered, employment in the construction sector at a standstill, many industries and businesses operating at far less than full capacity—could well be the single most dangerous rationale for imposing cosmetic reforms that leave the incestuous relationship between governance and business intact. Or worse, if the pro-democracy movement lets itself be stampeded by the "economic ruin" narrative, structures could be put in place by "technocrats" under the aegis of the military transitional government that would tie the eventual civilian government into actually quickening the pace of privatization. Ideologues, including those of the neoliberal stripe, are prone to a witchcraft mode of thinking: if the spell does not work, it is not the fault of the magic, but rather the fault of the shaman who performed the spell. In other words, the logic could be that it was not neoliberalism that ruined Mubarak's Egypt, but the faulty application of neoliberalism. Trial balloons for this witchcraft narrative are already being floated outside of Egypt. *The New York Times* ran an article on 17 February[53] casting the military as a regressive force opposed to privatization and seeking a return to Nasserist statism. The article pits the ostensibly "good side" of the Mubarak regime (privatization programs) against "bad old Arab nationalist statism," completely ignoring the fact that while the system of military privilege may preserve some public-sector resources transferred from the civilian economy under pressure of IMF structural adjustment programs, the empire of the generals is hardly limited to a ring-fenced quasi-underground public sector. Officers were also rewarded with private-sector perks; civilian political/business empires mixed public and private roles to the point that what was government and what was private were indistinguishable; both the military and civilians raked in rents from foreign aid. The generals may well prefer a new round of neoliberal witchcraft. More privatization will simply free up assets and rents that only the politically connected (including the generals) can acquire. Fixing a failed neoliberal state by more stringent applications of neoliberalism could be the surest way for them to preserve their privileges.

A neoliberal fix would, however, be a tragedy for the pro-democracy movement. The demands of the protesters were clear and largely political: remove the regime; end the emergency law; stop state torture; hold free and fair elections. But implicit in these demands from the beginning (and decisive by the end) was an expectation of greater social and economic justice. Social media may have helped organize the kernel of a movement that eventually overthrew Mubarak, but a large element of what got enough people into the streets to finally overwhelm the state security forces was economic grievances that are intrinsic to neoliberalism. These grievances cannot be reduced to grinding poverty, for revolutions are never carried out by the poorest of the poor. It was rather the erosion of a sense that some human spheres should be outside the logic of markets. Mubarak's Egypt degraded schools and hospitals, and guaranteed grossly inadequate wages, particularly in the ever-expanding private sector. This was what turned hundreds of dedicated activists into millions of determined protestors. If the 25 January Revolution results in no more than a retrenchment of neoliberalism, or even its intensification, those millions will have been cheated. The rest of the world could be cheated as well. Egypt and Tunisia are the first nations to carry out successful revolutions against neoliberal regimes. Americans could learn from Egypt. Indeed, there are signs that they already are doing so. Wisconsin teachers protesting against their governor's attempts to remove the right to collective bargaining have carried signs equating Mubarak with their governor. Egyptians might well say to America: *'uqbalek* ("May you be next").

17
Egypt's Orderly Transition: International Aid and the Rush to Structural Adjustment

Adam Hanieh[54]

29 May 2011

Although press coverage of the events in Egypt may have dropped off the front pages, discussions of the post-Mubarak period continues to dominate the financial news. Over the past few weeks, the economic direction of the interim Egyptian government has been the object of intense debate in the World Bank, International Monetary Fund (IMF) and European Bank for Reconstruction and Development (EBRD). US President Barack Obama's 19 May speech[55] on the Middle East and North Africa devoted much space to the question of Egypt's economic future—indeed, the sole concrete policy advanced in his talk concerned US economic relationships with Egypt. The G8 meeting in France[56] held on 26 and 27 May continued this trend, announcing that up to twenty billion US dollars would be offered to Egypt and Tunisia. When support from the Gulf Arab states is factored into these figures, Egypt alone appears to be on the verge of receiving around fifteen billion dollars in loans, investment, and aid from governments and the key international financial institutions (IFI).

The press releases accompanying the announcement of these financial packages have spoken grandly of "the transition to democracy and freedom," which, as several analysts have noted, conveniently obfuscates the previous support of Western governments for the deposed dictators in Tunisia and Egypt. This article argues, however, that a critique of these financial packages needs to be seen as much more than just a further illustration of Western hypocrisy. The plethora of aid and investment initiatives advanced by the leading powers in recent days represents a conscious attempt to consolidate and reinforce the power of Egypt's dominant class in the face of the ongoing popular mobilizations. They are part of, in other words, a sustained effort to restrain the revolution within the bounds of an "orderly transition"[57]—to borrow the perspicacious phrase that the US government repeatedly used following the ousting of Husni Mubarak.

At the core of this financial intervention in Egypt is an attempt to accelerate the neoliberal program that was pursued by the Mubarak regime. The IFI financial packages ostensibly promote measures such as "employment creation," "infrastructure expansion," and other seemingly laudable goals, but, in reality, these are premised upon the classic neoliberal policies of privatization, de-regulation, and opening to foreign investment. Despite the claims of democratic transition, the institutions of the Egyptian state are being refashioned within this neoliberal drive as an enabling mechanism of the market. Egypt is, in many ways, shaping up as the perfect laboratory of the so-called post-Washington Consensus, in which a liberal-sounding "pro-poor" rhetoric—principally linked to the discourse of democratization— is used to deepen the neoliberal trajectory of the Mubarak-era. If successful, the likely outcome of this—particularly in the face of heightened political mobilization and the unfulfilled expectations of the Egyptian people—is a society that at a superficial level takes some limited appearances of the form of liberal democracy but, in actuality, remains a highly authoritarian neoliberal state dominated by an alliance of the military and business elites.

'ACCELERATING STRUCTURAL ECONOMIC REFORMS'

The most important point to note about the aid packages promised to Egypt is that they do not in any way represent a break from the logic encapsulated in previous economic strategies for the region. In a report to the 26–27 May G8 Summit, the IMF clearly summarized this logic, noting[58] that:

> Overcoming high unemployment will require a substantial increase in the pace of economic growth...Achieving such growth rates will entail both additional investment and improved productivity. While some increases in public investment may be required, for instance to improve the quality of infrastructure and services in less developed rural areas, the key role will have to be played by the private sector, including by attracting foreign direct investment. Thus, government policies should support an enabling environment in which the private sector flourishes.

The core argument expressed in this statement is essentially the same message that the IMF and World Bank have been pushing in decades of reports on the Egyptian and Middle East economies. Egypt's problems stem from the weakness of the private sector and the "rent-seeking" of state officials. The solution is to open Egypt's markets to the outside world, lift restrictions on investment in key sectors of the economy, liberalize ownership laws, end subsidies to the poor for food and other necessities, and increase market competition. By allowing unfettered markets to operate freely, the private sector will be the key engine of growth and, through this harnessing of entrepreneurial initiative, lead to the creation of jobs and prosperity.

Of course these ideas are simply a restatement of the basic premises of neoliberalism, but it is imperative to acknowledge their continuity with earlier plans—the promised aid to Egypt consciously aims at achieving a specific outcome in line with previous neoliberal strategy. The concrete policy implications of this were most clearly spelt out in a flagship World Bank report published in 2009, *From Privilege to Competition: Unlocking Private-Led Growth in the Middle East and North Africa*.[59] The report prescribes steps to be taken by all governments in the Middle East, including:

1. opening protected sectors such as retail and real estate, which have barriers to foreign investors...;
2. reducing tariff bands and non-tariff barriers;
3. removing protection of state-owned firms by enforcing hard budget constraints and exposing them to open competition; and
4. eliminating anti-export biases.

In order to encourage foreign investment, governments should eliminate "high minimum capital requirements and restrictions on foreign ownership" and, in countries where state-owned banks exist, they should "engage in open and transparent privatization."

These are the types of policies that we can expect to see in Egypt as this aid begins to flows—in fact, they are the essential prerequisites for the receipt of this financial support. The mechanisms of this conditionality are discussed later; at this stage, it is simply important to note that there has been an unassailable link established between aid and the fulfillment of neoliberal reforms. As the Institute of International Finance (IIF), a policy and lobby organization that brings together the largest financial institutions in the world, noted[60] in early May:

As momentous as the current security and political restructuring challenges may be, it is absolutely critical that the transition authorities...place a high priority on deepening and accelerating structural economic reforms...transition and subsequent governments must articulate a credible medium-term reform and stabilization framework...[and] need to focus on creating the legal and institutional environment for fostering entrepreneurship, investment, and market-driven growth.

The IIF went on to bluntly identify this acceleration of structural adjustment as the "context" in which aid to Egypt would be provided.

"RED TAPE" AND INSTITUTIONAL REFORM

In addition to these standard neoliberal prescriptions, the other element to the policy logic guiding IFI financial support concerns institutional reform. This reflects a wider shift in the developmental strategy of the IFIs since the 1990s, in which more emphasis has been placed on linking the function of markets with their institutional governance. Within this context, the World Bank and other institutions have emphasized notions such as the "rule of law," "decentralization," "good governance," "separation of the legislative and executive," and so forth, which supposedly aim at reducing the rent-seeking capabilities of state officials, and guarantee greater transparency in economic affairs.

This emphasis on institutional reform partly reflects a problem of perception faced by the IFIs. The embracing of the issues of "governance" and "democracy" is explicitly designed to ensure greater legitimacy for neoliberalism, particularly in the wake of the disastrous decades of the 1980s and 1990s where the open advocacy of structural adjustment wreaked havoc on much of the South. This policy shift, however, does not represent a turn away from the logic of neoliberalism. Rather, it actually serves to reinforce this logic by tailoring institutions to the needs of the private sector, and removing any ability of the state to intervene in the market. In the Middle East, where authoritarian regimes have been the norm, these calls for institutional reform can be easily portrayed as democratic (and, indeed, they are explicitly framed within a discourse of democratization). In reality they are profoundly anti-democratic. By limiting democracy to the "political" sphere and expanding the notion of freedom to include "markets," they obfuscate the necessary relations of power within the market, and explicitly block the ability of states to determine the use, ownership, and distribution of their economic resources. Democratic control of the economy is thus precluded as a violation of "good governance."

In the case of Egypt, the discourse of institutional reform has allowed neoliberal structural adjustment to be presented not just as a technocratic necessity—but as the actual fulfillment of the demands innervating the uprisings. In this sense, neoliberal ideology attempts to reabsorb and fashion dissent in its own image, through rendering Egypt's uprisings within a pro-market discourse. This fundamental message has been repeatedly emphasized by US and European spokespeople over the last weeks: this was not a revolt against several decades of neoliberalism, but rather a movement against an intrusive state that had obstructed the pursuit of individual self-interest through the market.

Perhaps the starkest example of this discursive shift was the statement made by World Bank President Robert Zoellick at the opening of a World Bank meeting on the Middle East in mid-April. Referring to Mohamed Bouazizi, the young peddler from a Tunisian market place who set himself on fire and became the catalyst for the uprising in Tunisia, Zoellick remarked:[61]

> the key point I have also been emphasizing and I emphasized in this speech is that it is not just a question of money. It is a question of policy...keep in mind, the late Mr. Bouazizi was basically driven to burn himself alive because he was harassed with red tape...one starting point is to quit harassing those people and let them have a chance to start some small businesses.

In this discursive reframing of the uprisings, the massive protests that overthrew Mubarak and Zine El Abidine Ben Ali occurred due to the absence of capitalism rather than under its normal functioning. In an ideological sense, this reframing directly confronts the popular aspirations that have arisen through the course of the struggle in Egypt. The political demands heard on the streets of Egypt today—to reclaim wealth that was stolen from the people, offer state support and services to the poor, nationalize those industries that were privatized, and place restrictions on foreign investment—can be either disregarded or portrayed as "anti-democratic." Precisely because Egypt's uprising was one in which the political and economic[62] demands were inseparable and intertwined, this effort to recast the struggle as "pro-market" is, in a very real sense, directly aimed at undercutting and weakening the country's ongoing mobilizations.

THE MECHANISMS OF STRUCTURAL ADJUSTMENT

This understanding of the basic logic presupposed in the IFI financial packages allows us to turn to the precise mechanisms through which structural adjustment is unfolding. There are two common elements to all the financial support offered to Egypt to date: an extension of loans (that is, an increase in Egypt's external debt) and promised investment in so-called Public–Private Partnerships (PPPs). Both these elements are tied to Egypt's implementation of structural adjustment. Strategically, it appears that the initial focus of this structural adjustment will be the privatization of Egypt's infrastructure and the opening of the economy to foreign investment and trade through PPPs (these are discussed below). In addition to the US government, World Bank and IMF, the other main institutional actor in this process is the European Bank for Reconstruction and Development (EBRD).

Debt

Currently Egypt's external debt runs at around thirty-five billion US dollars and over the last decade the country has been paying around three billion dollars a year in debt service.[63] From 2000–2009, Egypt's level of debt increased by around fifteen percent, despite the fact that the country paid a total of 24.6 billion dollars in debt repayments over the same period. Egypt's net transfers on long-term debt between 2000–2009, which measures the total difference between received loans and repayments, reached 3.4 billion dollars. In other words, contrary to popular belief, more money actually flows from Egypt to Western lenders than vice versa. These figures demonstrate the striking reality of Egypt's financial relationship with the global economy—Western loans act to extract wealth from Egypt's poor and redistribute it to the richest banks in North America and Europe.

Of course, the decision to borrow this money and enter into this "debt trap" was not made by Egypt's poor. The vast majority of this debt is public or publicly-guaranteed (around eighty-five percent), that is, debt that was taken on by the Mubarak government with the open encouragement of the IFIs. Egypt's ruling elite—centered around Mubarak and his closest coterie—profited handsomely from these transactions (estimated in the many billions). This is indicative of the fact that much of Egypt's debt is what development economists call "odious debt"—debt that has been built up by a dictatorial regime without regard to the needs of the population. Mubarak does not hold sole responsibility for this process. The World Bank, IMF, and many other lenders continued to encourage this borrowing (and to praise Egypt's economic direction under Mubarak) precisely because it was such a profitable enterprise.

This is the essential background context to the discussions around Egypt's foreign debt. In his 19 May speech, US President Barack Obama made much of a promise to relieve Egypt of up to one billion dollars in its debt obligations. Obama described[64] this as the US government's attempt to support "positive change in the region... through our efforts to advance economic development for nations that are transitioning to democracy." In addition to this monetary support, Obama also promised to urge the World Bank, IMF and other countries to help "stabilize and modernize" Egypt and "meet its near-term financial needs."

Putting aside the hubris of this speech, Obama's offer needs to be understood accurately. Contrary to what has been widely reported in the media, this was not a forgiveness of Egypt's debt. It is actually a debt-swap—a promise to reduce Egypt's debt service by one billion dollars, provided that money is used in a manner in which the US government approves. This debt-swap confirms the relationship of power that is inherent in modern finance. The United States is able to use Egypt's indebtedness as a means to compel the country to adopt the types of economic policies described above. Obama was very explicit about what this meant—stating[65] that:

> the goal must be a model in which protectionism gives way to openness, the reigns of commerce pass from the few to the many, and the economy generates jobs for the young. America's support for democracy will therefore be based on ensuring financial stability, promoting reform, and integrating competitive markets with each other and the global economy.

This same policy language has been clearly articulated alongside the loans promised to Egypt by the World Bank and the International Monetary Fund (IMF). On 12 May, Caroline Atkinson, Director of the External Relations Department at the IMF, announced that the IMF was studying a request from the Egyptian government for three to four billion US dollars of loans and would "visit Cairo shortly to begin discussions with the Egyptian authorities on an arrangement."

Indicating that these loans would come with conditions, Atkinson noted[66] that "the size and scope of Fund support will be defined as discussions progress." An advisor to Egyptian Finance Minister Samir Radwan confirmed this,[67] declaring "How the money will be spent will undergo a process of negotiation." On 24 May this conditionality was set out following an announcement by the World Bank and the IMF that they would provide 4.5 billion US dollars to Egypt over two years. Noting that "reforms were as important as money," World Bank President Robert Zoellick explicitly linked[68] the initial one billion dollars "to governance and openness reforms with a further $1 billion available next year dependant on progress." The remaining 2.5 billion dollars would be invested in development projects and private sector loans (see below).

Unless these loans are refused and the existing debt repudiated, Egypt will find itself in a cul-de-sac from which there is little chance of escape. Foreign debt is not a neutral form of "aid" but an exploitative social relation established between financial institutions in the North and countries in the South. Trapped in this relationship, countries become dependent upon a continuous stream of new loans in order to service previously accumulated long-term debt. It is a means to deepen the extraction of wealth from Egypt and—precisely because of the continued dependency on financial inflows—serves to chain Egypt to further structural adjustment measures. The Egyptian people are being punished for an indebtedness that they did not create, and that punishment consists of being locked into even greater indebtedness by the institutions that put them there in the first place.

Foreign Investment and Public–Private Partnerships (PPPs)

Also in his 19 May speech, Obama pledged one billion dollars in investments through a US institution known as the Overseas Private Investment Corporation (OPIC). The OPIC's mandate is to support US business investment in so-called emerging markets; it provides guarantees for loans (particularly in the case of large projects) or direct loans for projects that have a significant proportion of US business involvement and may face political risk. Perhaps emblematic of the OPIC's activities was its first investment in Afghanistan following soon after the invasion of that country by NATO-led forces in 2001—a new Hyatt Hotel in Kabul that would be used as "a platform for business persons"[69] visiting the country. The OPIC was also a key partner[70] in encouraging the free-market ideology that underpinned the economic policy of the Coalition

Provisional Authority (CPA) in Iraq following the US-led invasion of 2003. A fundamental part of this process, which is likely to be replicated in the case of Egypt, was a focus on encouraging Iraqi business to become increasingly dependent upon US-owned finance capital through the support of US bank and finance lending to small and medium enterprises in the country. The US government openly asserts[71] the link between the OPIC's and US foreign policy's objectives. This is well encapsulated in the organization's slogan— "support[ing] U.S. investment in emerging markets worldwide, fostering development & the growth of free markets".

Because the OPIC's investment depends upon reducing barriers to foreign capital and accelerating the privatization of state-owned enterprises, its activities are predicated upon, and help to reinforce, the extension of the neoliberal program described above. In the case of Egypt, this is likely to take place primarily through the use of US government funds to establish Public–Private Partnerships (PPPs). A PPP is a means of encouraging the outsourcing of previously state-run utilities and services to private companies. A private company provides a service through a contract with the government—typically, this may include activities such as running hospitals or schools, or building infrastructure such as highways or power plants. For this, they receive payments from the government or through the users of the service (such as highway tolls). PPPs are thus a form of privatization, which, in the words of one of their foremost proponents, Emanuel Savas (in his *Privatization in the City*), is "a useful phrase because it avoids the inflammatory effect of 'privatization' on those ideologically opposed."

The OPIC's intervention in Egypt has been explicitly tied to the promotion of PPPs. An OPIC press release, for example, that followed soon after Obama's speech, noted that the one billion dollars promised[72] by the US government would be used "to identify Egyptian government owned enterprises investing in public–private partnerships in order to promote growth in mutually agreed-upon sectors of the Egyptian economy."

The focus on PPPs, however, is illustrated even more clearly in the investment promised by another international financial institution, the European Bank for Reconstruction and Development (EBRD). The EBRD was established at the time of the fall of the Soviet Union, with the goal of transitioning Eastern Europe to a capitalist economy. As the EBRD's President Thomas Mirow put it[73] in the lead up to the Bank's discussions on Egypt: "The EBRD was created in 1991 to promote democracy and market economy, and the historic developments in Egypt strike a deep chord at this bank."

The EBRD is shaping up to be one of the lead agents of the neoliberal project in Egypt. On 21 May, EBRD shareholders agreed to lend up to 3.5 billion dollars to the Middle East, with Egypt the first country earmarked for receipt of loans in the first half of 2012. This will be the first time since its establishment that the EBRD has lent to the Middle East. Catherine Ashton, the European Union foreign policy chief, has remarked that the EBRD could provide one billion euros annually to Egypt, which would give the institution an enormous weight in the Egyptian economy—as a point of comparison, the total investment value of all PPP projects in Egypt from 1990–2008 was 16.6 billion dollars.

Anyone who has any illusions about the goals of the EBRD's investment in Egypt would do well to read carefully the *EBRD 2010 Transition Report*.[74] The report presents a detailed assessment of the East European and ex-Soviet Republics, measuring their progress on a detailed set of indicators. These indicators are highly revealing: (1) Private sector share of GDP; (2) Large-scale privatization; (3) Small-scale privatization; (4) Governance and enterprise restructuring; (5) Price liberalization; (6) Trade and foreign exchange system; (7) Competition policy; (8) Banking reform and interest rate liberalization; (9) Securities markets and non-bank financial institutions; and (10) Overall infrastructure reform.* Only countries that score well on these indicators are eligible for EBRD loans. A research institute that tracks the activity of the EBRD, *Bank Watch*,[75] noted in 2008 that a country cannot achieve top marks in the EBRD assessment[76] without the implementation of PPPs in the water and road sectors.

The EBRD intervention thus likely augurs a massive acceleration of the privatization process in Egypt, most likely under the extension of PPPs. The current Egyptian government has given its open consent to this process. Indeed, at the EBRD Annual General Meeting on 20–21 May where Egypt was promised funds, a spokesperson of the Egyptian government remarked:[77] "the current transition government remains committed to the open market approach, which Egypt will further pursue at an accelerated rate following

---

* Belarus, for example, was rewarded for its "removal of price and trade restrictions on many goods and reduction of list of minimum export price" by a rise in its price liberalization indicator from 3 to 3+. Likewise, Montenegro received the same increase for privatizing parts of its power and port sectors.

upcoming election." The statement noted "that public–private partnerships have much potential as an effective modality for designing and implementing development projects, particularly in infrastructure and service sectors (transport, health, etc.). Therefore we will encourage PPP initiatives." Moreover, fully embracing the pro-market ideological discourse discussed above, the Egyptian government promised to relax control over foreign investments through committing "to overcoming the previous shortcomings of excessive government centralisation. In addition, we will build on existing initiatives to achieve a greater level of decentralisation, especially in terms of local planning and financial management."

CONCLUSION

The projects and investments mentioned above are not the sole aspects of the IFI-backed neoliberal project in Egypt.* But at the most fundamental level, this financial aid confirms a conscious intervention by Western governments into Egypt's revolutionary process. In the very short term, large infrastructure projects and other economic schemes may provide some employment creation, housing, educational training, and perhaps the appearance of a return to stability given the prevailing sense of "crisis." This investment, however, is premised upon a profound liberalization of the Egyptian economy. They will only be undertaken concomitant with measures such as a deepening privatization (undoubtedly in the form of PPPs), deregulation (initially likely to be connected to the opening up of more sectors to foreign investment), the reduction of trade barriers (connected to access to US and European markets), and the expansion of the informal sector (under the banner of cutting "red tape"). They will necessarily involve, furthermore, a rapid expansion in Egypt's overall indebtedness—tying the country ever more firmly to future structural adjustment packages.

---

* For example, another important vehicle is The Arab Financing Facility for Infrastructure (AFFI), established by the World Bank, International Finance Corporation and the Islamic Development Bank earlier this year to promote investment in the Middle East region. The AFFI aims to raise one billion dollars and will focus on infrastructure, explicitly around PPPs. The AFFI focuses on regional integration projects, and is thereby being used to promote the reduction of trade and tariffs within the region. It is as yet unclear what the AFFI involvement with Egypt will be, but it has been highlighted by the World Bank as a major component of its future activities in the country.

If this process is not resisted, it threatens to negate the achievements of the Egyptian uprising. As the decades of the Egyptian experience of neoliberalism illustrate all too clearly, these measures will further deepen poverty, precarity and the erosion of living standards for the vast majority. Simultaneously, the financial inflows will help to strengthen and consolidate Egypt's narrow business and military elites as the only layer of society that stands to gain from further liberalization of the economy. The expansion of PPPs, for example, will provide enormous opportunities for the largest business groups in the country to take ownership stakes in major infrastructure projects and other privatized service provision. Alongside foreign investors, these groups will gain from the deregulation of labor markets, liberalization of land and retail activities, and the potential access to export markets in the United States and Europe.

These measures also have a regional impact. Their other main beneficiary will be the states of the Gulf Cooperation Council (Saudi Arabia, Kuwait, United Arab Emirates, Bahrain, Qatar, and Oman) who are playing a highly visible and complementary role alongside the IFIs. Saudi Arabia has pledged four billion dollars to Egypt— exceeding the amounts promised by the United States and the EBRD. The Kuwait Investment Authority announced in April that it was establishing a one billion US dollar sovereign wealth fund that would invest in Egyptian companies. Kuwait's Kharafi Group,[78] which had won PPP contracts in the power sector in Egypt in 2010 and is estimated to have seven billion dollars invested in Egypt already, announced that it was taking out an eighty million dollar loan[79] for investments in Egypt. Qatar is also reportedly considering investing up to ten billion dollars, according to its ambassador in Egypt.

As with the investments from Western states, these financial flows from the GCC are dependent upon the further liberalization of Egypt's economy, most likely through the mechanisms of PPPs. Indeed, Essam Sharaf, Egypt's interim prime minister, and Samir Radwan, its finance minister, have both travelled frequently to the GCC states over recent months with the aim of marketing PPP projects, particularly in water and wastewater, roads, education, healthcare, and energy. One indication of the direction of these efforts was the announcement[80] by the Dubai and Egyptian Stock Exchanges to allow the dual listing of stocks on their respective exchanges. This measure will allow privatized companies or investment vehicles to be jointly listed on both exchanges, thus facilitating the increased flows of GCC capital into Egypt.

In essence, the financial initiatives announced over recent weeks represent an attempt to bind social layers such as these—Egypt's military and business elites, the ruling families and large conglomerates of the GCC, and so forth—ever more tightly to the Western states. The revolutionary process in Egypt represented an attack against these elements of the Arab world. The uprising cannot be reduced to a question of "democratic transition" precisely because the political form of the Egyptian state under Mubarak was a direct reflection of the nature of capitalism in the country—the uprising implicitly involved a challenge to the position of these elites. The inspiring mobilizations that continue on the Egyptian streets confirm that these aspirations remain firmly held. Western financial aid needs to be understood as an intervention in this ongoing struggle—an attempt to utilize the sense of "economic crisis" to refashion Egyptian society against the interests of Egypt's majority, and to divert the revolution from the goals it has yet to achieve.

Section IV
Libya

The "initial spark" for the Libyan uprising was the combination of the 15 February 2011 arrest of a prominent human rights lawyer and the violence meted against civilians who almost immediately gathered to protest the arrest. Libyans then called for a "Day of Rage" on 17 February, during which mass protests broke out in Benghazi, Tripoli, as well as other neighboring cities. The regime responded by violently suppressing the mobilizations, at times using live ammunition. Less than twenty-four hours later, the protesters had overwhelmed both police and army forces in Benghazi. By 19 February there were widely circulating reports of an escalation in both protest tactics and regime violence.

As with other Arab authoritarian states, the regime attempted to dismiss the protesters as Islamic fundamentalists, agents of the United States and Israel, and even pill-popping youth with no sense of responsibility. However, unlike Tunisia, Egypt, Bahrain, and Yemen, Libya was peripherally located, politically, academically, and geographically. This facilitated the emergence of a number of questions, debates, and interventions around the Libyan uprising that did not emerge with as much vigor in other cases. These included the issue of tribal feuds, the question of race, and the mobilization of the "international community" and "universal justice." Further setting the Libyan case apart was the Qaddafi regime's historic demobilization of state institutions as a means of buffering itself against any potential oppositional threat, including that of a military coup. This effectively meant that the armed forces, as an institution, lacked the capacity for collective action—even to simply maintain its existence—once the regime was threatened.

It is important to recall the dread and horror with which many Libyans lived as Muammar al-Qaddafi and his son, Saif al-Islam, addressed the Libyan people with both a complete detachment from the realities of the country, and direct threats of murder, massacre, and mayhem. Perhaps what was most horrifying about developments in Libya before the emergence of a full-scale civil war and an international military campaign against the regime, was that the "chaos card" was no longer a mere threat. Not only had it very quickly become the regime's only strategy for holding on to what little power it had left, but it also demonstrated the extent to which the regime would go to avenge its break up by punishing Libyans. Despite the sometimes over-exaggerated capacity of Qaddafi to inflict mass violence and the eleventh-hour nature of international concern over that potential mass violence, one cannot but have been in awe of the courage of the Libyans who continued to take to the streets. In the face of unwavering demonstrators and various defecting elements, it was unclear what amount of death, injury, and trauma would accompany the final collapse of the regime. Yet, the Libyan people continued to turn out in larger numbers. As the uprising transformed into a civil war, and eventually gave way to a post-Qaddafi state-building process, the new center of contestation is rooted in questions of incorporation, cooptation, and various political and economic arrangements that will give life to the new system of rule.

18
The Arabs in Africa

Callie Maidhof[81]

1 March 2011

As Libyans rise up against the forty-one-year-old dictatorship of Muammar al-Qaddafi, one of the most striking claims of state violence has been the hiring of "African mercenaries" to crush the revolt. Like Husni Mubarak's "thugs" (or *baltagiya* in Arabic, terms that gained widespread currency almost instantly), the mercenaries represent the anti-populist face of violence, those who are willing to take to the streets not for reasons of personal conviction or national duty, but for compensation from the embattled regime.

The mercenaries and the thugs provide a contrast to the non-violent, impassioned politics of the protesters. One point further distinguishes Qaddafi's mercenaries from both the revolutionaries and Mubarak's thugs: that they are continuously referred to as "African." This should be an empty signifier, like saying that European mercenaries were hired to crush a revolt in Spain; after all, Libya is an African country and Libyans are Africans. But those of us who are watching the news know what is "meant" by this, and some reporters have been quick to correct themselves with either "black Africans" or, less frequently, "sub-Saharan Africans."

Although it is just one aspect of the current situation in Libya, I suggest that it should give us pause to consider the stakes of this conceptualization of a basic Arab-African or Arab-black antagonism—one that not only formulates these as mutually exclusive categories but also pins them against one another in the context of the Libyan revolution.

This formulation is taking place both "on the ground" in Libya as well as in its representation outside its borders, and the generalized media blackout has severely compromised understanding of the situation. Just a handful of commentators have questioned the veracity of the "African mercenaries" charge while maintaining their support for the uprising.

Evidence of these mercenaries has largely consisted of photographs and video footage of foreign passports[82] and documents, as well as black bodies—both alive and dead, the former inevitably surrounded by angry or even violent protesters. However, there is scant evidence that these people are, first of all, participating in state-sponsored violence against the popular uprising, and, second, were brought into Libya for this explicit purpose. On the contrary, we know that Libya was already home to a significant number of foreign workers—including some two million black African migrant workers. We should also note Libya's documented history of racial discrimination. Almost one year to the day before the 17 February Day of Anger that jump-started the revolution, UN Watch, an independent organization monitoring the UN, issued a statement[83] entitled, "Libya Must End Racism Against Black African Migrants and Others."

In light of this recent history, the videos and photographs of "African mercenaries" raise disturbing questions. Are the men we see pictured here perpetrators of state-sponsored violence, are they victims of racism, or is it possible that both of these things may be true at the same time? Are they being attacked in retaliation or in the course of a battle, or are they taken for mercenaries simply on the basis of their skin color? Is this just one more instance of non-citizens falling victim to a conflict that is not their own?

Whether or not al-Qaddafi has recruited foreign mercenaries, it is clear that none of us—in Libya or abroad—are getting the full story. However, the speed with which this charge has been accepted as true should call into question our own assumptions about relations between Arab and black Africans.

This is not the first time that Arab and black Africans have been tragically opposed; rather, this has been integral to policymaking in the United States and beyond, as well as to numerous think-tanks and international organizations, humanitarian, and otherwise. For a far more extreme example, we can look to Sudan. In his work on that topic, Mahmood Mamdani (2009) has argued that the perceived dichotomy between Arab and black Africans is a false one, relying on colonial-era tropes of settler and native which additionally sought to retribalize and reify Sudanese social (and ethnic) divisions. Mamdani holds that anti-genocide campaigns focusing on Darfur, such as Save Darfur, depoliticize the insurgency/counter-insurgency by shifting the discourse into the moral realm in order to: (1) link the conflict to the War on Terror; and (2) instigate a military response on behalf of the United States and other Western powers. This move also includes Sudan in the political geography of the Middle East.

But the same narrative techniques of depoliticization play on existing conceptions of Africa and the kinds of problems that Africans, as a generalized populace, encounter. The depoliticization of an insurgency/counter-insurgency in Darfur not only places it in the rank of terrorism, but it also situates it among other (supposedly) non-political evils that have besieged the African continent, such as HIV/AIDS, poverty, and innumerable other instances of seemingly interminable, incomprehensible violence.

This is crucial to our understanding of Libya and the question of "African mercenaries" in particular. What we can learn from the framing of violence in Darfur is that Arabs are not considered "Africans" by policymakers, journalists, and organizations, and that Arabs and Africans may be seen by these same groups as fundamentally different, and consequently face fundamentally different kinds of problems—suffering differently, inflicting harm differently, and handling politics differently—in a manner that hinders "our" own consideration of them together.

The story in Libya diverges considerably from that of Sudan, with black Africans and Arabs playing very different kinds of roles. Nonetheless, there is a recurring theme of the antagonism between (black) Africans and Arabs, one that reflects an inability of popular or even scholarly analysis to assimilate Arabs to the African continent. This is the continuation of a Cold War area studies paradigm, as well as a colonial politics of race.

The ongoing revolution in Libya has been rightly interpreted in light of what is now a succession of regional revolutions moving from Tunisia to Egypt and now to Libya, with continuing unrest in Yemen, Jordan, Bahrain, and elsewhere. The area that is considered vulnerable to this regional unrest stretches at least from Algeria to Iran and has been called the Arab world or the Middle East, despite the fact that Iranians are not Arab and most of Algeria lies west of France. This geography does not, however, appear to reach far south of the Mediterranean, at least where Africa is concerned. Although the two successful revolutions thus far lay on the African continent, there has been an overall failure to consider their effect in terms of sub-Saharan African politics and places such as Gabon, Mauritania, Djibouti, and Uganda.

This is not for lack of substantial historical involvement of these countries in African politics. Libya has long played a critical role with regard to its neighbors, and al-Qaddafi himself has been heavily involved in African politics. In his 22 February speech, he further reinforced his ties to Africa, calling into question the consonance of something called the Middle East when he claimed that without him, Libya would undergo US occupation or incorporation by the United Arab Emirates. Additionally, while the Arab League has suspended Libya for its brutal treatment of civilians, the African Union (of which al-Qaddafi used to be the chairman) has remained silent on the matter.

The use of the term "African mercenaries" points to African-ness as a site of difference. But al-Qaddafi's career has been characterized by a loud and memorable involvement in African politics—even taking on the title "the King of Kings" of Africa or in Arabic "*malik al-mulūk.*" This would suggest that if he has deployed non-citizen mercenaries, it would highlight his and Libya's regional embeddedness rather than its absolute difference.

Given this embeddedness, we may account for the use of the word "African" to suggest "foreign" in a number of ways. One answer would be the radical break this uprising has produced in our conceptions of "Libya" and "Libyans" versus al-Qaddafi himself, who has until recently been regarded as almost selfsame with his state and people. In contrast with al-Qaddafi's African ties, one could argue, that Libyans have determined that they will stand in concert with other Arab revolutions.

Although this view might have some truth to it, I want to suggest something else about what I may clumsily call the politics of geopolitics. First, what we should recognize is that terms such as "Africa" and "the Middle East" function not only on the basis of geography or actual political ties, but as stand-ins for racial signifiers. Despite a shared history of European colonialism in its different manifestations, Africa and the Middle East nonetheless bear extremely different histories of representation or historical imaginaries within the European continent (which is, I would point out, also not a continent, but something like a subcontinent).

Furthered by an area studies paradigm that is a remnant of the Cold War, these deeply rooted histories have frankly hindered our understanding of the recent revolutions—especially that of Libya—and even more so of their effect on politics on the African continent. While we stand in solidarity with the uprisings in Libya and beyond, we must nonetheless be more vigilant than ever in critiquing the role that race has played in shaping this revolutionary moment.

19
Tribes of Libya as the Third Front: Myths and Realities of Non-State Actors in the Long Battle for Misrata

Jamila Benkato[84]

2 May 2011

Recent news reports originating from Libyan state media have Libyan tribes sending representatives to the rebels in Misrata, hoping to negotiate for peace and for control of the city. A 24 April article in *The Guardian* quoted Libya's Deputy Foreign Minister, Khaled Kaim, as threatening[85] a "very bloody" assault against the rebels in Misrata if they fail to negotiate. "I hope to God we can avoid this," Kaim lamented to *The Guardian*.

Why do al-Qaddafi's tales of "tribal" identities mobilizing against rebels gain traction in the international media, whereas other Libyan government pronouncements (about ceasefires and civilian casualties, for example) are greeted with skepticism?

One significant cause of tribal rhetoric in Western media and academia is forty years of al-Qaddafi propaganda. The autocratic regime has an interest in depicting Libya as a (non)state of fragmented warring factions unified by a benevolent and beloved leader. Saif al-Islam argued in a February speech[86] that "if there is a disturbance, Libya will split into several states." If Libyans would not accept the government concessions, he warned, "be ready to start a civil war." Considering the source of this most recent story, we must take note of the regime's historic exploitation not only of tribal relationships but also of divisive tribal language. Many of al-Qaddafi's policies in the last four decades have been aimed at reducing the influence and power of tribal networks. Libyan scholar Mansour O. al-Kikhia, for example, discusses[87] how the "gerrymandering" of administrative districts broke up the historical power bases of Libya's largest and most influential tribes. Land once under the influence of powerful, but resistant, tribal shaykhs was redistributed to supportive tribes, such as parts of the Warfalla, Qadhadfa, and Megarha. Favoritism toward certain families, tribes, regions, and towns all served to create inequality and the perception of deep divisions. Today, for example, towns such as al-Qaddafi's hometown of Sirte (the stronghold of the Qadhadfa tribe) and the capital of Tripoli are noticeably more modern and developed, while Benghazi and many eastern towns, historically bases of tribal and popular resistance, have been starved of resources, infrastructure development, and state investment for the last four decades. In fact, as noted in several news sources including *The National*, accusations of regional and tribal favoritism were present from the very start of the current Libyan conflict.

Indeed many of the regime's policies have served to create social chaos, including the use of state-controlled television to disseminate misleading or manipulative information about everything from promised reforms to socio-political dynamics. Divisive tribal language has been used by the Qaddafi regime to spread dissent and create fear; a chaotic populace—especially one with as tumultuous a history as Libya's—is more easily forced to rely on the state for employment, income, and protection. For example, see al-Qaddafi's February speech claiming, "All the tribes support me." In the same speech he warned Libyans against joining the opposition, claiming that people should remain with their tribes and not succumb to outside influence. "It's the people of the tribes [that] will help them, not the agents of the Americans, or of Bin Laden, or Zarqawi." Al-Qaddafi claimed the opposition wore "turbans and long beards," clear signifiers of outside radical Islamists. By contrast, real Libyans are not radical, belong with their tribe, and were not participating in any agitations. Saif al-Islam uses similar rhetoric. In his own February speech the younger al-Qaddafi described[88] the opposition as "drunks" funded by "millionaire businessmen." By contrast, the real "Libya is tribes, not like Egypt. There are no political parties; it is made of tribes."

The most alarming example of this discourse is the construction of a false "tribe vs. rebels" dichotomy. This is not only inaccurate but, at a time when Libyan civilians are dying in the streets, it is also dangerous. There is, in fact, no tribe–rebel division. Historically, most Libyans are born into a tribe that predates the modern Libyan state. Tribal structures have held different importance during different eras and under different rulers and systems of governance. Nevertheless, it follows that all Libyans involved in the opposition are therefore just as "tribal" as any supposed leaders who are on the opposite side of the negotiating table. Actually, this construction plays directly into al-Qaddafi's own twisted narrative: he has long been claiming that opposition forces are outsiders or members of al-Qaeda. In *The Guardian*, Khaled Kaim describes "foreign fighters"[89] in Misrata. This is regime propaganda—especially cynical in the face of mounting evidence that the regime has employed non-Libyan African mercenaries to kill its own people. Considering the source of this story, there is a significant chance it is more of the same familiar regime tactics.

In another example, an article published in *The New York Times* on 21 April asks,[90] "Is the battle for Libya the clash of a brutal dictator against a democratic opposition, or is it fundamentally a tribal civil war?" These juxtapositions are fallacies: that the opposition cannot be both democratically-oriented and consist of tribes, that the fight must either be against a brutal dictator or simply be between two competing tribal alliances. None of these supposed binaries are actually mutually exclusive, although they do seem to echo the regime's party line. Knowingly or not, media reports and news analysis over the last several decades have often parroted al-Qaddafi's own rhetoric.

Tribes in modern Libya have not been institutionalized; they have no real formal role, but do remain significant social support structures. As Hasni Abidi, director of the Study and Research Centre for the Arab and Mediterranean World, explained[91] to *France 24*, "tribal chiefs represent a sort of moral and social support, and a refuge, given the total absence of Libyan political institutions." An April statement[92] signed by sixty-one Libyan tribal leaders explains it this way: "Every Libyan has certainly had [his] origins in a particular tribe. But he has complete freedom to create family ties, friendship, neighborhood or fellowship with any member of any other tribe." This is very relevant to the most recent reports of a tribes vs. rebels stand-off. Khalifa al-Zwawi, a judge who heads Misrata's transitional council, is one opposition leader that has dismissed[93] recent reports of tribal negotiators. "This is simply one of Qaddafi's plots to save time, " he told *The Guardian*. "He is not dealing with tribes, but with individuals within tribes." This is an essential point to remember both when analyzing the current Libyan conflict and when speculating on the role of tribes in Libya's future government.

Certainly there are variations in the strength of individual tribal identity depending on age and region, among other demographic indicators. An increase in urbanization and education has meant that tribes are no longer purely—or even marginally—territorial institutions. Perhaps most important at this historical moment is the remarkable demonstration of Libyan nationalist feeling, most dramatically illustrated in March by men in a liberated Benghazi who were training to help free cities in central and western Libya. These two areas are often painted in simplistic articles and television reports as having irreconcilable historical tensions. In fact, the April statement mentioned above is a statement of unity between tribes of varying sizes, regions, and prominence. The sixty-one tribal leaders specifically point to al-Qaddafi as the source of much of tribal discord or division: "It is the dictator, trying to play the Libyan tribes against each other, dividing the country to better conquer. There is no truth in this myth, it has fed an ancestral opposition and, today, a rift between tribes of Fezzan, of Cyrenaica and Tripolitania." These elders are united in denouncing al-Qaddafi and supporting the opposition movement. One specific demonstration of regional and tribal unity is found in al-Zwawi's comments to *The Guardian*. After securing Misrata, he claims,[94] "We want to go to Tripoli and set it free, and Libya free."

Unsophisticated language about tribes can be found everywhere. A recent report[95] from Reuters quotes Alia Brahimi, head of the North Africa program at the London School of Economics. "In Libya, it will be the tribal system that will hold the balance of power rather than the military, " he says. "I think you will see defections of some of the main tribes if that is not happening already." This particular analysis is lacking in a few ways. Of course we must note that it has, in fact, been the military that has held the balance of power in Libya. The opposition, "tribal" or not, is pushing back against the regime only because they, too, now have some degree of military capability. But most notably for the purposes of this discussion, the "main tribes" are offhandedly discussed as monolithic entities. How reasonable an assumption can this possibly be? Consider only one example, that of Warfalla, a tribe of an estimated one million Libyans. As encouraging as the April tribal declaration is, how likely is it that one Warfalla signatory represents the desires or political leanings of one million people who live all over Libya? Brahimi's description suggests that Libyan tribes are monolithic groups who were all part of al-Qaddafi's regime in some respect (or why would they need to "defect"?). Tribes are not military units, who act in one accord and move en masse throughout the political and social structure of Libya.

However, this trope is present even in popular political analysis. In *The Middle East Quarterly*, McGill University's Philip Carl Salzman argues:[96] "The propensity of Arab states and Iran to dictatorship... has roots in tribal culture. There is an inherent conflict between peasants and nomads. Peasants are sedentary, tied to their land, water, and crops while tribesmen are nomadic, moving around remote regions." This description, in a widely read (if conservative-leaning) journal, creates a false peasant/tribe binary. "Tribesmen" are stereotyped as isolated, landless, and in constant conflict with more civilized landed peoples. This smacks of language used to describe Native Americans during the American Western expansion. Further, Arabs are "tribal" and therefore prone to violent, autocratic regimes. Is there no hope for Arabs, then? Accurate analysis of the Libyan situation absolutely must dismiss scholarship along these lines. The reality is much more nuanced than is reflected in the current rhetoric, academic or otherwise.

Simplistic and un-nuanced language is given the sheen of legitimacy in particular when used by famous public scholars such as Benjamin Barber. Barber, the American political theorist, has repeatedly predicted[97] that the "tribal society" that is Libya will descend into "tribal war." "Blood trumps principle," Barber declared[98] to *The Huffington Post* in February. Al-Qaddafi's attacks against the Libyan people represent "his tribal struggle to uphold the 'honor' of his clan, the Qadaffa [sic], against rivals like the Zuwayya in the East or the Warfalla in the South." Geographical inaccuracies aside, what are the implications of dismissing war crimes and the shooting, bombing, and torturing of civilians as a "tribal" dispute? The answer can be found in the title of this article: "Why Libya Will Not Be Democratic." In the same vein, Samuel Huntington describes[99] the "structure of political loyalty" of Arabs and Muslims as "opposite that of the modern West." He strangely and dismissively notes that "at least eighteen tribes have played major roles in Libyan development." Aside from the few historical questions that these statements raise, simple generalizations in reference to tribes are once again evident. So too is a casual dismissal of Arab and/or Muslim political structures as "un-modern." Tribes are unruly, backwards, violent, anti-modern, and generally unregenerate, according to this discourse. The same connotations have been used for centuries to justify all manner of invasion, occupation, exploitation, and disenfranchisement.

Of course, Barber (the "long time advisor to Saif al-Qaddafi," according[100] to *Foreign Policy*) is looking after his reputation and defending his questionable relationship with al-Qaddafi's brutal regime. Nevertheless, it is important to point out the remarkably simplistic analyses that have unfortunately been given such a public platform (most egregiously in a March 2011 article[101] in *Foreign Policy*). Recent articles in *The Huffington Post*,[102] *The New York Times*,[103] and *The Guardian*[104] are only the most recent examples of this "tribal" discourse.

This discourse can be very damaging, especially when used by notable scholars in public forums. These words have a real effect on foreign policy, intervention strategy, and public perception of "other" people half a world away. And, needless to say, public perception affects aid money and the pressure (or lack thereof) that politicians feel to shape policy in one way or another. Western audiences especially hear "tribal" and think "backwards, savage, and unreformed." A recent article in *The New York Times* uses alarmist language to question the legitimacy of the Libyan opposition. The journalist David Kirkpatrick wonders[105] if the transitional council will use "rough tribal justice or a more measured legal process" in dealing with al-Qaddafi's spies. When did the "secular-minded professionals—lawyers, academics, businesspeople" that Kirkpatrick describes become "rough," and "tribal?" This comment blatantly ignores not only important Arab and Islamic justice traditions, but also the education and agency of the modern Libyans trying to better their country. This tribal discourse paints Libyans—even those progressively forming a new government—as constantly on the verge of devolving into violence and savagery.

To conclude, there is no tribe vs. rebel stand-off in Libya. This is not a tribal war, but one fought by Libyans of all affiliations against an exploitative and brutal regime. There are almost certainly massive amounts of coercion and manipulation going on to maintain military support and the limited tribal or regional support that al-Qaddafi still has. The current hot tribe-related story comes from the most questionable of all Libyan sources and has inexplicably received uncritical treatment from even the most reputable news outlets. Most importantly, especially considering the evolution of the tribal structure over the last few decades, any discourse that relies on the tired "tribal war" trope is almost guaranteed to be inaccurate. Tribe is not the primary identification for many Libyans, and Libyan nationalist feeling is running very high in many areas, regardless of any other affiliations. Although tribes and historical tensions are very real and deserving of attention, a much more nuanced understanding of Libyan history and society is required for any responsible presentation of the current Libyan conflict. As renowned Libya scholar Ali Ahmida told[106] *Mother Jones* in late February, "There's a huge vacuum in our knowledge about Libya. We reduce it to tribes and clans, or to Qaddafi, or to oil. There's nothing about Libyan society. I find that appalling, even among our commentators and our scholars." Indeed. The question is: How do we accurately and responsibly discuss Libyan tribes in this context?

20
Solidarity and Intervention in Libya

Asli Ü Bâli and Ziad Abu-Rish[107]

16 March 2011

The Libyan uprising is entering its fourth week. The courage and persistence of the Libyan people's efforts to overthrow Muammar al-Qaddafi have been met with ongoing regime brutality ranging from shoot-to-kill policies to the indiscriminate use of artillery against unarmed civilians. When we last wrote[108] on this subject, we already recognized that the situation in Libya was dire. Since that time the violence of the regime's unhinged bid to subdue the armed insurgency has only escalated. The mounting civilian death toll resulting from regime brutality has amplified previous calls for international intervention. The Security Council unanimously issued a resolution[109] imposing tough measures against the Libyan regime including an arms embargo, asset freeze, travel ban, and a referral of the situation in Libya to the International Criminal Court for investigation. More recently, the Arab League has called[110] on the Security Council to impose a no-fly zone over Libya. The issue of a no-fly zone is only one of several proposals now being loudly advocated.[111] Others include funneling arms[112] to Libyan rebels and proposals to coordinate with Egyptian commandos allegedly already operating in Libya to provide logistical assistance and training to the rebels. Despite the intuitive appeal of the argument that something must be done, we write again now to oppose calls for the types of international intervention that are currently under discussion.

The desire to act in solidarity with the Libyan people demands that we assess the available options against the core principle of legitimacy that any intervention must satisfy: do no harm[113] (that is, do not do more harm on balance by intervening). The likelihood that any of the current proposals involving coercive intervention would satisfy the "do no harm" principle is severely constrained when evaluated against the historical record, logistical realities, and the incentives and interests of the states in a position to serve as the would-be external interveners. Put simply, coercive external intervention to alter the balance of power on the ground in Libya in favor of the anti-Qaddafi revolt is likely to backfire badly. The attendant costs would, of course, be borne not by those who call for intervention from outside of Libya but by the Libyan people with whom we hope to show solidarity. In what follows we argue that embracing the call for solidarity requires a much more careful appraisal of the interventionist option, precisely because the potential risks will be borne by Libyan civilians.

MIXED MOTIVATIONS AND REGIME CHANGE

Of the arguments against intervention, the most straightforward draws on an assessment of the long history of external intervention in the Middle East and North Africa. There is no need to rehearse that history here since the failure of such past interventions to advance the humanitarian welfare or political aspirations of local populations is well-established. But because the possibility of intervention is debated in some circles as if the starting point is a tabula rasa,[114] it is important to begin by recalling this dismal history. For instance, the imposition of a no-fly zone on Iraq did little in and of itself to shift the balance of power against the Saddam Hussein regime, but it did result in the deaths of hundreds of civilians. Further, the no-fly zone served as a predicate for the subsequent invasion and occupation of Iraq insofar as the ongoing use of this coercive measure against the regime from 1991 until 2003 was cited in support of the argument that there was "implied authorization" to forcibly topple the regime. Indeed, in some ways the modes of intervention that are currently being suggested—including a no-fly zone—should be understood precisely in the register of regime change (rather than humanitarian) intervention.

While humanitarian considerations are often invoked in defense of intervention, humanitarianism is far from the only issue on the table. Other reasons that have been adduced in favor of intervention in Libya include vindicating[115] international norms, re-establishing the leadership[116] of the United States in the region, preventing the spill-over[117] of the refugee crisis into Europe, and the stabilization[118] of world oil markets. The Libyan people are struggling to change their regime on their own terms and there is no reason to presume an overlap between these various logics of intervention and their interests. The historical record clearly establishes that an external regime change intervention based on mixed motives—even when accompanied with claims of humanitarianism—usually privileges the strategic and economic interests of interveners and results in disastrous consequences for the people on the ground. Indeed, the discord currently evidenced among Western powers concerning intervention in Libya is precisely based[119] on their doubts as to whether their strategic interests are adequately served by such a course.

The incongruence between the interests of external interveners and those on the ground in Libya is already apparent. Beyond their eleventh-hour timing,[120] serious mobilizations for intervention on the part of Western powers were issued only after most Western nationals had been safely evacuated from Libya. The fact that outside powers were unwilling to act while their nationals were on Libyan soil demonstrates their understanding that treating the regime with coercion may lead to civilian deaths either directly as a result of an intervention or indirectly through reprisals against civilians identified as opponents. Furthermore, the evacuation channels made available to Western nationals—airlifts across the Mediterranean—were not and are not being offered to Libyan civilians nor African migrant workers trapped in Libya. If the humanitarian welfare of civilians in Libya were paramount, they, too, would have been offered this secure escape route. Instead, once Western nationals were safely out of harm's way, coercive measures were adopted without any effort to protect or evacuate the civilians that were left behind in Tripoli and beyond.

NO-FLY ZONE, LOCAL CALLS, AND SOLIDARITY

To be clear, we are not categorically rejecting any and all forms of intervention irrespective of the context. Instead, we reject forms of intervention that, on balance, are likely to produce more harm than benefit. This is a context-specific determination that requires an assessment of the foreseeable consequences of particular proposed interventions. With respect to the context in Libya today we are critical of current proposals for intervention in light of the identities and interests of would-be interveners and the limited understanding of intra-Libyan political dynamics on which they rely. There are circumstances under which a no-fly zone might conceivably serve a humanitarian purpose. In particular, if air strikes were the principal means by which the regime was inflicting civilian casualties there would be a much stronger case for a no-fly zone. Though the military situation within Libya remains unclear, the empirical evidence that is available suggests that al-Qaddafi's artillery poses a more serious threat to both civilians and rebels than air strikes. In addition, the regime's aerial assaults have primarily employed helicopter gunships, which would be difficult to counter[121] through a no-fly zone because they fly lower and are harder to target than warplanes. Further, a no-fly zone imposed either through the Security Council or NATO would involve an attack on Libyan runways, radars, and anti-aircraft artillery installations with the potential for significant "collateral damage" against civilians and civilian infrastructure. A no-fly zone that risks killing Libyans would also run the risk of strengthening the regime's hand by enabling al-Qaddafi to style himself as an anti-imperialist defender of Libyan sovereignty. Rather than persuading elements of the military and air force to defect, such a move might produce a counter-productive rally-round-the-flag effect in parts of Libya still under the control of the regime. The fact that for logistical and political reasons a no-fly zone poses a serious risk of backfiring is an important consideration. But it is not the only reason to question whether heeding local calls for a no-fly zone necessarily represent an act of solidarity.

Unlike many other parts of the Middle East, Libya is a relatively unknown political context for outsiders whether they are progressive activists or conventional analysts. In a context where intervention is based on the logic of regime change rather than the well-being of the people on the ground, the absence of on-the-ground knowledge about local actors is especially worrying. Elsewhere, for instance in the Palestinian context, much is known about the different parties on the ground. As a result, activists, scholars, and analysts are able to disaggregate different calls emanating from local actors and determine which they deem to be "representative" of the civilian population or entitled to "solidarity." By contrast, little is known about the groups that now comprise the Benghazi-based National Transitional Council of Libya and the degree to which they represent the wider demands and interests of the Libyan civilian population. Libyans from other regions of the country (whether liberated or regime-controlled), who experience allegiance to different tribal leaders and/or political factions among Libyan social forces, may or may not be represented by those currently calling for no-fly zones. Furthermore, a response to calls emanating from one region may risk fragmenting the country. The fact that we know so little about the domestic context among non-regime actors in Libya is precisely the reason that the types of external intervention currently being proposed are so likely to backfire.

The desire to act in solidarity with local Libyans struggling for their liberation is important. But without a clear sense of the consequences of a particular intervention—or the interests and diverse actors likely to be impacted—there is no way to satisfy the do-no-harm principle. Notwithstanding the provenance of the calls for a no-fly zone—whether within Libya or the Arab League—and their attendant "authenticity" or legitimacy, we cannot justify intervention unless we can appraise its likely consequences for the civilian population with whom we are allegedly acting in solidarity. This difficulty is further compounded by the fact that neither the Western nor Arab powers currently calling for intervention have a record of privileging particular domestic partners based on the interests or aspirations of local populations. There is little reason to expect that Libya will be exceptional in this regard, particularly in light of the mixed motives of any potential intervener.

We do not argue that the international community has no obligation to support Libyan civilians. To the contrary, we strongly believe there is such an obligation, but that current coercive options pose serious risks to the Libyan population with little concomitant benefit in terms of humanitarian protections. The interests of potential external interveners are not well aligned with those of Libyans on the ground beyond that of regime change. This is evidenced both by the eleventh-hour nature of current discussions about strategies of intervention and by the fact that the policies under consideration are largely symbolic, such as a no-fly zone that would offer little concrete support to Libyans on the ground. Further, the identities of those contemplating intervention reinforce concerns about such proposals. Many members of the Arab League are currently undertaking repression of democratic uprisings against their rule. The legitimacy and representativeness of any call they issue should be called into question by their own internal anti-democratic practices. As Saudi troops enter Bahrain to shore up the defenses of an authoritarian ruling family against its own people, the bankruptcy of calls for intervention in Libya by members of the GCC and the Arab League is evident. Members of the Group of Eight, who met in Paris to discuss a no-fly zone this week, are also compromised by their ambivalence toward democratic demands met with repression by their regional allies and their own long history of brutal interventions and direct support of authoritarian regimes.

Libyans have already made great inroads on the ground and without external support toward a goal of regime change in which they will determine the day-after scenarios for their country. To date, measures adopted by the international community have done little to aid, and may have undermined, Libyan efforts at liberation. For instance, the call for an ICC referral in the measures adopted by the Security Council was most likely counter-productive. The first priority should have been a negotiated exit strategy for al-Qaddafi and his family, not unlike the path already paved for the other recently deposed Arab despots, Ben Ali and Mubarak. Instead, by immediately referring the regime for investigation by the ICC the international community has signaled to al-Qaddafi that neither he nor his children will be allowed to go quietly, potentially redoubling his resolve to fight to the last. Allowing a negotiated exit to exile in an African or South American country would not have precluded a subsequent ICC referral, but might have facilitated an early end to the violence currently ravaging Libya. Further, the same resolution that referred Libyan authorities to the ICC contained a specific exemption from ICC jurisdiction for foreign interveners not party to the Rome Statute, anticipating and providing impunity in some cases for civilian deaths that result from possible Security Council-authorized operations in Libya down the line. The ICC referral has been described as an attempt to incentivize those around al-Qaddafi to defect. Rather than vindicating international accountability, this logic of incentives suggests impunity for last-minute defectors notwithstanding decades of crimes against the Libyan population. At its most basic, the ICC referral represents the triumph of a set of international goals (vindicating a constrained conception of international accountability through the Libyan regime) over the immediate interest in an early resolution of the Libyan crisis through the provision of a regime exit strategy. This privileging of international over local interests is typical of external intervention and would only be exacerbated by options involving the use of force.

We argue for forms of international assistance that reverse this privileging and begin from the known interests of Libyan civilians. At a minimum, resources must be mobilized to offer relief supplies to the Libyan population that is currently outside of the control of the regime (bearing in mind some of the problematic dynamics also associated with such forms of "aid"). Urgent priority should be given to addressing the shortages of medical supplies and the provision of essential foods and clean water. Beyond these basics, an evacuation corridor for civilians—including non-Libyan African workers trapped in the territory—should be secured and responsibility for shouldering the burden of refugee flows should not be restricted to Tunisia and Egypt. To the contrary, rather than imposing these costs on Libya's poorest neighbors—in the early stages of transitions of their own—Libya's relatively wealthy northern neighbors in Europe should be absorbing a much larger share of the costs, human and material, of offering refuge to fleeing civilians. The fact that the airlifting of Libyan and other African civilians to safety out of Tripoli is an option that is not currently on the table speaks eloquently to the misalignment of priorities between those who would potentially impose a no-fly zone—NATO countries—and the local population. Dropping the xenophobic European rhetoric on the "dangers"[122] of African immigration would also have the benefit of removing one of the Libyan regime's major levers with the EU. As al-Qaddafi threatens to terminate the agreements by which he has been warehousing African migrants at Europe's behest, he lays bare the cruel logic of tacit alliances (based on immigration,[123] energy,[124] and security[125] interests) that has long lent support to his rule. A Europe willing to take concrete steps to facilitate the evacuation to its own shores of civilians who wish to leave Libyan territory regardless of nationality would at least have broken with its record of shameful complicity in regime brutality.

Acting in solidarity with the Libyan people within a do-no-harm principle presents many constraints and frustratingly few options. This is not because of an absence of concern for the interests of the Libyan population but because there are few good options beyond the provision of relief supplies and evacuation channels. There may be other alternatives short of external coercive intervention that might be considered—such as sharing tactical intelligence with Libyan rebels or jamming regime communications—though such options would have to be carefully evaluated in light of potential risks. By contrast, overt and covert coercive options ranging from no-fly zones to arming Libyan rebels or using regional commandos to train them all implicate external actors in altering the balance on the ground in unpredictable ways. To engage in such coercive strategies without being able to evaluate the full range of consequences amounts to subordinating the interests of the Libyan people to our own sense of purpose and justice. As of this writing, reports from Libya suggest that the tide may be turning against the rebels. We are deeply concerned about these developments, though they do not alter our assessment. We strongly advocate creative strategies of solidarity with the Libyan people while underscoring that calls for coercive external intervention do not qualify. Indeed, it is possible that demands for Western support to the rebels may already have done more harm than good.[126]

In the end, we argue for humility in imagining the role we might play in the course of Libyans' struggle. The international community is neither entitled to take the reins today nor dictate the post-regime scenario tomorrow. Further, those of us who wish to stand in solidarity with Libyans from outside of their country must recognize that we may not be best placed to identify which local actors enjoy broad-based support. Solidarity cannot be reduced to the diplomatic politics of recognition nor to arguments for external intervention. In the end, we counsel acting from the outside only when our actions are clearly aligned with the interests of Libyan civilians. Imaginative strategies to offer much-needed relief and refuge to Libya's vulnerable population represent a challenge the international community has yet to meet. That is a good starting point for transnational solidarity.

Section V
Bahrain

More than any other contemporary Arab protest movement, Bahrain's February 14 Uprising—which itself began on a day that marked the ten-year anniversary of the country's 2001 National Action Charter—is an extension of previous, decades-long popular struggles to institute constitutional rule, the separation of powers, social justice, and citizens' basic rights. Rooted in the 1930s anti-discrimination strikes at the Bahrain Petroleum Company and the attendant anti-colonial, anti-monarchical liberation movements that continued until the turn of the century, the February 14 Uprising has reiterated some of these same popular demands that call for freedom, justice, and political participation. The twentieth-century struggles went through various iterations, from compromise and negotiation with the Bahraini monarchy to non-violent mobilizations and calls for action. As with the current uprising, the Bahraini regime, then largely aided by British security forces, responded to each with systematic oppression, violence, intimidation, imprisonment, torture, and the deployment of sectarian tactics.

Despite fresh memories of this counter-revolutionary violence, the first few months of the 2011 Bahraini uprising witnessed a seemingly unstoppable momentum of cross-class, regional, and sectarian solidarity. The regime's brutal response created divisions among the ranks of the protesters, mainly along sectarian and class lines, yet the uprising continued. A generation who had been raised on the steadfast struggles of their parents and grandparents took to the streets, filled with hope for a better, more egalitarian, and democratic future. Against all odds, they stood up to an armed counter-revolutionary campaign determined to keep the uprisings from reaching the shores of the oil-producing states. American and Western European governments stood idly as Bahraini security forces and their imported mercenaries unleashed an arsenal of violent tactics against peaceful, unarmed protesters. The uprising continued. Saudi Arabia, supported by the United Arab Emirates, Qatar, and Kuwait, deployed the GCC Peninsula Shield Forces to occupy Bahrain and accomplish what the Bahraini regime had seemingly failed to do on its own: crush the uprising. A concerted campaign of mass violence, destruction, and silencing ensued. Over seventy Bahrainis have been killed since. Hundreds have been injured, illegally detained, and tortured. Thousands of students, journalists, doctors, and teachers have been the target of campaigns of intimidation, consequently losing their economic means of livelihood. Religious, urban, and historical landmarks have also been completely destroyed in an attempt to subdue even the infrastructure of revolution.

Despite, or perhaps in spite of, the unprecedented scale of indiscriminate regime violence meted out against peaceful protesters, Bahrain's revolutionaries quickly reorganized themselves and took to the streets again after a relative lull in late March 2011. While some opposition parties called for an end to the violence through negotiations and dialogue with the regime, most rejected such empty calls. Instead, they escalated their revolutionary demands to include the overthrow of the Al Khalifa regime. In particular, the Coalition of February 14th Youth, a largely decentralized network of political activists, has rejected superficial attempts by the regime for "reconciliation" and reform, and is steadfast in its demands for revolutionary, democratic change. For now, it seems as though Bahrain's uprising is here to stay.

21
Let's Talk about Sect

Tahiyya Lulu[127]
24 February 2011

"This was an affluent crowd, far different from the mostly low-income Shiites who took to the streets to demand a constitutional monarchy, an elected government and a representative Parliament. The air was scented with perfume, and people drove expensive cars," writes Michael Slackman[128] of *The New York Times*, describing a pro-status quo government self-described "Unity" demonstration held in Bahrain on Monday, 21 February 2011.

With repeated[129] reference to Bahrain's sectarian divide in local and international media (some variation of the tagline "Bahrain has a seventy percent Shi'a population ruled by a Sunni ruling family" has rolled along the ticker of almost every major television news network), and anti-government protesters insisting on Shi'a–Sunni unity (a cry also parroted by pro-government crowds), it is worthwhile then to follow the trail of this mysterious scent a little further.

First, some facts. The majority of Bahrainis are Shi'a, who are estimated[130] to make up seventy percent of the local population. The majority of pro-reform/anti-government demonstrators at the Pearl Roundabout are Bahraini Shi'a. True, also, that Bahrain is ruled by a Sunni royal family, and that the majority of participants at pro-government rallies[131] held over the past week appear to be Bahraini Sunnis.

As Slackman and a few other commentators have pointed out, the "Sunni" and "Shi'a" hashtags certainly reflect a disparity in wealth while suggesting only a difference in sect. The BBC[132] describes the Mercedes and Humvees at the "luxury car protest" pro-government rally, while a discerning tweeter[133] from the Pearl Roundabout asks, "Most of the cars here in #lulu[134] are pre-2000 models, I wonder what was the case in #fateh[135] [site of pro-government rally]?"

This is not to say that being Bahraini and Shi'a is always synonymous with being poor or disenfranchised. As many pro-status quo commentators will point out, Bahrain is home to economically powerful Shi'a families and high-ranking Shi'a government officials. It is also not to say that all Bahraini Sunnis are rich; a drive to the Huneiniyah valley bordering the affluent area of Riffa (where much of the royal family resides) will take you through neighborhoods characterized by the issues raised by pro-reform demonstrators, including poverty, bad infrastructure, inadequate housing, and poor school facilities.

But the facts of the matter speak for themselves. Corruption, crony capitalism, and lack of transparency add up to uneven development and a vast disparity[136] in wealth in a country so small, that five minutes away from glass towers of international banking centers and royal palaces you find yourself among the crumbling walls and crowded streets of Bahrain's villages. By and large, Bahrain's Shi'a[137] are losing out on the country's economic boom, which affords it one of the highest GDP per capita in the world. But if the current uprising is just a matter of the underclass, how come the hundreds of thousands of migrant workers[138] who make up the socially invisible strata of Bahrain's working class, along with Sunni have-nots, have not joined the pro-reformers at Pearl Roundabout?

What this reflects, to a large extent, is the success of the Bahraini regime's strategy to deal with challenges to its legitimacy by promoting and reinforcing identity politics[139] within a system of privileges where certain groups and individuals are favored over others. In a word: discrimination.

So yes, the Shi'a represent the majority of pro-reform anti-government protesters because they are the majority of the population—but also because the government actively discriminates against them. The big pearl elephant in the living room would tell you if it could that while Bahraini Shi'a make up around two-thirds of the population, their rulers, the majority of the government, military, and business leaders are Sunni.[140] Bahrain's political, social, and economic system operates by offering privileges and *"wasta"* to some, at the expense of the rights of others. In this way, the government maintains a separation between Bahrain's communal groups (Baharna, Arab, Howala, Ajam, and Asians) and discourages citizens from associating with each other on a national basis—which has posed a real challenge to the regime in the past.[141]

This "divide and rule" politic was developed by the Al Khalifa and its allies after they settled in Bahrain in the eighteenth century, when they appropriated land from the indigenous Shi'a owners and effectively made them into peasants. Even then, the regime operated with the assistance of a number of Shi'a families who they employed as ministers or tax collectors. Still today, high-ranking government positions are disproportionately awarded to members of the Al Khalifa family, or other Sunni allies, and a few hand-picked Shi'a representatives are given seats of power.

Continuing the discriminatory tradition set by imperial Britain during Bahrain's time as a British protectorate (when police were recruited[142] from British-colonized India), the Bahraini regime today relies on defense from imported mercenaries,[143] while the Bahraini Shi'a are denied the right to serve in their own armed forces. The Bahraini Defense Force remains the domain of the royal family and the descendants of its tribal allies, as well as the foreign mercenaries. Contention over discrimination has now developed into a row over illegal political naturalization of these personnel as well as others.[144] Government statistics from 2008 show an annual population increase[145] of forty-one percent, and a fifteen percent increase in the number of citizens (13.6 percent higher than the previous year).

Another form of discrimination practiced by the Bahraini government is electoral gerrymandering.[146] In past elections, the Shi'a-dominated Northern Governorate of more than 91,000 voters elected nine members of parliament. In the Sunni-dominated Southern Governorate only 16,000 voters elected six members. This is in addition to the already weighty tome: the detention of hundreds of Shi'a protesters last year, and the prolific[147] arrest of twenty-three Shi'a citizens charged with forming a "terror network" to overthrow the government. The twenty-three men, many of them members of the Haq Movement of Liberties and Democracy (an opposition group that boycotts elections), were charged under the widely criticized anti-terror law. The highly publicized[148] trial was preceded by the release of the suspects' names and photographs to national media outlets by the governmental Bahrain News Agency. They have been released as of Tuesday (22 February) in a concession to the current uprising, confirming suspicions that the case was politically motivated and gives another example of the government's oppressive policies toward its opponents.

The sectarian divide therefore stems from economic disparity and the denial of civil rights. A better way to understand the current uprising is as a movement for civil rights and liberties. The demands are for a transition from a system of privileges for a few at the expense of the many toward a system of greater rights for all. That is presumably why the Shi'a-dominated "cannot-haves" of the anti-government, pro-reform crowds appear to have crossed the sectarian rift and drawn in Bahrainis from a range of political platforms including liberals, seculars, and human rights activists.

This is not to say that there are no sectarian elements within both the anti-government camp and the pro-government rallies. But at this point there appears to be a larger calling for less economic disparity and more rights, which has to some extent managed to cut through the boundaries of the Shi'a-Sunni political divide in Bahrain. A good illustration of the class element is the position of the affluent upper-middle class "Nido"[149] youth. While some are part of the Pearl Roundabout pro-reform opposition, many more it seems have awoken from their apolitical reverie to participate in the pro-government rally, in bewildered protest that, "this [complaints of the protesters] is not the Bahrain we know,"—well, because, it is not.

Suffice to say then, that it is not so much the "haves" and "have-nots" but the "haves" and "cannot-haves" battling for Bahrain's future today.

CAVEAT EMPTOR

In terms of "conciliatory gestures" by the government, what Bahrain needs now is not publicity stunts supported by the privileged and grateful supporters of the government proclaiming "unity." This is little more than a PR exercise to relegate the issue of a deeply flawed and potentially failing political system, by window-dressing real sectarian discrimination with a glossy banner (book and video[150]) calling for Sunni and Shi'a to unite. It has been a long winter of discontent in the wider Middle East, and the sweeping changes this spring have not escaped Bahrain's imagination. The outcome right now looks uncertain, but one thing is for sure, it is not the demands of the pro-reform protesters at Pearl Roundabout, but the Bahrain government's rule by repression and discrimination that is pushing this country toward a "sectarian abyss."[151]

22
Distortions of Dialogue

Tahiyya Lulu[152]

10 March 2011

"I've had nothing yet," Alice replied in an offended tone, "so I can't take more."
"You mean you can't take less," said the Hatter, "it's very easy to take more than nothing."

Recent news reports on the current uprising in Bahrain are all talking about the talk; we hear, or read, that, "Clinton, Saudi minister support Bahrain dialogue,"[153] and that "UAE-Qatar support Dialogue Initiative."[154] Days later, US Assistant Secretary of State for Near Eastern Affairs "Feltman praises initiatives by HM King Hamad,"[155] and according to Bahraini authorities, "Bahrain has also received support from the Governments of France, Jordan, Russia, and Turkey for the national dialogue."

So how come the protesters are not at the negotiating table? Clearly, that miserable lot munching on popcorn at the Pearl[156] are just unwilling to talk, defiantly refusing "civilized" methods of reform, right? Well, allow me to suggest that perhaps it is because the table they are being invited to does not have a leg to stand on. And this is why:

Not long after the Bahraini regime gained great fortune from Bahrain's 1932 discovery of oil, there emerged a movement[157] for judicial reform that called for an end to employment discrimination against locals at the Bahrain Petroleum Company and to the growing disparity of wealth between the ruling family and ordinary Bahrainis. Strikers were arrested and dismissed from employment in order to quell the movement—and the government later created a Labour Committee.

Then came the 1950s. Socio-political grievances merged with nationalist and anti-imperialist street action and heralded several strikes. A Higher Executive Committee[158] emerged and led strikes that called for political participation, an elected legislative council, a codified criminal and civil code, and the establishment of a trade union and a court of appeals. The government, with help from the British, suppressed this popular movement. Security forces killed three Bahrainis, which then led to a general strike. In a conciliatory attempt, the then-ruler Shaykh Salman bin Hamad Al Khalifa allowed the Committee to establish itself as the Committee for National Unity. But when spontaneous demonstrations after the British-French-Israeli invasion of Egypt erupted in Bahrain in 1956,[159] the government exiled Committee members and imposed a state of emergency.

Public discontent in Bahrain erupted again in 1965[160] in the face of increasing government suppression that was bolstered by the British Royal Air Force. Not quite there yet? Following newfound independence from Britain and the March 1972 uprising,[161] a National Assembly was established in 1972. Two sessions later, a polarizing disagreement led to the dissolution of the Parliament in 1975 and the creation of the Prime Minister's Cabinet. Yes, the same prime minister who is in power today.

Soon after, the winds of change in Iran inspired disenfranchised Bahrainis. In 1981 the government staged secret trials[162] and jailed seventy-three Gulf nationals for receiving military equipment and training from Iran. The same year, Bahrain entered a "bilateral security" treaty with Saudi Arabia, and joined the (newly-formed) Gulf Cooperation Council.

Following the 1991 Gulf War, intense state oppression[163] and violence continued amid economic disparity and social tension, and a Consultative (Shura) Council of thirty men was appointed in 1992. On the streets, a "petition"[164] movement emerged, asking for the re-institution of the 1972 Constitution and National Assembly, the release of political prisoners, and the annulment of the State Security Law. Not surprisingly, the government responded by imprisoning, arresting, and exiling many. It then expanded the Shura Council membership to forty members and increased its "advisory powers."

Stifled unrest continued until 1999, when the current King inherited his father's throne and held a referendum on a National Action Charter[165] promising to reinstate an amended constitution, an elected legislative assembly, and an appointed advisory council. Riding a wave of hopeful public enthusiasm (and US-led calls for "democracy in the Middle East"), he then introduced a new constitution ratified in 2002 that instated an elected legislative assembly—one that would be superseded by an appointed Shura Council. Greater freedoms of expression and assembly, the abolition of the State Security Law, re-entry of exiled Bahrainis, and the release of political prisoners were, however, marred by the amnesty also granted to their torturers.[166]

In 2002, most opposition groups refused to participate in the elections[167] in protest of the King's reneged promises. But in the 2006 elections, opposition groups, including the al-Wefaq National Islamic Society and the Liberal Democratic Action Society, did participate. Meanwhile, democratic reforms were consistently being either eroded or ignored.[168] Several developments further aggravated the already mounting complaints: (1) accusations of electoral gerrymandering;[169] (2) illegal naturalization;[170] and (3) the leak of government documents purportedly showing a 2.7 million dollar government conspiracy[171] to rig elections, spy on citizens, and fund NGOs and media outfits to discredit activists and rights workers.

By round three, the 2010 elections, the issues on the table were piling high. The government was accused[172] of appropriating public land worth sixty-five billion dollars, continuing illegal naturalization, conducting mass arrests, and closing down websites belonging to political societies as part of a pre-election crackdown.[173] Twenty-three Shi'a citizens were arrested on accusations of a terrorist plot[174] to overthrow the government, and assertions of rampant torture and maltreatment in jail resurfaced. Amid claims of irregularities, the Parliament was essentially hung between al-Wefaq (former opposition) representatives and supporters of the government. The general sense was that the regime could rest easy[175] in the face of demands for change as the Parliament effectively and conveniently neutralized itself.

So back then to January of this year: Egypt rose once again—hot on the heels of the Tunisian Revolution. Inspired, a popular call for a "Day of Rage"[176] in Bahrain was disseminated across social media forums—an event which developed into the current uprising. The details are already known, but in summary, the Bahraini government once again answered demands for change with lethal[177] force leading to the deaths of seven protesters, and then drew up its own agenda for reform, which brings us back to the issue of "dialogue." After using violence to silence its challengers, the government's repositioning of itself as "open to dialogue" seems disingenuous, to say the least.

The implication of all this talk about "dialogue"[178] is that the government appears to be open to expressions of discontent and reform, while the protesters are the ones responsible for dragging Bahrain into the economic slump and high social tensions of the last three weeks. The 140-character memory of a tweet allows us to forget that Bahrainis have been expressing the desire for social change for several decades. Conventional wisdom about "dialogue" now places the onus on protesters to end the current stalemate.

While popular anti-government demonstrations continue at various strategic locations, the government has effectively given[179] rise to a new social "movement"—a self-described "Unity Gathering" of pro-government forces which has staged mass counter-demonstrations criticizing the pro-reform protesters and calling for dialogue "without conditions."

What this does is effectively de-legitimate the demands of the protesters. It forecloses the desires for change that Bahrainis have expressed time and again at least since the 1950s. It also conveniently repackages the government's response to these demands: erasing the violence that the government has unleashed at all calls for change, and exaggerating the self-imposed, superficial[180] changes that include little concession or sharing of power. All this is made possible, of course, with backing from the regime's powerful neighbors[181] and friends.[182]

Emile Nakhleh wrote that the ruling family's concession to form a Parliament in 1972 was "an expression of royal benevolence,"[183] rather than the recognition of citizens' legitimate demands for political participation. Whether in 1938 or 2011, this attitude is still the same. But what the royals need to know now is that what has changed is that people are no longer asking for benevolence; and they know, to paraphrase, that the hour is getting late, and this table just offers false talk.

23
When Petro-Dictators Unite: The Bahraini Opposition's Struggle for Survival

Rosie Bsheer and Ziad Abu-Rish[184]

19 March 2011

For at least several decades, geopolitical, economic, territorial, and ideological considerations have led to serious tensions, if not outright feuds, between the Gulf Cooperation Council (GCC) member states. In recent weeks, however, the regimes of the GCC states have shown their citizens that when their authoritarian rule is at stake, they will put aside their differences and put up a united front. Exceptional times, it seems, do call for exceptional measures. As such, the GCC endorsed[185] UNSC Resolution 1973– authorizing "all measures necessary" in Libya, including a no-fly zone. Indeed, while some GCC states have agreed to send troops to help overthrow one brutal dictator in Libya, others have already sent their US-trained and armed troops to uphold the rule of another entrenched and equally brutal dictator in Bahrain. But what exactly happens when some of the world's most oppressive dictators unite, not to fight a well-known regional adversary further up North, but to put down a peaceful and democratic popular uprising?

The GCC's Peninsula Shield Forces—composed mainly of Saudi,[186] but also Qatari and Emirati[187] troops—officially entered Bahrain on Monday, 14 March 2011. While their stated[188] goal is to protect the Bahraini government and oil facilities, the level of indiscriminate state violence against unarmed civilians in the last few days has been unprecedented. First-hand accounts[189] and video footage of Bahraini state security personnel using tear gas, rubber bullets, machine guns,[190] tanks, and other weapons against unarmed civilians and journalists[191] without warning have emerged from many villages,[192] mainly Sitra[193] and Qadham,[194] and not just from the capital, Manama. In one reported incident, an Indian national working for a private security firm in Bahrain was killed[195] while on duty on Wednesday night by a stray bullet from a military helicopter that was firing at protesters.

Bahrain's Foreign Minister Shaykh Khalid bin Ahmed al-Khalifa held a press conference[196] on Friday night in which he denied that his regime is involved in any systematic violence against civilians. He rendered the escalation of violence in Bahrain as an expected consequence of the "volatile situation" as security forces try to "restore order." While some sense of "calm" has reportedly been restored to a few areas in Bahrain, many neighborhoods and villages are suffering from extreme police and military brutality. Especially alarming has been the shootings at medical facilities as well as the harassment and detention of medical staff. According to the Bahraini *Al-Wasat* newspaper, the Salmaniya Medical Complex remained under siege for days, and at least two of its doctors have been detained[197] so far. Dr Nada Dhaif, who appeared on *Al Jazeera* last week, has also been confirmed as missing by her relatives. So was Dr Mohamed Saeed, member of the Bahrain Center for Human Rights (BCHR) and one of the twenty-five political detainees that were released earlier last month as a concessionary attempt by King Hamad. Dr Saeed has been reported missing[198] since the morning of 17 March. Several attacks against medical staff have also been reported, including an attack[199] by thugs against nurses on the campus of Bahrain University. Hospitals in Bahrain have issued pleas for help from the international community, given the alarming number of casualties. However, medical staff traveling to Bahrain in response to a call by the Red Crescent have been denied entry to Bahrain, including a Kuwaiti thirty-plus medical team that was turned away at the Bahraini airport.

While the Bahraini regime purports to still be committed[200] to dialogue,[201] its forces have launched a systematic attack[202] against many members of the formal opposition, protesters, and those who have publicly criticized the ruling family. Security forces have already raided[203] the homes of the members of the "group of twenty-five." According to the BBC,[204] sixty people have been missing since Wednesday, whereas the *Al Manama Voice*[205] puts the total number of those missing at 115, thirty-five of whom have been found while eighty remain unaccounted for. As a recent tweet by @Nabeelrajab put it, "As Bahrain arrests the opposition leaders, no one is left for dialogue." Activists Abdul-Jalil Alsingace[206] and Mohammad Sultan—a BCHR member who is suffering from a brain tumor—were both arrested. Ali Abdulemam,[207] the Bahraini "blog father," and Ali al-Yaseen, who called Bahrain television accusing[208] it of inciting sectarianism and maintaining a media blackout in Bahrain, are both missing. Isa al-Radhi had been missing for five days, when on Friday the military hospital contacted his family to collect his body. Many others, whose names are not known, have suffered the same fates. So far, Amnesty International[209] and Human Rights Watch[210] have condemned the detention of at least eight activists and protest leaders. As details of disappearances and detentions continue to emerge, there seems to be a systematic attempt at torturing some of those in the regime's "custody" both to deter them from further political activity as well as to extract information on others deemed threatening by the regime.

Bahraini forces, taking cue from their Saudi counterparts, have also escalated sectarian-based harassment and violence. Reminiscent of ID-based killings in Beirut during Lebanon's protracted civil war, Bahraini officers are reportedly beating up[211] and holding civilians at checkpoints based on their accent (which indicates their sect). Shi'a neighborhoods have also been singled out for random police and military attacks, and several accusations have been leveled at Bahrain television for inciting[212] sectarianism and sectarian violence. It seems that the predominantly Sunni GCC states will stop at little to prevent what they perceive[213] as a Shi'a takeover of one of their own member states. One of the consequences of the GCC intervention has been the escalation of blatantly sectarian state and security policies against all Shi'a civilians, even those who did not partake in the democratic uprising.

This week's shootings, torture incidents, arrests, and disappearances are far from collateral damage of the regime's attempt at "restoring security." They are part and parcel of its plan to terrorize, silence, and in some instances, eliminate the democratic opposition within its borders. Yesterday's destruction of the Pearl Roundabout,[214] which in the last month was transformed from a symbol tying the monarchy to Bahrain's historic pearl diving industry to one indexing the histories of protest against the authoritarian rule of the Al Khalifa, is yet another example of state violence even against the memory and infrastructure of the uprising. By redesigning the space on which the Pearl Roundabout once stood, the Al Khalifa regime is able to write this momentous month out of its national history while ensuring the future life of the space will not be as welcoming to public gatherings as the previous one was.

Today, the Bahraini people's resolve is strengthened[215] in the face of the regime's escalated retaliation against their popular democratic uprising. Today, as Bahrainis defied[216] the State of Emergency and the ban on public gatherings and took to the streets, we are reminded of the currency that the word "*samidoun*" (resilient) had during the 2006 Lebanon War. Then, "*samidoun*" emerged as a lynch pin symbol of civilian defiance in the face of Israel's brutal attack on Lebanon and (some of)[217] its people. Today, the word symbolizes the resolve of Bahrain's peaceful movement for democracy and justice against the brutal attack by "its" own government, which in turn is aided and abetted by a conglomeration of the world's most authoritarian petro-regimes and their Western clients. Whether the Bahraini opposition survives this systematic campaign to destroy it remains to be seen. The implications are not just local, but regional as well in that the Bahraini uprising represents the first major manifestation of the "Arab Spring" in one of the Gulf monarchies. That journalists, writers, and bloggers are being harassed and intimidated into silence does not make their struggle any easier. Neither will the UN Secretary General Ban Ki Moon accusing[218] the Bahraini regime of possible violations of international law, or those in the White House who are "deeply troubled"[219] by the treatment of Bahraini activists and protesters. As Bahraini civilians bear the brunt of the GCC's sectarian military machine on their own, we stand humbled by their resilience.

The following list[220] of those killed by the Al Khalifa regime in its brutal suppression of the Bahraini people's peaceful, democratic uprising continues to grow:

Ali Mshemi', twenty-four years old, killed in al-Dayya on 14 February 2011;

Fadil al-Matruk, twenty-one years old, killed in al-Mahuz on 15 February 2011;

Mahmud Abu-Taki, twenty-three years old, killed in Sitrah on 17 February 2011;

Ali Mansur Khudayr, fifty-three years old, killed in Sitrah on 17 February 2011;

Isa Abdul-Hasan, sixty years old, killed in Karzakan on 17 February 2011;

Ali al-Umin, twenty-two years old, killed in Sitrah on 17 February 2011;

Abdul-Ridah Muhammad Hasan, thirty-two years old, killed in al-Malkiyyah on 21 February 2011;

Ali al-Dumistani, eighteen years old, killed in Dumistan on 13 March 2011;

Ahmad Abdullah al-Farhan, thirty years old, killed in Sitrah on 15 March 2011;

Ahmad Abdullah Hasan, twenty-two years old, killed in Hamad Town on 16 March 2011;

Jafar Muhammad Abd Ali, forty-one years old, killed in Karranah on 16 March 2011;

Jafar Abdullah Ma'yuf, thirty years old, killed in 'Ali on 16 March 2011.

Section VI
Yemen

In addition to Bahrain and Libya, the uprising in Yemen further highlights how specific state-building legacies, regime-opposition dynamics, and a state's location within regional and international alliances combine to structure the constraints on anti-regime collective action. The starting point of much discussion on Yemen is the political and geographic disjunctures between its northern, central, and southern regions. On the one hand, this effectively meant that activists and analysts had to speak of different uprisings in different parts of Yemen, and thus the major obstacles to unifying the protests under the banner of common demands and objectives. On the other hand, there were particular junctures during the first few months of the uprising in Yemen whereby such unity and coordination was indeed achieved. Regional anxieties about revolutionary contagions and spillover violence, however, meant that such success was short-lived, as the Gulf Cooperation Council (GCC) and the United States applied immense political and financial pressure to undermine the uprising. The Arabian Peninsula was deemed a no-go zone for the toppling of a regime.

Within these two contexts of geopolitical fragmentation and high regional stakes, the various forces that made up the opposition (both formal and informal) in Yemen mobilized to assert their presence in the street, solicit the support of various military factions and tribal formations, and strike alliances with other anti-regime movements and civil society groups. Simultaneously, these mobilizations also featured attempts to position themselves in proximity to leadership figures of the uprising and prospective beneficiaries of the post-conflict political spoils. This competition speaks to the degree of investment that various social and political forces currently have in the ongoing "negotiated settlement" in Yemen.

24
Yemen's Turn: An Overview

Lara Aryani[221]

20 February 2011

To begin to understand the trajectory of recent political developments in Yemen, it is necessary to cast one's eye back further than the heady days of 2011. Undoubtedly, the events in Egypt and Tunisia have lent considerable force to demonstrations in the capital, Sanaa. However, it would be unfair to the thousands of Yemenis who for years have organized daily protests throughout the country and the thousands who have been killed, imprisoned, injured, and tortured by the state to say that the widespread popular organizing against the regime of Ali Abdullah Saleh had its genesis anywhere but Yemen.

There have been street protests throughout Yemen, and especially in the south, since 2007. While the southern protesters are now demanding secession, their initial demands included grievances similar to those articulated in Egypt and Tunisia, including complaints of unemployment, increasing economic destitution, as well as political repression and under-representation. It was unsurprising that the grievances articulated by the southern protesters became anti-northern and secessionist in nature. A majority of Yemen's resources flow from oil fields, fisheries, and ports in the south into the coffers of the national government that largely favors infrastructure projects and government patrons based in Sanaa. Eager to isolate southern grievances from similar rumblings in the north, the government framed the southern protests as a regional nationalistic agitation held over from 1994, when the former north and south Yemen states fought a post-unification civil war. The government's efforts were successful as southern grievances slowly evolved into calls for secession and the popular northern reaction was of anger and defensiveness against the southerners who came to be perceived as people who were seeking to destroy national unity and who "have wanted to secede since 1990."

While there have been sporadic protests throughout the north—and a rebellion north of Sanaa that has been ongoing for almost a decade—it was the protests in Tunisia and then in Egypt that triggered the larger and more persistent protests in Sanaa and Taiz (the second largest city in the north); these have been primarily organized by university students and other middle-class activists. The protests in Sanaa overtly seek to learn from and replicate the protests in Egypt, including calling themselves "the youth movement," the use of slogans ("the people want the fall of the regime"), the emphasis on peaceful protests, setting up a public projector screen to broadcast *Al Jazeera* (in Taiz) and the use of Twitter, Facebook, YouTube, and other sites to publicize protester actions and government responses.

The emphasis on non-partisanship is also an important feature of the protests in Yemen. While early protests in January were organized by the opposition coalition, the larger more recent protests have emphatically denied partisan affiliation. Most significantly, members and supporters of Islah, the Islamist/reformist party and largest opposition party in Yemen, have largely refrained from the use of their regular Islamist slogans.

REGIME RESPONSES

The government has been closely watching developments in Egypt and Tunisia. The day after Zine El Abidine Ben Ali fled and only hours before Yemen's first planned "Day of Rage," Saleh convened an emergency session with Parliament and the Shura Council where he offered several major concessions: he would not amend the constitution to effectively permit him to be president for life; he would not run for president in the September 2013 elections; he was "against hereditary rule" (referencing what was widely expected to be his eventually handing power over to his son Ahmed); and he would increase civil service wages and cut income taxes. The government also reached out to the coalition of opposition parties, the Joint Meetings Parties (JMP)—made up of Islah, the Socialist Party, and a number of other minor parties—urging them to accept a dialogue on terms that the government had previously refused.

Days after the fall of Mubarak, as protests in Yemen, and the north in particular, began to gain steam, the regime also sent out "*baltaga*," soldiers and thugs hired to be the "pro-ruling party protesters," to attack anti-Saleh protesters with sticks, knives, and guns. The government has also continued to use its regular tactics of arresting and harassing activists and journalists. They are targeting *Al Jazeera* news crews in particular, and one rumor is that an *Al Arabiya* journalist was attacked because he was thought to be an *Al Jazeera* reporter.

One of the most vulnerable activists has been Tawakul Karman, chairperson of Women Journalists Without Chains and one of the most high-profile protest organizers. In protests of hundreds or thousands of people, mostly men, Karman is often leading the protesters' chants. While her high profile may have provided her some security thus far, she has been arrested, threatened, and harassed by the government on numerous occasions and it seems that the *baltaga* have been targeting her for attack.

THE TRANSFORMATION OF PROTESTS

There have been several key developments in the protests so far (in addition to the events described above). A day after large protests started in Taiz, a major city located in the central highlands, the regime commanded its *baltaga* in Sanaa to chant slogans against the "*burghuli*" or "*baraghila*" (pl). This is a pejorative term that was used by northern tribesmen in the 1960s and 1970s to refer to the people of the central highlands after large numbers of people from these areas moved to Sanaa to work as civil servants and businessmen. The government's effort to sow regional strife between the peoples of the northern highlands and the central highlands (as was successfully done between the peoples of the former north and south Yemeni states) seemed to backfire as public opinion against the regime was further inflamed in Sanaa and Taiz, the latter becoming a major flashpoint for protests in the north.

Another key development is the declaration by Hussein al-Ahmar, the head of a major tribal grouping, that his tribe would protect the protesters in Sanaa against a government crackdown. Other tribes in Marib also declared that they would be joining the protests and/or shielding protesters in Sanaa from attack. Hussein al-Ahmar has not yet fulfilled his promises to the protesters of Sanaa, and he, his brothers, and his late father (whom they succeeded) have played a crucial role in supporting and perpetuating Saleh's regime. Nevertheless, the al-Ahmar brothers, their late father, and their constituents have historically been a key ally of Saleh and a true defection would be a significant blow to Saleh.

Lastly, and probably most significantly, is the decision by the groups composing al-Hirak, the southern secessionist movement, to abandon the call for secession and join the call for a revolution. Al-Hirak has been organizing for secession for years now, and they are arguably as close as they have ever been to achieving this goal. Nevertheless, certain leaders within al-Hirak and the Houthis, the latter of which have been fighting a rebellion in the north of the country, have declared their support for a unified nationwide revolution to overthrow the Saleh regime.

The protests in Yemen have not yet reached the critical mass tipping point that was reached in Egypt and Tunisia. Foremost among the barriers to a surge in the number of protesters, particularly in the north, is the widespread fear of the political vacuum that would follow Saleh's removal. There is no single institution in Yemen with a monopoly over power and violence, like the Egyptian army. The armed forces are split into several factions, two of which have already faced off against each other while fighting the Houthi rebellion in the north. One faction is the army led by Saleh's rival Ali Mohsen, two significant others include the republican guard and internal security forces led by Saleh's son and nephews, respectively. In the north, the third major player is the Hashid tribal confederacy, which is both politically and militarily powerful, and is commanded by the sons of the late Shaykh Abdullah al-Ahmar (mentioned above).

THE QUESTION OF UNITY

At the time of writing, there is no unified protest movement. The most significant division is that between the north and the south, but the gap seems to be narrowing as the southern movement becomes convinced of the north's commitment to regime change. There is a formal opposition (the JMP, referenced above), but it does not seem that the protesters consider the JMP representative of their interests and demands. On 13 February, while the largest of protests were being organized in rejection of the regime and its call for dialogue, the JMP announced its acceptance of the government's terms to enter into dialogue. The JMP has since then retracted its acceptance.

Generally, the protesters seem to be composed of members of formal opposition parties, large informal activist groups that have been organizing for years throughout the south, unions, small activist groups that have been organizing in the north, and regular people who have not previously been involved in political organizing but have participated in the protests.

However, thus far, beyond the demand for Saleh's resignation, the protesters have not yet formulated a concrete set of shared demands. The impetus for the protests in each of the various regions have been the grievances related to political and economic disenfranchisement, but it is not clear that they would all agree on the nature and degree of the restructuring that would be required to adequately address their respective demands.

25
How it Started in Yemen:
From Tahrir to Taghyir

Nir Rosen[222]

18 March 2011

On 11 February after the Friday noon prayers, Yemeni students and activists organized a demonstration in the capital city of Sanaa in solidarity with the Egyptian demonstrators who were frustrated with Mubarak's refusal to resign. At about one in the afternoon they met in front of the small roundabout by the new campus of Sanaa University and marched through town chanting slogans and carrying pictures of Gamal Abdel Nasser, the Egyptian hero of Arab nationalism. Less than two hundred people took part and only two were women. They sang an excerpt from a poem by Abu al-Qasim al-Shabi, a Tunisian poet of the early twentieth century: "If the people will to live, providence is destined to favorably respond; and night is destined to fold, and the chains are certain to be broken." This song had been heard in Tunisia, Egypt, and then throughout the Arab world as popular mass uprisings spread.

The small group of demonstrators walked by throngs of Yemenis ignoring them or looking bemused while they continued their purchase of Qat, the mild stimulating narcotic nearly all Yemenis chew. One onlooker asked another who the guy in the picture was. "Gamal Abdel-Nasser," said the other man. One traffic policeman spat out that the demonstrators were sons of whores and nobodies. "What does Egypt have to do with our mothers?" asked a boy contemptuously. "Fuck them they're gay!" said another man. Some people watching shouted "Long live Husni Mubarak!" and laughed.

A Yemeni Red Crescent car with about six people in it followed the protesters from start to finish. I asked why they were there. "For them," one of them told me, gesturing at the demonstrators. A lone policeman on a motorcycle and two sanitation trucks full of young men with plenty of sticks and rocks also followed.

When the demonstrators reached the cemetery for Egyptian soldiers who died fighting against Yemeni royalists many more security forces arrived in several cars and one bus. Now there were at least thirty uniformed security men along with others in civilian clothes. Some had clubs. The two sanitation trucks full of at least twenty men also pulled up. They were obviously there to attack the demonstrators if it became necessary. After a couple of minutes in front of the cemetery it ended and people walked home. One of the female demonstrators, Tawakul Karman, smiled and shouted in front of the security forces "Down down with Ali Saleh!" She was referring to President Ali Abdullah Saleh whose rule started in 1978.

Saleh, who rules the poorest Arab country, seems poised to be the next dictator to fall in the popular revolutions spreading from Tunisia on to Egypt. Though each country is different, many of the complaints demonstrators voice are the same, and thanks to *Al Jazeera* and social media, activists are able to learn effective tactics. Yemen today is an uncomfortable amalgam of North Yemen and South Yemen, united in 1990. Yemen receives attention for the small al-Qaeda presence but this is the least of its problems. In the north Saleh has been brutally fighting Houthis seeking autonomy by massively bombing their villages, displacing hundreds of thousands and then attacking displaced civilians. In the south he is at war against secessionists. The peaceful southern movement which demonstrated for a more just access to power and resources was violently crushed, leading some of its members to turn to armed resistance. Saleh delegates control of much of the country to tribal shaykhs whose loyalty is tenuous. Yemen's powerful Saudi neighbors are deeply involved in its internal affairs, their money purchasing officials and spreading Wahabi Islam. Saleh has instrumentalized al-Qaeda against domestic foes while using the threat of al-Qaeda to extort money from the US government, which sees the Muslim world only through the prism of the war on terror. As with Egypt, Tunisia, and Bahrain, the United States has had a close relationship with the Yemeni dictatorship thanks to the war on terror. US President Barack Obama increased military assistance for Yemen from sixty-seven million dollars in 2009 to one hundred and fifty million dollars in 2010. Documents released by Wikileaks exposed the cozy relationship between senior US officials and the Yemeni dictatorship. In one document we learned about America's beloved General David Petraeus conniving to lie to the Yemeni people about who was killing Yemeni civilians in the name of the war on terror. Instead of fighting the al-Qaeda bogeyman, Saleh's

US-backed security forces fight Houthis, southerners, journalists, and students.

The Joint Meeting Parties, or JMP, formed in 2002, served as a loyal opposition composed of parties with divergent goals and constituencies. The regime has been able to exploit this and the JMP has had little success. On 2 February, in response to Egypt's revolution, Saleh promised not to run again in 2013 (a promise he also made and broke before the 2006 elections too) and that his son would not succeed him. In Sanaa it was not the establishment parties who started the revolution, but youth, just as in the rest of the Arab world. In defiance of those who predicted that Yemen was "not Tunisia" or "not Egypt," that it was too poor, or uneducated, or tribal, the protests have been spreading there, finally threatening Saleh in his capital city. In response to the surprising and powerful showing of the non-aligned youth, the Houthi rebels in the north promised their cooperation while southern demonstrators stopped calling for secession and only for "*suqut al-nidham*," or the fall of the regime, the same words shouted throughout the Arab world.

The small al-Qaeda franchise in Yemen is known as al-Qaeda in the Arabian Peninsula (AQAP). The American industry of terrorism experts has dubbed AQAP the greatest terrorist threat facing the United States and has wrung its hands over AQAP's threat to the Yemeni regime. This is despite the fact that AQAP's international successes amount to a failed underwear bomb and a package bomb that failed to detonate. In fact the regime does little to pursue AQAP because it does not perceive it as a threat. Rather than being too weak to fight AQAP, the regime has focused its various security forces attention on fighting domestic political opposition, killing or wounding hundreds of demonstrators. Likewise the demonstrators have not been concerned about al-Qaeda except as a pretext for the regime's security forces to target innocent people or receive international support. Al-Qaeda is a marginal phenomenon in Yemen (as in the rest of the Middle East). While it is the primary concern of the United States government and hence the United States media, it is far from the real problems facing Yemen, which the demonstrators express in a near blackout of international media attention.

Later that night on 11 February, Husni Mubarak resigned. "You should do something," one activist said to another, who called up several other activists and suggested a candlelight vigil in front of the university to show support for the Egyptian victory. By eight-thirty in the evening hundreds of Yemeni students, academics, activists, and citizens gathered in front of the new university. Their numbers grew to the thousands. Chants included:

"The Egyptian people brought down Mubarak!"
"Long live the Egyptian people!"
"Revolution until victory!"
"One thousand greetings to *Al Jazeera*!"

The Yemeni popular opposition wanted the powerful satellite network to focus on them as it had on their brethren in Tunisia and Egypt and they knew that without *Al Jazeera* none of the revolutions could have succeeded.

Soon the chants' theme shifted from Egypt to Yemen:

"Yesterday Tunisia, today Egypt, tomorrow Yemen will open the prison!"
"Down with the regime!"
"The people want the regime to collapse!"
"Revolution oh Yemen from Sanaa to Aden!"
"The Yemeni people is fed up with Ali Abdullah Saleh"

The demonstrators were eventually met by soldiers guarding the Egyptian embassy and they turned around and gathered in Sanaa's Liberation Square. Most of the square had already been blocked off by Yemeni security forces and tribesmen with whom they were collaborating. By about ten-thirty in the evening several trucks full of heavily armed soldiers began to arrive. At least ten army trucks carrying dozens of men in civilian clothing, who were probably members of the Yemeni security forces, arrived as did many security force pick-up trucks and jeeps. Hundreds and hundreds of men in civilian attire carrying sticks, and knives as well as automatic weapons arrived carrying pictures of President Saleh. They attacked some demonstrators with knives and sticks and at this the majority of the anti-regime demonstrators dispersed. Hundreds of uniformed members of the Yemeni security forces were present facilitating the arrival of those chanting support for Saleh. The security forces also closed off the roads in the area of Tahrir Square, allowing only pro-regime demonstrators in who came running with signs, sticks, knives, and automatic weapons. The remaining few hundred anti-regime demonstrators lasted for a while with a few dozen of them sitting on the street. There was some pushing back and forth as the columns of pro- and anti-regime demonstrators met, and some water bottles were thrown back and forth. But dozens of police in riot gear separated the two sides. Anti-regime demonstrators burned pictures of Saleh. They shouted at the pro-regime demonstrators "army wearing civilian clothes!" Pro-regime demonstrators shouted "with our spirits with our blood we sacrifice for you oh Ali!" Anti-regime demonstrators responded by chanting "Oh oh leave oh Ali" and "Oh God oh God down with Ali Abdullah!" Demonstrators on both sides danced and sang. Then hundreds more pro-regime demonstrators charged the opposition youth, forcing them all to flee. This happened under the eyes of the chief of security for the area, hundreds of various security forces and the General Secretary for Sanaa, Amin Juman. In the end thousands of pro-regime demonstrators had occupied the square singing, banging on drums, and dancing. At least ten anti-regime demonstrators had been arrested.

President Saleh's people were very wise to pre-empt the Yemeni youth opposition and seize Sanaa's Tahrir Square, preventing the opposition activists from occupying the square in the way that their Egyptian counterparts had occupied their own Tahrir Square. For the Yemeni opposition it would have been both a symbolic and strategic victory. Symbolic because it would obviously associate them with the Egyptian people's victory, and strategic because it is basically the only such large public square in the city. The government denied the demonstrators any location to call their own. At night around the outskirts of the square dozens of Yemeni security force members are sprawled on steps or on the street, their Kalashnikovs on their laps, tapping their large clubs on their palms or swinging them. Thousands of men in tribal attire fill the square, pacing in boredom or standing indolently, their cheeks swollen like tennis balls from the qat paste in their mouths. In addition to their Gambia decorative daggers, many of them have clubs. It is widely believed their tribal leaders have ordered them to the square. Security forces gather some of them during the day to oppose anti-government demonstrators and intimidate them. At night, corn is roasting for them, and they are given other meals. There are several long tents in the square. Above one is a banner that says "International Support Destruct Terrorism." Inside are a few dozen men sprawled on the floor chewing Qat. In another tent dozens of men watch a circle of men dancing in a circle to a drumbeat and waving their daggers. People eye me suspiciously. It is a tense mob and I feel like I am in some mix of tribalism, fascism, and drug-induced stupor. A few hundred men stand around in a crowd and listen to various tribal poets shouting speeches into a loudspeaker. Whoever fights the eagle of Yemen will go down, they are told, and President Saleh made Yemen a leader among nations. "Long live our leader the struggler!" he shouted. Another poet denied the widespread belief that they were in the square for money. "If it wasn't for our president you would be crushed like Iraq," a poet said, asking where were Saddam's sons Qusay and Uday. "See how blood is flowing in your country!" he called to Iraqis. "We are yours Abu Ahmad," he addressed the president, "with our guns and our soldiers."

"This is the real problem in our demonstrations," Tawakul Karman told me on Saturday 12 February, "that they send these *baltaga*. Since the Tunisian revolution we have organized eleven demos and they send these guys with their Gambia knives. The revolution is starting and gets bigger and bigger, we just need to decide." Tahrir Square had never had tents before, she told me. "These thugs and national security members can protest whenever they want and build tents without permission and we are not allowed to protest. These tents are there since 3 February. They occupy the place so we can't take it. But we will sleep there one day." Karman runs an NGO called Women Journalists Without Chains. She is also part of the younger more rebellious generation of the Islah party, ostensibly an opposition party but one close to the regime. Twenty-one demonstrators had been arrested the night before, she told me. "Sometimes we don't know about the prisoners until some time after." She could hardly contain her excitement about the freedom she anticipated to arrive following the Egyptian victory.

We call Houthis and the movement in the south and the GNP to get along with us in one national struggle to make this ruler fall down and the response is strong. But practically the revolution was started by students and young people, specifically Sanaa University students, and it's proceeding by very well studied steps under the slogan of peaceful performance and Jasmine spirit. Unlike Mubarak the international community hates Ali Saleh.

Karman's arrest on 22 January helped mobilize the activist community. At one o'clock in the morning that day she was driving home with her husband when several cars cut them off. They asked her to get out but she demanded an arrest warrant. Five men from the National Security Forces took her by force inside their car. She shouted that she was being kidnapped and neighbors came out but the police drove off with her.

They released me because of the protests all around the country. They expected to silence my voice by putting me in prison but the popular protests surprised them as did the international protests. Because of the huge anger and the pressure on them internationally and locally they released me.

Karman was charged with attacking the regime and calling for an uprising through protests and demonstrations as well as calling for prohibited demonstrations and protests. She was released with her home as a guarantee. "At any moment I can be arrested again I don't know what the next stages are," she said. This was Karman's second arrest.

It's unusual for them to treat women like this but women annoyed them very much before Tunisia's Jasmine Revolution. We have been organizing weekly protests for human rights and freedom of speech, for prisoners, every week since May 2007. After the Jasmine Revolution we realized that all of our previous struggles, fighting corruption and for human rights won't lead to any result. Three years of struggle and the human rights situation keeps falling down, we have released tens of reports about human rights and freedom of the press and corruption in Yemen. Now we believe there is no solution for human rights except the departure of this regime.

Karman's brother Tariq is close to the regime and recites poetry in official events. The day after Karman was released she attended another demonstration. Tariq received a phone call from President Saleh. "You have to control your sister and put her in house arrest," the president said, adding an Arabic expression, "otherwise whoever splits the stick of obedience, kill him." Tariq was pressured to deny that this ever happened but he sent his sister a text message on her phone apologizing for his recantation. "This threat and the arrest before it and the arrest before that one keeps empowering the human rights movement and enabled me and strengthened my will," she said,

I used to receive hundreds of threats by SMS, email and Facebook, but this threat came from the president of the country. Before and after that threat I saw signs telling me that they might carry out that threat. In one of the protests a woman was behind me and she was holding a knife but the guys noticed her and captured her and handed her to the police. And now at most demonstrations and protests these thugs go directly towards me with the daggers. You can see on YouTube a video they put up called "the escape of the agent Tawakul Karman." When I walk all the men are around me protecting me, before I used to go alone. The *baltaga* come and cheer our slogans and suddenly they raise their daggers in front of us and attack us but for sure we will make the regime fall. As it fell down in Egypt it will fall down here in Yemen.

Karman complained about American financial support and training for the security forces who attack the protestors while wearing civilian clothes. Some of them were members of the Central Security's counter-terrorism unit. "The National Security Agency was founded after September 11 to fight terrorism in Yemen but it left its job to struggle against journalists, human rights activists and began overseeing terrorism instead of struggling against it."

Karman's arrest helped galvanize the opposition. Khalid al-Ansi, a lawyer and activist explained to me that the post-Egypt demonstrations were the largest independent ones yet, not organized by the official opposition parties. He told me:

They went out by themselves not following political parties, young people started to call for them on their own, not through political parties or famous people. There was a demonstration in Yemen to support Tunisia. On Facebook I called on youth and my friends not to raise the Tunisian flag but to raise the Yemeni flag if you are serious about demanding this regime to fall.

The security forces brought *baltaga* to provoke riots and attack the demonstrators.

They had sticks and pictures of the president. They came with their knives. They were cursing us. The police was between us and them and they allowed them in and provided them with space to bring them into our protest. That day they closed university gate. We tried not to be provoked. They threw stones, soda cans. The police arrested one of the protestors. I was asked to give a speech that day. My speech was directed to police and army. I told them that we go out for you because you are suffering more than us. Your presence here is against your will. And I said Ali Abdullah Saleh has to fall and he will fall. I asked the protestors "do you agree to be subjects, animals?" and they said "no," and

I said "how can you accept that Ali Abdullah Saleh bequeaths us to his son like animals?" Then I talked about the suffering in Yemen. The prices in Yemen are higher than Saudi Arabia and Saudi Arabia is an oil rich country and we are a poor country.

Al-Ansi also complained about corruption in the universities. The free openings for qualified students had been reduced to make more space available for unqualified students who paid in US dollars. He said:

I spoke about how they changed our republic into a monarchy, we have the Saleh Mosque, Saleh Institution, Saleh Foundation, Saleh Projects for Unemployment, if we remain silent he will change it from Republic of Yemen to Republic of Saleh. Instead of starting a charity foundation he just needs to stop corruption. There was a microphone, everybody was silent, even the security forces. I wanted to remind the forces and police about their problem. Even political parties don't talk to these people. I discovered we get wide respect from these people.

That night I dreamed I was arrested. In the morning I found many calls, early calls, one of them from Tawakul Karman, I read the news about her arrest. I start to think what we have to do. I spoke to her husband, her organization called me. I said we have to go demonstrate. I felt that they arrested Tawakul because she was a head of these demonstrations and if they arrest her there will be no more demonstrations, and if there is no demonstration they will keep her in jail. I called the youth to go demonstrate, we were about two hundred and then the older people followed us. We made our way to the new university. We found many police cars trying to surround the place. They arrested one of the youth who led chants in the demonstration so I started to lead the calls. They sang the poem by the Tunisian al-Shabi and chanted "with our spirits, with our blood, we sacrifice for you oh Yemen!"

Bystanders joined them. Two policemen arrested al-Ansi. "I don't use violence," he said, "I want to show to these people 'we know you are only a tool.'" In the police car one policeman shouted at him demanding to know why they were demonstrating. "For you," al-Ansi said, "my life is better than your life." He talked to them about their low salaries. "Why don't you go out in the thousands?" one of the policemen asked, "you are too few." Twenty-one other demonstrators were arrested. One of them was beaten. A journalist was also arrested. "After I was arrested people got angry and continued demonstrating," al-Ansi said. Because he was a prominent lawyer the prosecutor general wanted al-Ansi released.

I said I will not go out unless you release all the youth with me and after you release Tawakul Karman. Many people came to visit us. I told them to go protest, not to focus on trying to release me, continue demonstrating, look after Tawakul Karman, she is a woman, it's hard for a woman to be in jail. If there is a demonstration we will be released. The government thought if they arrest us there won't be demonstrations.

Ahmad Seif Hashid is an independent member of parliament who has served for eight years. He helped lead the demonstration demanding the release of Karman and the other activists. Hundreds took part and were met by the police and the Central Security forces. Hashid could not be arrested because of his status and some of his colleagues clung to him to avoid arrest as well but Hashid and others were beaten with fists and clubs. Major Raed Kamal, head of the May 22nd police station led the attack against the demonstrators, telling his men that they were paid agents of the West. "The Yemeni regime is a stained copy of the Egyptian regime in its policy and maneuvers," he said, "what's happening in Egypt had a big effect."

The demonstrations soon started to attract common people on the street outside the network of activists. Muhammad Ali al-Muhamadi is a thirty-eight-year-old mechanic. He did not belong to a political party and he did not own a television. He had six children and worked illegally in Saudi garages. He saw the demonstration while walking to work.

I joined because I am against the regime. I faced difficulties from shaykhs and others and these problems destroyed my family. They even shot at my children while I was working in Saudi Arabia. I went to the justice institutions and despite all the confessions and proof they increased injustice, in addition to what we suffer economically. From this I concluded that the Yemeni government uses the law to serve the strong and doesn't serve the poor class and labor class and as one of the Yemeni people that is persecuted it's my right to express my feelings and defend our rights and our freedom and our honor. The Egyptians suffered from the same thing we suffer here and they have the right to choose their destiny. I encourage any persecuted person to demand their rights democratically because human was born free and human is human not animal, he can't be guided by a stick. And I want from the regime to treat us like humans and make the law serve everybody equally without discrimination. We don't feel like humans, we feel like animals. We don't have health or security. I met people demonstrating. I found them suffering from the same thing I suffer. So it's my right to express my opinion and express what I suffer by this current regime.

On Saturday 12 February Muhammad joined the demonstrators at the new university at ten in the morning. From only one hundred at first, the crowd of mostly students grew to over one thousand demonstrators calling for the fall of the regime. Before the march began police arrested a man making signs. A group of *baltaga* attempted to provoke a clash with the demonstrators so they withdrew to a different location. When the demonstrators got to Qasr street they were attacked by *baltaga* with daggers, clubs, and axes as well as security forces with electrical stun guns. Muhammad was caught and stunned several times while his hand was stabbed and he was beaten on his head and leg with a club. He was slapped and punched and insulted. He maintained that the man with the electrical stun gun was a member of the security forces wearing civilian clothes. Undeterred, Muhammad vowed to attend more demonstrations.

The next day, 13 February, saw larger demonstrations. The demonstrators met at Sanaa University's new campus at ten in the morning and marched for about three hours, their numbers exceeding one thousand.

Importantly, tens of thousands of people saw the demonstrators march. Observers included young students in green or brown uniforms coming home from school, buses full of passengers, taxis, and people in their cars. Many cheered and waved as they sat in traffic. One taxi driver with a picture of President Saleh on his windshield also shouted "down with Ali Saleh!"

When they passed the home of the president's son Ahmad they shouted:

"Oh Ahmad tell your father Yemen is not your father's property!"
"Oh Hamada (nickname for Saleh's son Ahmad) tell your father Seventieth road doesn't belong to your father!"
"Oh Hamada tell your father, all the people hate you!"

"Oh free ones! Oh free ones! No to Ahmad and no to Amar!" they shouted, referring to Saleh's sons.
When they walked past the Saudi embassy "Oh King Abdullah, prepare a space for Ali Abdullah!"

They arrived at Seventieth Street, leading to the main parade grounds as well as the president's mosque and the president's residence. Security forces hastily formed a row and had lined the road with barbed wire. CNN had their footage confiscated by plain-clothed security agents. Uncertain of where to go next, the demonstrators debated if they should go to Tahrir Square or back to the university. They ended up at the Rowaishan Roundabout. Some students sat on the street, causing traffic jams while other students tried to direct traffic. At one in the afternoon several trucks full of Central Security men in green uniforms arrived as did pick-up trucks with Central Security men in riot gear. They all carried clubs. Some had tear-gas shotguns, electric stun guns, or automatic rifles. Emergency response police in blue uniforms and many security men in civilian clothes also arrived. Several security men in civilian clothes had been taking pictures of various demonstrators from the beginning of the day's events. The security men charged, swinging their batons at demonstrators who fled. At least twenty demonstrators were beaten with batons on their heads and backs. Others were beaten with fists and kicked. At least two demonstrators were attacked with electrical tasers. Mizar Baggash Ghanem a student leader at Sanaa University was shocked from behind. They also attacked leading activist Khaled al-Anisi with electrical stunners and arrested him, though he was later released. Female activist and journalist Samia al-Aghbari was attacked by Central Security men who threw her on the ground, causing her head to hit the curb. She lost consciousness and was taken to the hospital. At least one Central Security man loaded his rifle prominently to intimidate men trying to protect Tawakul Karman. Several youth were arrested including one who was first severely beaten at the intersection. Also beaten with batons on his back and wrist was Faez Nu'man a youth activist and member of the Communist Party youth committee. Another youth was beaten on his head in front of the nearby Happy Land supermarket whereupon he started to bleed. He too was arrested. A civilian security official from the area coordinated the Yemeni security response.

Later that day I met with Baggash and Nu'man. Baggash is a thirty-one-year-old activist and student at Sanaa University's trade faculty. He was a member of the executive office of student unions for Sanaa University and Amran University. Most of the demonstrators were unemployed young people and students, he told me. He said:

> Tunisia was the start, we went out on the sixteenth of January. Our first activity was to support the Tunisian Revolution and the fall of the regime of Yemen. We are the peaceful youth and student revolution. Hundreds of people organize it. Forty-eight youths have been arrested. They tried to arrest me more than once. The officers came to get me and the guys surrounded me and prevented it. Today the director of the 22nd of May police station came to arrest me specifically. This officer is the one who arrested thirty-two guys in one day. He focuses on the youth and activists.

Since Tahrir Square was denied to them, Baggash and his colleagues renamed the square in front of their university Taghyir, or change, Square. To avoid being attacked by the *baltaga*, they left the square that morning. In Rowaishan Roundabout Mizar gripped Ahmad Seif Hashid to avoid being dragged away. Security men used the electrical stunner on him and he was beaten but Hashid held him tightly so the police could not take Mizar away.

Faez Nu'man is a thirty-year-old graduate of Sanaa University who studied civil engineering. "We are inspired by Tunisia's and Egypt's revolutions that these dictatorial regimes shall leave because they oppress their people and their sons inside their country," he said. Nu'man had never been arrested but he had been beaten in previous demonstrations by security forces and *baltaga*. The *baltaga* phenomenon started in 2008, he told me. On that day's demonstration Nu'man saw emergency response police beating at least one man with their fists and legs and Nu'man was also among the victims of the security forces.

The next morning, on 14 February Nu'man was arrested while gathering for a demonstration in front of the university and taken to the May 22nd police station. Ahmad Seif Hashid and other students led the demonstration. Several members of Central Security and the emergency response police had electrical stun guns. One security officer filmed the demonstrators on his iPhone. Many security men had clubs. There were several army officers including one from special forces and numerous security men in civilian attire along with young *baltaga* who looked like high school students. "He starves you all year and pays you one thousand riyals today so you support him," one university student said to the *baltaga*. Police stood between the two sides as they shouted back and forth at each other.

Protesters shouted:

"We won't chew qat and we won't sleep until the regime falls!"
"Oh Hamdi return return, your people is begging at the borders!"
they shouted, referring to the president who preceded Saleh.
"Our demands are clear, leave oh Saleh!"
"No dialogue, no dialogue, resign or escape!" shouted the demonstrators, in response to the *baltaga* shouting in support of dialogue with the president.

The stand-off continued until suddenly about five hundred men from the lawyers syndicate came marching into the roundabout. The *baltaga* found themselves surrounded on both sides and the crowds mixed chaotically. Khalid al-Ansi and other lawyers led the demonstrators toward the Ministry of Justice. On the way, by the Kuwaiti hospital, security forces stopped them, but the lawyers pushed through the club swinging security men. In front of the National Institute of Administrative Science the demonstrators were met by high school students holding sticks and raising pictures of the president. The young students tried to attack the lawyers but were stopped by the police. Eventually the demonstrators turned back and walked to the university.

Near the university roundabout, Abdullah Ghorab, a BBC Arabic correspondent, was attacked with sticks and beaten harshly by *baltaga* pro-government thugs under the gaze of security men and he had to cut short his transmission. Security men shouted to the thugs that he was a spy and they should attack him. The thugs called him a mason, a spy, a dog, and said he was selling the country for dollars. "I showed them my ID," he told me, "I said 'I'm from BBC, I'm a professional, I show all sides.' They told the *baltaga* that I am an agent 'beat the spy.' I saw more than one hundred and fifty people with sticks, if they caught me I would be dead. I ran for two hundred meters to a small alley and sat to hide for a minute." Ten *baltaga* found him. They head-butted him, leaving a large bloody scar from top to bottom. His shirt and hands were covered with blood. They beat him on his back with sticks. The thugs took him to a white Land Rover belonging to Hafidh Ma'ayad. Ma'ayad is President of the Yemeni economic association, one of the biggest goverment associations. He is also one of the financial leaders of the country and a senior leader in the ruling party. Ma'ayad was sitting in the front passenger seat and called Abdullah a spy. "Shame on you!" Ghorab shouted at them, "this issue will grow bigger." Ma'ayad threatened Ghorab with tribal vengeance. Ghorab asked him how he could threaten him when there was blood on Ghorab's face. Central Security officers came and advised Ma'ayad to let Abdullah go. Some of the thugs who attacked him left in Ma'ayad's car. The day before *baltaga* had also tried to attack Abdullah during the demonstration but he escaped. "I am not ok, and the country is not ok," says Abdullah angrily, "this is the result of speaking the truth." Later that day Ma'ayad called a tribal shaykh related to Ghorab so that their two tribes could reconcile. "This is the tribal system that stinks that we are suffering from it," he told me.

In the morning near the Beit Bus roundabout, where day laborers gather and wait for long hours to find work, about one hundred day-laborers began to demonstrate and call for the president to resign because there was no work. Policemen and general security men arrested the man who was organizing them as well as about seven laborers. At least fifteen riot police came and attacked the protestors, forcibly dispersing them. Six or seven were arrested. Later on pro-government thugs attacked anti-government student demonstrators with bottles and stones near the new campus. The students called for restraint and retreated to the university. Campus police officers opened the gates for them. Inside seven or eight students were beaten by six or seven university police and there was a group standing watching. A senior university security officer was in charge of the attack.

On 16 February hundreds of judges protested in front of the Ministry of Justice. The Yemeni student union called for a demonstration that day and hundreds of new demonstrators came out. The university gate was closed by authorities, forcing them to change the direction of their march. At least four police pick-up trucks dropped off dozens of *baltaga* by the demonstrators. When they approached the Foreign Ministry the demonstrators were attacked by *baltaga* and security forces. Students were beaten with chains and clubs and stabbed with daggers. The *baltaga* threw stones as well. Three students were arrested and taken away in a military vehicle in the same area. Foreshadowing what was to come, some of the *baltaga* had pistols and fired shots into the air. Radhwan Masud, head of the student union, maintained that police officers in civilian clothes attacked students. "We know them and their faces," he said, "they have attacked students in the past. We know them very well. Some students who were hurt didn't go to hospitals because they were afraid they would be followed by the police."

Just as the demonstrators were grateful to *Al Jazeera* for its support and its populist reporting, governments throughout the Arab world and their hired thugs hated the satellite channel. The *baltaga* searched the crowds for *Al Jazeera*'s correspondent, Ahmad al-Shalafi and attacked the station's cameraman.

Amir al-Gimri, a first-year medical student with a hypertrophied leg was unable to escape. He was attacked by police and *baltaga*. They called him a traitor and a spy, slapped his face, and threw him on the ground. They beat his head and his legs, including his bad leg, with clubs. They left him on the ground unable to get up. Activists carried him to the hospital.

Suheil al-Kherbash, a twenty-five-year-old electrician attended a demonstration for the first time on 15 February after seeing a call on Facebook. "We went to demand removing the regime," he told me, "the general situation is bad, corruption, bribery, the government is seized by a few people." Egypt's revolution was a historic achievement, he said, "it gives us inspiration." He took part in the next day's demonstration. The police who were blocking the *baltaga* moved away to allow for the *baltaga* to attack. "We tried to convince the *baltaga* that what they are doing is not ethical and everybody should express themselves and we should not collect at the same place." Then the emergency police attacked. Suheil was beaten with clubs and electrically stunned in his kidneys. They beat his back and head with their rifle butts. His friends wrapped a bandage around his head and it quickly was soaked in blood. "I will definitely demonstrate again," he said.

That day I was sitting in a taxi when a young man at an intersection throwing leaflets into car windows threw one into ours. It said:

> The Yemen Youth Organization with the cooperation of the Yemen Change and Reformation Youth and Future Youth are organizing demonstrations to request more rights and freedom and to remove the representatives of corruption on Thursday and Friday the 17th and 18th of February. Please be with us and on time. The first meeting is in front of the gate of the new Sanaa University. The slogan is peaceful youthful and independent.

The role of independent youth was a new phenomenon, which had gained a crucial fillip from Tunisia and Egypt. "We've never had real street mobilizations," Yemeni political scientist Abdulghani al-Aryani told me:

> Tunisia and Egypt were massively significant. Before Tunisia the opposition had a demonstration of two hundred. After Tunisia they came in the thousands. After Egypt it became an avalanche. There is a new appreciation of collective power. What the formal political establishment could not do, to bring the people together, the youth protest has succeeded in doing.

Things continued to escalate on Thursday 17 February, when demonstrations started at eleven in the morning. Because the *baltaga* were waiting by the university the demonstrators marched to Sanaa's Ribat street. Their numbers exceeded two thousand that day. Security forces and *baltaga* attacked them on the intersection of Ribat and Sixtieth streets. The attackers used stones, clubs, and fired many shots into the air. At least thirty demonstrators were injured, some with serious injuries. Samir al-Nimri, an *Al Jazeera* cameraman, was badly beaten and his camera was shattered.

The Yemeni regime responded like Arab dictators in Tunisia, Egypt, Bahrain, Libya, and elsewhere. But the people's fear was gone, and the regime's days were numbered.

That day I took a taxi. It was three in the afternoon and the driver already had a mouth full of Qat. I asked him if there were any demonstrations today. "In Tahrir Square," he said, referring to the pro-government sit-in the Yemeni government has arranged. "He has to go," he said matter of factly, "like in Egypt." I asked if he expected a revolution in Yemen. "There has to be one," he said. "How will he go?" I asked. "In a revolution," he said. "Do all the people think like this?" I asked. "Yes," he said. "What about the army and security forces?" I asked. "When there is a revolution there is no fear," he said. "But Tahrir Square is full of government supporters," I said. "We'll remove them," he smiled, showing me how with his hand. "He has to go, to Saudi Arabia, or France."

"God grant you victory," I said as I left. He smiled a big green-toothed Qat grin.

The Yemeni Qat-chewing habit was evinced as a factor militating against revolution there. In Yemen the daily cycle for most people seems to revolve around Qat, which they start chewing in the early afternoon, halting other activities and often gathering at "Qat chews." In fact these sessions are where people discuss issues very passionately, and they can be seen as a grass roots democracy, a place where debates are continuous, especially when the press is not free. Thanks to Qat-chewing there are no secrets, everybody talks, even ministers participate, and the information travels and spreads. Qat is a stimulant. It is not like being in an opium den. It makes you want to do things; it leads to agitated discussions; it does not prevent activism. Unlike some of their Gulf neighbors, Yemenis are not spoiled and are willing to put up with the hardships of a revolution. When holding sit-ins Qat can actually help, keeping you awake. Unfortunately Qat is also a way for the government to attract *baltaga*.

The demonstrations continued to grow, forcing the establishment opposition parties to take a more aggressive stance against the regime and leading to defections of major tribal leaders. Taghyir, change, became the semi-official name for the demonstrator's camp, and even *Al Jazeera* referred to it as such.

Taking advantage of the lack of any strong US response to his regime's abuses and the earthquake in Japan distracting the world's attention, Saleh's forces increased their violent crackdown over the weekend of 12 and 13 March, killing at least seven protestors while injuring hundreds of others. In a pre-dawn raid the youth demonstrators camped by Sanaa University were ambushed with live automatic rifle fire, rubber bullets, electrical stun guns, and some form of gas that caused terrible convulsions. The regime also began to expel the few remaining foreign correspondents covering the protests. Obama's silence on Saleh's escalating attacks on demonstrators and its tacit support for his tactics makes it likely that when Saleh falls the government that succeeds him will be less friendly to the United States. President Saleh has offered reforms but as in Tunisia, Egypt, Bahrain, and Libya, once the dictator declares war on his own people his days are numbered. The recent Arab revolts have also shown that once a dictator concedes to the demands of the people he is transferring legitimacy to them, and their victory is inevitable. The chants in Yemen are now "After Qadhafi, oh Ali!"

[This is a longer version of a shorter article appearing in the 21 March issue of the New Statesman*]*

26
Saleh Defiant

Ziad Abu-Rish[223]

23 March 2011

In the face of popular protests as well as defections by Yemeni diplomats, government ministers, and military leaders, President Ali Abdullah Saleh yesterday invited the Yemeni youth to participate in a "transparent and open dialogue." He also announced that he would step down as president by the end of this year, and not—as he had promised earlier—when his term expires in 2013. It is tempting to understand Saleh's obstinance as detached from reality given the protests and defections. However, a closer examination of these developments might offer a different take on both Saleh and the nature of his regime. Studying the context in which protests and defections are taking place—without undermining the legitimate aspirations of the Yemeni people—points to a rational calculation and gamble on Saleh's part as he continues to cling to power.

Of the litany of defections that have occurred, the most important in terms of the structure of Saleh's regime are those of his former allies and political partners General Ali Muhsin Saleh al-Ahmar (including his military commanders) and Abdul-Majid al-Zindani. Also important is the publically declared opposition of Hamid al-Ahmar—a long-time opposition figure—as well as Sadeq al-Ahmar and Hussein al-Ahmar—both of whom, while not part of the official regime structure, were certainly not considered members of the opposition prior to this week. The significance of such defections and declarations can only be appreciated within an understanding of the nature of political and social organization in Yemen.

As was the case in Tunisia, Egypt, and to a certain extent in Libya, the loyalty, unity, and coordination of an authoritarian regime's coercive institutions are central to its longevity in the face of massive popular uprisings. In the case of Yemen, these coercive institutions can be divided into the Armed Forces (that is, the army, air force, and navy), the Special Forces, the Republican Guard, the

Counter-Terrorism Forces, and the various intelligence apparatuses (including the Central Security Forces and the National Security Bureau). While the renouncement of General Ali Muhsin al-Ahmar precipitated the defection of several military brigades and their leaders, President Ali Abdullah Saleh continues to command the remaining loyal brigades, as well as the Special Forces and the Republican Guard (both headed by his son Ahmad Saleh), the Central Security Forces and the Counter-Terrorism Unit (headed by his nephew Yahya Saleh), and the National Security Bureau (headed by another nephew, Ammar Saleh).

This division of military forces, both loyal and opposed to the Saleh regime, helps to explain the increasing frequency of clashes between different military factions. It also appears to be setting the stage for a military showdown between the regime and the opposition, the likes of which we have yet to see in the region. While Libya immediately comes to mind, the unfolding of events there were/are different in terms of a popular uprising-turned-armed-rebellion primarily fought on the outskirts of cities. There currently are a number of tanks in the capital Sanaa that have been deployed by both the regime and those defectors that have joined the opposition. In the absence of some political settlement, this situation could very well lead to a military confrontation that would take place as much within urban centers as it would on their outskirts and other areas.

However, military elites are not the only players involved—neither in terms of defections nor in terms of mobilizing for an urban war. The al-Ahmar brothers are key political elites who have also declared their opposition to the regime. Collectively, they represent one of the wealthiest families in Yemen, having benefited greatly from the economic privatization and liberalization measures of the past twenty years. They are also one of the most politically influential families, which partly explains how they were able to benefit so much from the economic reforms that were part of the IMF and World Bank restructuring policies, and are able to call on significant numbers of well-armed and organized tribesmen. Each having inherited one of the many powerful positions held by their father, Shaykh Abdullah al-Ahmar, these brothers represent the core political party and tribal forces that have joined the opposition.

Hamid al-Ahmar heads the Islah Party, a pillar of the formal opposition in Yemen, and was an early supporter of the uprising there. Sadeq al-Ahmar is the Shaykh al-Mashayikh of the second largest tribal confederacy, Hashid, which is also the most powerful in terms of its unity and capacity for collective action—meaning that when its leadership declares a position or calls for an action, its membership can be relied on to mobilize toward such decisions. Initially quiet, the Hashid Confederacy declared its opposition to the regime on Sunday 21 March—the same day Ali Muhsin al-Ahmar did. Beyond the numerical membership and capacity for collective action, one important feature of the Hashid Confederacy is that it includes the Sanhan tribe from which President Saleh hails. The delayed defection of the Hashid Confederacy, as compared to other tribal groups—such as the tribal council headed by another al-Ahmar brother, Hussein—can be explained as an internal process of reconciling the allegiances of the Sanhan and other pro-Saleh tribes and perhaps even their potential transfer to Ali Muhsin (who is also from the Sanhan tribe) and the al-Ahmar brothers. Another important factor in explaining the timing of the defection of the Sanhan tribe and Hashid Confederacy is the Friday massacre by regime forces in which fifty-two fatalities and over two hundred injuries were reported, many of whom were members of the Hashid Tribal Confederacy.

Finally, there is the defection of Abdul-Majid al-Zindani, a Salafi cleric who has wide appeal in Yemen. He has long been a prominent ideological leader for certain factions of the Islah Party and has extended his influence through the establishment of al-Iman University. His ties to Islamist militants are well known and he has been a key ally of President Saleh. When the mass protests first emerged on the streets of Sanaa, al-Zindani issued a statement condemning them and instructing people to return to their homes. Ignored, he has since pledged his opposition to Saleh and solidarity with the protesters. This is a crucial loss for Saleh, but it also highlights the challenge of maintaining a diverse oppositional coalition composed of marginalized poor and political elites, southern secessionists, urban progressives, and Salafis—a point that will be addressed in our next update.

Up until Sunday, President Saleh did not seem to be phased by the uprisings his regime faced. However, Sunday featured the resignation of his Minister of Human Rights, Saleh's sacking of his cabinet, and then the announcement of major military and tribal defections. While an authoritarian leader's sacking of his cabinet is usually a move meant to placate protesters (a la Jordan and Egypt), it seems plausible that it was an attempt to pre-empt the humiliation of additional cabinet defections. Furthermore, any defections from the sacked cabinet can always be described as a function of revenge on Saleh as opposed to genuine opposition. Thus, in many ways, Sunday's defections were a sort of wake-up call alerting him to the fact that he does not have the broad-based support he might have assumed he had. Saleh's realization of this fact is perhaps best represented by the dispatching of his foreign minister to Saudi Arabia on Tuesday to allegedly ask the Al Sauds—and through them the United States—for assistance. In fact, how the United States and Saudi Arabia choose to proceed will be a crucial determinant of if, how, and when Saleh steps down.

Section VII
Syria

After more than one year, the status of Syria's uprising seems to be as intractable as it was on day one, in March 2011. More than eight thousand Syrians have been killed (primarily by the regime) and many more arrested or disappeared. Although all uprisings are complex, the Syrian uprising has more than its share of complexity, largely because of the pivotal role Syria plays on various levels. This complexity explains, for the most part, the protracted nature of the Syrian uprising, and the undesirable trade-offs involved. In fact, what Syria faces today is a trade-off between the horrible and the catastrophic, as the increasing violence—mostly by the regime—and external interference has raised the stakes for all parties involved. We are no longer witnessing a local event. The Syrian scene is enmeshed in regional and international power-plays that have little to do with the best interests of the Syrian people. Regionally and internationally, the uprising involves the question of Palestine, the question of resistance, of balance of power in the region, and it involves international forces that are attempting to leverage their power in a changing region.

However, two stubborn facts continue to animate this uprising at the outset of its first anniversary on 15 March 2012. First is the fact that this is an opposition to decades of dictatorship in Syria. This fact cannot be compromised simply because the opposition is being infiltrated or compromised. It might affect what courses of action are better or worse, but it should not give the regime a carte blanche. Secondly, we can no longer take this uprising for granted, or at face value. We are no longer witnessing a clear-cut event where a pro-democracy movement is facing a dictatorship. This has become a war of position in which the opposition's moral high ground has diminished considerably as a result of some of its tactics and alliances—despite the fact that the opposition is not monolithic. In other words, we have passed the point where the opposition can depend on the fact that it is fighting a dictatorial regime. In and of itself, this constitutes a failure of the opposition in general hitherto.

Finally, in keeping with the theme of this book, it is important to note the conflicting analysis and predictions at the outset of the uprising. While most analysts were quick to sound the death knell of the regime, *Jadaliyya* was careful not to jump to conclusions based on the structural and strategic dimensions of the Syrian case, as some of the articles herein attest. Many say we are back to square one a year after the uprising in Syria.

27
Why Syria is Not Next...So Far

Bassam Haddad[224]

9 March 2011

As millions of Arabs stir their respective countries with demonstrations and slogans of change and transition, certain Arab states have been generally spared, including some oil rich countries and Syria. Syria stands out as a powerful regional player without the benefit of economic prosperity and with a domestic political climate that leaves a lot to be desired. Some say it combines the heavy-handedness of the Tunisian regime, the economic woes of Egypt, the hereditary rule aspects of Morocco and Jordan, and a narrower leadership base than any other country across the Arab world. Why, then, is all relatively quiet on the Syrian front?

We can delude ourselves by resorting to facile explanations related to the threat of severe coercion facing a potential uprising in Syria—which certainly does exist. But the reality of the matter is more complex. To begin with, one must account for the unexpected: a clumsy incident involving a disproportionately brutal reaction against civilians, even in Syria, will spin structural variables out of control.

"SYRIA IS NOT EGYPT"

Any cursory review of the Syrian press, or the press on Syria, reveals that many Syrians empathize with the grievances of their rebellious Arab brethren and share many of them. This includes those who actually protested in small numbers and were harassed and/or beaten on Friday, 4 February, the planned "Day of Anger" in Syria, and during the few days prior. Other sporadic incidents[225] took place in the past few weeks, but none rose to the level of an explicit anti-regime demonstration, as happened in Egypt and elsewhere. This puts Syria in stark contrast with Egypt.

Egyptian protesters grew in courage gradually as civil society snatched gains such as degrees of freedom of the press, freedom of speech, and freedom of organization and contestation by truly independent political parties, not least among whom is the Muslim Brotherhood, even if by proxy. On the other hand, Syrian civil society does not enjoy nearly the same measures of liberty. Syrian President Bashar al-Asad was correct in saying that Syria is not Egypt in a 31 January *The Wall Street Journal* interview.[226] The reverse is equally true.

As repressive as the government of former President Husni Mubarak might have been, Egypt's public space was much more open than that of Syria. Independent papers, parties, and political activists have proliferated in Egypt for the better part of the past decade, gaining adherents and mobilizing supporters via various forms of networking. With time, the components of, and room for, collective action have broadened considerably. Between 2004 and 2010 more than six thousand small- and medium-sized protests took place throughout Egypt, most of them labor protests. Over the past decade in Egypt, these led to a level of individual and group empowerment—as well as re-politicization of the society—from which Syrians are quite removed.

In addition, while social polarization and poverty are increasing in Syria and social safety nets are deteriorating, the overall socioeconomic conditions are nowhere near those endured in Egypt. Furthermore, the heterogeneity of Syrian society (in terms of politics, region, community, sect, and ethnicity) exacerbates divisions among those affected and discourages cohesion among the opposition. Snowballing demonstrations that would dramatically raise the cost of brutal reaction in Syria are thus unlikely for the time being. As matters stand today, the calculus of the ordinary Syrian does not favor going to the streets—in the absence of an unexpected incident of regime brutality, of course.

...NOR IS IT TUNISIA OR LIBYA

Individual and group decisions are not motivated solely by social connectivity, legal permissiveness, and collective action. Otherwise, Tunisia's revolt would have not seen the light of day, as Tunisians dwelled in a security atmosphere intolerant of independent organization and collective action, much like Syria's today. But Tunisia's state, regime, and government did not overlap nearly as much as those of Syria do, and certainly the Tunisian coercive apparatuses and army were not as closely knit around the heights of power as they are in Syria. As a result, expecting the Syrian army/

security services to jettison al-Asad as their Tunisian counterparts did to Zine El Abidine Ben Ali is simply a non-starter.

At the same time, despite the existence within both the Libyan and Syrian regimes of a will and rationale to fight for survival, state–society relationships in Syria are much thicker than those of Libya, where detachment at the top has reached delusional levels. For instance, the Syrian regime has promoted a new cross-sectarian business class often with considerable roots in traditional city quarters. If something is afoot in Syria, however, it is likely to come from the northern cities.

THE "RESISTANCE" FACTOR

Discussions of Syria's vulnerability to internal protests often posit Damascus's resistance status to explain why Syria will be spared: that is, because of Syria's confrontational stance toward Israel and the United States' brutal policies in the region, the regime enjoys a form of Arab nationalist legitimacy. In particular, Syria's support for Hizbollah and Hamas is considered a unique and legitimate tool for manifesting such confrontation to imperialism. After all, President Bashar al-Asad polls quite well throughout the region compared to other Arab leaders, and enjoys significant popularity among various segments of Syrian society.

Still, overemphasizing the regime "resistance legitimacy" is problematic on two counts: first, even in Egypt, where Mubarak was viewed as a US protégé and Israel's accomplice, the demonstrators did not make that point a major issue. Second, the region is entering a new era in which Syria's confrontational stance might become less unique, as Egypt and other Arab governments take more independent positions and withdraw from the strong US orbit.

It is difficult to make blanket predictions due to the constant dynamism of the factors involved. While Syria's confrontational positions regarding Israel and the United States might be increasingly popular in the region, the citizens of democratizing Arab states will want governments that are more responsive to them regarding domestic as well as foreign policies. The Syrian government will face this growing demand in due time. For now many factors weigh against revolution in Syria, barring an extraordinary event such as an excessively violent regime reaction to a demonstration or other incident. Observers would be wise not to hold their breath.

28
Fear of Arrest

Hani Sayed[227]
6 August 2011

The author of the following text is anonymous. But his deeds have rocked the foundations of our world in Syria. He is one and he is everyone. I do not know his whereabouts. He is probably already dead or in prison. Or maybe he is still roaming the streets of cities and towns in Syria trying in all earnestness to get the frame of his next picture right where it is supposed to be. At this very moment I imagine him cursing his laptop because it froze a few seconds before the video was successfully uploaded; or struggling to figure out why his Skype cannot work with the new VPN software even though he was told that it should configure itself automatically. But he could very well be spending the night in the basement of the *mukhabarat* headquarters in Kafar Soussa: unable to stretch his leg in the crowded prison cell, unable to rest his back because his wounds from the afternoon beating session are still burning and bleeding; unable to close his eyes because the screams of tortured bodies are whirling in his head like a tornado. But wherever he could be, he knows that he has already won.

I picked up the text from one of the Facebook pages administered by a "local coordination committee" in one of the neighborhoods of Damascus. The text is written in colloquial Arabic. I could tell that he is probably in his early twenties with a clear Aleppo accent. On how a youth from Aleppo ended up in a Damascus neighborhood we can only speculate. Few sleep in their houses these days or in the same place for long.

The text has this ordinary, almost technocratic, quality that makes it extraordinary considering the circumstances. It is not written for political propaganda. It does not theorize, it does not make too many claims, it is not poetic, or confessional. The author addresses his "buddies" to neutralize the effect of a paralyzing fear of arrest that may have made some of them too cautious to participate in demonstrations. The rhetorical posture is descriptive. His goal is to demystify the experience of arrest as an antidote to fear. The premise of the text is that his destined reader should expect arrest and torture, and should therefore stop wasting time to avoid it. The fact that one is arrested has nothing to do with the relative strength of the *mukhabarat*. It has also little to do with how cautious you are. A revolution is taking place, and if you are there in the regime's field of projections of power, arrest is a matter of time—an absurd game of probabilities. Knowing what an arrest entails will make it more bearable, and the fear of it less debilitating.

There is an immense distance separating you, the reader of this translation, and the author of the original text. There is perhaps an even more inexhaustible distance that separates *me*, a native speaker, who is presumed to share a "hermeneutic environment" with this author. This distance is not about culture or language, or any other plausible marker of identity. I translate this text not to bridge or mediate difference, but to paint the horizons of our distance. I translate because the work of translation on a text is like the dream work in psychoanalysis—a desperate attempt to represent an experience when words are at the edge of language. I translate this text because translation forces me to interrogate his words, to explore a consciousness from afar, the way scientists interrogate the many shades of light picked up from a distant star in the hope of understanding a cosmic event.

The distance is this—for you and me this text is an artefact, something that I have the luxury to write about and for you to gloss over while sipping your coffee. But for our anonymous author this text is a catalogue for *survival*. A great deal hinges on whether his destined readers can in fact shed their fear of "it"—because their fear might kill him, because our silence is killing him, because "whomever engages in half revolution, he would be in fact digging his own grave."

Our middle-class, liberal cosmopolitanism struggles with a text like this. Our author is *irrational*, in exactly the same way as when we understand why no single rational maximizer in a competitive context would choose to bear the cost of building and operating a lighthouse. Our author is unethical, because in Syria we all know that the consequences of merely playing a tune in a public garden thousands of miles away is the pain and humiliation inflicted on your beloved by the infamous pro-regime thugs for hire—the *shabbiha*. Because you know that if you are arrested by a security branch, and your dead body turned up a couple of days later showing the traces of torture, your father will be intimidated, beaten, and humiliated until he agrees to go on state-run television to "thank" the President for it and to plead for more stringent treatment of those infiltrators. It is unethical, that is, to the extent that we know that the consequences of our "irrational" actions will be suffering inflicted on others who chose to act rationally. And yet, in his mind, more people should take the streets. There is one additional move he makes that is inaccessible to us. Our author knows the relative weakness of one individual before the security apparatus of the regime. He is resigned to the idea that during arrest, his interrogator can break his bones; heal them, to break them again. His arrest could be for hours, or could be for decades. Our author knows all that, and he understands that during his arrest there is nothing he can do about it. He is resigned in his fear. But something paradoxical happens at that very moment of the resignation of his intellect. His will refuses to surrender because he believes—because in some surreal way he knows that he has already won. In our liberal cosmopolitan comprehensive worldview, our author's final move is absurd. It is absurd to believe that a peaceful protest can bring down a regime. But where we are inclined to stop on the force of the absurd, our author moves on. He understands the meaning of what is absurd, and he grasps his next move by secular *faith*.

The distance, to reiterate, is between the resignation of a whole generation, and his "fear and trembling." It is between what Kierkegaard called the "knight of resignation," and the "knight of faith." It is crossed silently, instantly, almost the way a ray of light activates the few sensitive cells of the macula. Faith, Kierkegaard says, "is no aesthetic emotion, but something far higher, exactly because it presupposes resignation; it is not the immediate inclination of the heart but the paradox of existence."

We cannot speak for him. We can only admire him.

Before proceeding to the text, a few remarks about this translation.

The text is written in a colloquial language that is difficult to translate. I hope the bi-lingual reader would indulge my inability to bring into full force the nuances of the text. I have opted to keep some words in transliterated Arabic. This is particularly the case when discussing the methods of torture used in Syrian prisons. In the remaining space of this note, I shall explain these words.

In the late 1980s, Amnesty International documented approximately thirty-eight methods of torture, pervasively, and systematically used in Syrian prisons.* From the many accounts of what is happening in Syrian prisons during the revolution, it is obvious that the cruelty and systematic spread of these practices did not abate during Asad Jr's reign. The following methods were mentioned in the text:

> *dulab* (tire): "hanging the (detainee) from a suspended tire and beating him/her with sticks, clubs, cables or whips";
> *falqa*: Beating the soles of the feet;
> *bisat al-rih* (flying carpet): Strapping the victim to a piece of wood shaped like a human body and either beating him or her or applying electric shocks all over the body. The description of *bisat al-rih* provided in the text makes it look more like a hybrid with *al-kursi al-almani* (the German Chair). This method described in the 1980s consists of "a metal chair with moving parts to which the (detainee) is tied by the hands and feet. The backrest of the chair bends backwards, causing acute hyperextension of the spine and severe pressure on the detainee's neck and limbs. The author describes a device that is used to create pressure on the spine and neck accompanied with the beating all over the body.

The text reads as follows:

FEAR OF ARREST

A lot of our friends are becoming paranoid and afraid of the reach of the hands of the *mukhabarat*.

They constantly feel as if the *mukhabarat* private is waiting behind the door, under the bed, or about to hack into their Facebook accounts. They have four fictitious accounts, six pseudonyms, and they only participate in demonstrations when it is a safe thing. Like some kind of aristocrats! Why do they do all that? Because they do not want to get arrested. Really?! If that is the case, then you can kiss this revolution goodbye. And so we will write what could happen to you if you get arrested, and what you need to know to prepare yourself. I pray to God to inspire me to write all that correctly.

OK, here we go in the name of God we start:

Arrest is never as scary an experience as many might suspect. Arrest is a medal that you will wear on your chest, and one whose stories you will tell to your children.

---

* Middle East Watch, *Syria Unmasked: The Suppression of Human Rights by the Asad Regime* (1991), in particular Appendix A: Types of Torture in Syria—The Amnesty International List, 149–155.

Arrest is a mixture of a strange, unknown, honorable, and incredible experiences. The more diverse the circumstances of your arrest, the more extended your stay, and the more people you meet, the richer and more exciting your experience will be. This is why it is important that you do not forget to write your account as soon as you are out.

When you get caught the unknown will terrify you. But be reassured. The most difficult part has already passed—these are the moments of arrest and the first beating. Try in moments of calm to regain your self-confidence and to raise your own morale, and to enjoy while you are receiving this honor—because there isn't much time left until this regime will fall, and you may not get another round.

In prison try to adapt to everything except to the humiliation and to the blasphemies that you will hear. Pray—no matter in what position—and try to keep your relationship to God strong—spirituality will be very high when your soul is completely bare.

And so we begin:

Arrest

First of all you may be arrested from home or during a demonstration.

From Home

They will confiscate a lot of things and they will search the house really thoroughly. If you have any suspicious items like spray paint, leaflets, pepper spray, hide them in the roof or in the basement or anywhere else.

They will confiscate the computer, your laptop and mobile phone, your camera, passport, ID card, etc. Relax! Everything will be returned. They will not take anything for good. Seriously, I am not kidding.

If you are caught from home this means that one of your friends or acquaintances has been caught before you, and had to give your address under torture.

Or it is possible that your Excellency did not use the well-known safety measures when using the internet or your mobile.

Facebook

What I have seen during my arrest, which lasted for one month, and after mingling with many people who were interrogated by different interrogators, is that the interrogators are completely out-of-touch when it comes not only to Facebook but the whole internet, if not computers also.

But the interrogator will tell you: Now the "engineer" or the "specialist" will come. This one will also be a donkey but from a different breed :) they will call him only to scare you.

The engineer or the specialist: he is most probably a high-school graduate and may understand a little; he may be a graduate of a technical school or an employee in telecommunication. Personally I did not think he understood anything like an engineer would.

The specialist asked me once for passwords...unfortunately I did store them once in a file that I deleted, but with file recovery, the file was discovered and I was not able to hide anything.

You can take them for a ride if you feel like it, especially if you felt that the reason for the arrest has nothing to do with the net or hacking; this means that they have no clue what accounts you have.

Incidentally, my passwords were with the "specialist" and he was unable to enter my account and he brought me many times thinking that I was fooling him—so this is how tech-savvy they are.

It would be a good idea that you give the password for your fictitious Facebook account to one of the guys that come with you to the demonstrations or to your brother so that when you get arrested he will immediately access Facebook and clean the account completely.

The inspection of your account on Facebook will take time; I imagine it could be a couple of days. During that time they will interrogate you orally—and whatever scenes horrible to the regime you have published, it will not change much for them; perhaps the guys are getting used to it by now.

Example: Before the revolution, I made a video for publication and I deleted it because it was not well done. They recovered the file and landed in the hands of the interrogator, and I refused to confess about this film—not heroically—but because I did effectively forget about it. The interrogator brought me and brought a laptop and played the scene and it was horrible with direct speech against Hafez and Bashar (and note that it was before the revolution). I thought that they would skin me, but at the end nothing really came out of it :) only the regular beating like every day and then "drag this dog to the cell."

The important thing, and we return to the "specialist," he will take the laptop, the mobile, and the camera (if confiscated) and he will inspect for any materials that might be of interest to them.

The Mobile

Erase all Islamic, struggle, and revolutionary chants, and all the private pictures of your family because the *mukhabarat* are just scoundrels. Erase or change all the suspicious names of your friends, such as Abu Qoutada, Abu Obada, Abu Al-Q'aq'a, that is, any name that sounds Islamic, or names that refer to "revolution" and any derivative word.

Inspect your pictures to verify that they do not contain anything that might draw their attention, such as the picture of a street or a neighborhood.

Do not keep anything that has to do with the revolution, whether it is a demonstration a caricature, a song, a slogan, etc.

Do not forget to delete the call log after every call. Although, if they take the trouble they can get the call log, and messages log from the Makhlouf company. In any case, do what you have to do and erase.

Concerning messages, erase whatever might be used against you. In any case, if messaging ever happens between the revolutionaries, it gets erased on the spot.

Your mobile now should be clean. Correct? No! Wrong!

Because it is very easy to retrieve data from the memory card. Therefore, and in order to get your peace of mind with respect to the camera and the mobile, change the memory card. Hide the old one in a hole in the ground, or under some tree, even on the surface of Mars. Do this even if the memory card has nothing about the revolution. You really do not want these scoundrels to see the pictures of your family.

I did address the camera. The issue will be solved with the memory card.

The Computer or the Laptop

They can recover data. Try to format and fragment your drives to make sure that the data are truly erased. Set your internet browser NOT to keep browsing history or cookies. In all cases, use Chrome Google's invisible browser to get some peace of mind.

Facebook and Passwords

The specialist will ask you about passwords. If you are a university student, he would not buy that you do not have an account, especially if you were caught through Facebook or if a friend of yours was caught before you and he talked.

Maintain two accounts: One normal and peaceful as if the revolution is taking place in Mozambique. When asked you will confess that you have a Facebook account and show this account to them. It would have your real friends and you log in everyday to chat normally. The second account is where you do all the real work under a pseudonym without any personal information. Of course none of this is any news to you.

On your normal account use an ambiguous profile picture, like the picture of the flag with blood on it, or expressions of grief, etc. But do not exaggerate, you do not need to put the picture of a frog.

After all this time, they have probably accumulated some expertise in Facebook, and these tricks will not get past them. Here a fundamental question presents itself: What information can I hide, and what information would I have to divulge under pressure by hook or by crook?

"The Golden Rule"

You can keep to yourself and hold on very strongly to every bit of information that no one other than you knows, or information that only you and another person, who is impossible for them to reach, know. Never divulge that information easily. And so where is the problem? The problem is that if you get arrested from your house, you would not know how they got to you. Did they get to you through Facebook? A snitch? One of your friends was caught before you, etc.? Here you have to use your ingenuity to deduce how they got to you from the interrogations.

Example: The smart-ass interrogator asked me once about one of my old friends. This old friend and I both knew another friend with whom I did some coordination before the revolution. I concluded from this question that this common friend was caught before me, and he was the one that spoke about my old friend. And so I managed to figure out how they got to me and I behaved on that basis.

From the Street

If you get arrested from the street, you will receive a bad beating at the moment of arrest. In all honesty, I do not know how they will treat you when you are first taken to the security branch. If they have arrested you from the house, they will tell your family that it is a matter of a half-hour, some questions and answers, or mere verification.

When you arrive to the security branch, they will start talking nicely to you (like what happened to me) a man-to-man conversation. They will make you feel safe and secure. Be careful! Do not be fooled and become enthusiastic to give them everything you have. In a short while, they will start the real interrogations and they will pick it up from where you stopped.

Every time they take you from the prison cell to the interrogation, the prison guard (that is, a security private) accompanying you will speak to you. He will whisper in your ears with the voice of the merciful, compassionate, and advising father: "Confess my son! I swear you will feel relieved. Listen to me! Everyone brought to this branch, ended up forced to say everything. Save us the efforts and do not make yourself go through the torture."

Do not listen to him. He is a blabber. When you are out pretend that you trust his words, that all the time you have understood the rules, that you want to be freed from the beating and that you want to tell about everything.

The first whip on the sole of your foot will shock you—it is unbelievably painful—you will feel soft and think that you will inevitably confess to everything. This is wrong. Guys! Everything is a matter of habit. The first strike only has the greatest effect, the rest is whatever. A lot of people endured the first strike, and they did not utter any unnecessary words. Read Mustafa Khaliefa's novel the *Shell** to make your heart for sure stronger.

After a period in detention, especially if there was repeated torture (like what happened to me), you will enter the *dulab* almost with a smile on your face, and the whole matter becomes a farce. And so whatever information there is, that they can only get to because you talked, keep to yourself.

For everything else, it is up to your ingenuity.

Do not listen to them if they try use your family to blackmail you—no matter how much they curse, no matter how much they threaten. They have stopped using this method, except in very rare circumstances.

If you get caught in the street, you can try to bribe the security operative with a thousand pounds to escape, like one of the guys once told us. Other than that, do not waste your money. Once you are in the security branch, this will have no effect.

---

* Al-Qawqa'a *The Shell*, Beirut: Dar al-Adab (2008). Mustafa Khalifa was detained in the infamous military prison of Tadmur (Palmyra) between 1982 and 1994. The novel recounts in detail the horrors of torture, intimidation, and humiliation experienced by political prisoners at the hands of the security forces in Tadmur.

If you get caught in the street, try to play dumb and deny any relationship with the group. In the worst case, you can try to claim that you saw people marching so you followed the crowd. Remember that the one who organizes the demonstration will have a bonus treatment, so try to play dumb.

In general, the following is certain, all those arrested who spent considerable time in detention did learn one thing: They stopped fearing them. They turned out to be not as smart as we imagined. In addition, they are dead afraid, clueless, and are barely able to keep-up. In mid-March, when I was arrested, we were in the car heading to the security branch. The security private told his friend. "I'll pay five hundred SYP just for one hour of sleep!!" This was four months ago, when Syria was still asleep.

INTERROGATION

When the interrogator demands the name of your friends and you were forced to speak, start with those who are already well known, that is, the probability that they will get caught is already high whether you mention their names or not. Try to stay clear of collectivities and groups, and continue to maintain that you got enthusiastic to participate simply because you saw the rest of the guys marching.

Do not give up names of people who belong to different groups (university, neighborhood, Facebook). If the chain of arrests start rolling, it will go then in different directions and you end up implicating too many people. Keep in your mind one group of friends and every time you are forced to leak a name you pick one from the same group. After all every group is limited in numbers and the matter would never expand like an arthimatic sequence.

When it comes to the beating and the torture, it is important that you have to know how they are done (!) and to get the idea—the element of surprise is half of the terror.

Beating and Torture

It ranges from: (1) a slap on the face or a kick; (2) *dulab* (tire); (3) electricity; (4) *bisat al-rih* (flying carpet).

The slap on the face, the kick, and the butt—these are a form of pampering. In other words, don't get sad; to the contrary you should be happy that it was over with these.

The *dulab* is the first stop in the interrogation. Usually, before they start the interrogation, they will treat you to a "show of muscles" round. In terms of duration this first round will be: (1) the longest after which you are out from between their hands "well done"; (2) he will tell you that this was just a joke, we haven't even started; and (3) He is lying. Do not let him win the psychological war.

The positioning of the *dulab* is a type of *falqa*, and it varies depending on what materials they use (rubber), a tank's belt, an electric cable, a regular belt, or a bamboo stick.

Thank God I did not get to try electricity. They may use the old instrument with the two positive and negative poles, or the Iranian electric sticks—shame on them. They may use electric sticks to make noises and to threaten you. But its sound is louder than its effects.

Bisat al-rih is used in Damascus when they want to force the detainees to confess to false charges. They did it for instance with M. I., the lawyer, when they forced him to confess that he received millions from Saudi Arabia to distribute leaflets. *Bisat al-rih* consists of a wooden board on which the body of the detainee is spread. The board is then bent upward causing excruciating pain in his back, not to mention the side dish of beatings.

I am just bringing up the most terrifying piece. But do not be afraid! The most they will probably use is the *dulab*, that is, if they chose to use it.

Another thing that I should mention, to avoid any surprises after the arrest. When they took me from and back to the prison cell, my hands were tied behind my back and my eyes were covered with *tammasha* (or *tummesheh*) to prevent me from seeing anyone or anything. The interrogator will shout, and you will be surrounded by more than one. The *dulab* could be accompanied by someone stepping on your head or some forms of humiliation, including cursing and blasphamies. There are mere sound effects. They are worth a nickel. In any case, all the slaps on the face, the kicks and the fists, no matter how sensitive the areas they target, will not hurt as your adrenalin is too high. The *falqa* however is a little painful. I pray to God for your endurance. The swelling of the feet will vanish in two days.

Why did you get so terrified?! I swear it is not worth it. Consider it like atonement for your past sins, and a way to rise to a greater position with God. After a little while, we will be treated to a *falqa* without making a sound, and we considered the ones who screamed too soft. We were with two young men from Douma, seventeen years of age in the eleventh grade. They were beaten so hard, that beasts could not have stood it. But I swear they did not scream or open their lips. It was surprising. They looked too innocent and childish and not anything macho. They made us feel ashamed, and from that day we did not complain. So, stay strong and remember everything is for God and for Syria. In God's will—no one will be arrested. But, and seriously, if anyone gets arrested, they ought to enjoy it.

Prison Mates

(Only applicable when you are put in a communal cell) You will spend the best of your days with them, and become one soul in many bodies. It is very likely that you will be stuffed into a really small place. Rest assured! You will not feel disgust from the incredible smell, and you will not feel bothered from the feet that will bump your face no matter how you turned. Most of your companions in the cell would be fellow demonstrators. Those who have no relationship to the revolution are detained by mistake and prisons have had so many people by mistake. Try to adapt and get along with them very quickly, and favor your sense of the collective, and embody the ethics of revolutionaries. Do not get into fights with anyone because the prison guards will gloat after they punish you if your voices become too loud.

Stay away from infiltrators—as they always try to plant one among you or with you alone to verify that you have repented and to "check-up" your truthfulness during the interrogation. Pretend that you believe him, and express remorse before him, and that you are the first *minhebakgi* (colloquial reference used to describe, after 15 March, the supporters of the President) and that you were brought here by mistake. Of course you will have no difficulty discovering him because he is a *mukhabarat* private, who consists of a mass of stupidity with a stinking smell.

Remember that the prison is a world of little things. Your dreams will become a little more modest. In other words, you will forget a little the freedom and pluralism that you fought for outside the prison, and you will start dreaming of a nice shower, new change of underwear, to sleep on a mattress, and sometimes even more modest: the privilege to stretch your legs (for the place is really small), the privilege to sleep while you are sitting, and the privilege to drink water without worrying about the possibility of going to the bathroom, seeing sunlight, etc.

These are things that you will use to weave stories to tell your kids before they go to sleep. So do enjoy them with a smile.

Some Vocabulary Used in Prison with Explanation

Seidi (Master):
The infamous word for addresses. It is imposed for humiliation purposes. You use it to address both the private, and the head of the security branch. Be careful not to call anyone *Oustadh* (a polite colloquial mode to address strangers who are university graduates) or brother, so that you will not get surprised with a constantly accelerating vertical slap on your face.

t'al'oh 'al khat (Take him to the line):
This means take him to the bathroom.

al-sajjan (the Prison Guard):
The security private in charge of dragging you to the interrogator, taking you to the bathroom, or of bringing you food: This one also you address as *Seidi* (Master). Depending on the situation you can ask him to take a shower, when your stay becomes extended, to bring you cover when you feel cold, or salt for the boiled potato, or, to take you to the bathroom outside regular hours and so on. Do not ask for a Qur'an—FORBIDDEN.

tasyeef (packing the swords):
It is a wonderful position to sleep—may you one day experience it. It would be used when the prison cell is tight, in such a way that each one will sleep on his side by alternating the direction of the head (that is, like a box of sardines, head-feet-head-feet). You will be able to use your friend's feet as pillows. Especially with the swelling from *falqa*, your friend's feet would be soft just the way you like it.

Note: Sometimes, even *tasyeef*, is impossible. In this case God only help you. It is difficult for me to explain in writing the possible sleeping positions.

tammasha (or *tummesheh*):
A piece of leather or cloth used to cover the eyes during interrogation. This will increase the degree of your fear, and will reassure the interrogator in case you want to avenge yourself. Sometimes, depending on the rhythm of the beating, the *tumeesheh* may shift a little. Use this opportunity for example to take a look at his evil face, or to guess the time of the day. Take a look, do not be afraid.

Food

Three meals.

In the morning *Labneh*, olives, *Halawa*, jam. Do not get too excited, it is of a lower quality than what you think :)

Lunch: *Burgol* (cooked ground wheat) with potatoes and tomato sauce (hmmm, very filling!), or sometimes rice and chicken, and most of the time rice and lentils, green peas, and billed carrots.

Dinner: Boiled potato (without salt!), sometimes with a tomato. Some days they might bring a boiled egg or lentil soup, which consists of a yellowish, tasteless liquid.

Just shut your eyes and swallow—bon appetit—with the compliments of the chef with navy blue suspenders. When you are done eating, be nice to the guys and make a wish that the next meal you will share outside, and try not to forget yourself and say *Daimeh* (may we always eat like this) for the food will get stuck in their throats. Do not be too hasty in deciding to go on a hunger strike. Study the situation carefully, because it is forbidden. In some branches, they will sodomize whoever attempts to strike. Do not think you are a Gandhi.

Finally

Some specific circumstances of the arrest, like duration, whether they beat detainees in a particular security branch, vary depending on the situation. You are now on the ground, and your friends who were arrested can be more useful than me.

The difference between me and some of the newly arrested guys is that I was arrested for one month at the beginning of the revolution. I spent some part of the detention in state security in Aleppo, and after that I was sent with the heavy-weight organizers to the Central Headquarters of the *mukhabarat* in Kafar Soussa in Damascus. In there I met dozens of incredible detainees, and we exchanged stories and experiences, some of which are not necessarily known by the guys.

In detention raise your head high (in your head only), and remember the prophet Yusuf (Joseph) and sing:

You with your bloody eyes and hands remember that the night will not last, like the detention room and the rustling of your chains.

Stay optimistic and carve your name on the wall of your prison cell. When they ask you to stamp your statements with your thumbprint—think really hard about how you want to use the ink traces and what you would want to write on the wall.

When you get out safely, do not spread terror about your heroism as you are resisting the severest of cruel torture. This you say to the media, but not to the demonstrators on the ground.

When you are out do not fear that much from the pursuit of the *mukhabarat*. Try to spend each night in different places if you can, especially if you are still an activist, like all the other guys that were released, especially when you anticipate an arrest campaign.

When you taste arrest and are then released, one thing will leave your heart forever: Fear.

This is what I could think of so far. For more information please visit our branches in all Syrian governorates and cities. Hurry up, time is short, because when the regime falls there will not be anything left.

By: local coordination committee in xxxxx neighborhood.

29
Syrian Hope: A Journal

Amal Hanano[228]

MIND THE GAP   28 June 2011

I begin to lose sleep weeks before I leave—waking in the middle of the night, my mind racing with anxiety. My insomnia may be the obvious sign that I have no business going to Syria while the country, as my close friend likes to remind me, "is on the brink of civil war." Although I plan to visit Aleppo, where apparently "nothing" is happening, Bashar al-Asad's forces have been steadily marching north in the last few weeks, creeping closer to my hometown. Moving from southern Daraa to the central cities of Homs and Hama, and along the coast through Banyas and Latakia, the latest frontier against the Syrian Revolution has settled on the Turkish border.

Advice against my trip is repeated many, many times by frantic relatives and friends in the United States who have cancelled their summer reservations since the Arab Spring erupted in Syria on 15 March. But each warning is offset by phone calls and Facebook chats with friends already in Syria, their voices cheery (with only a hint of sarcasm), their tan lines already deeply defined, and their children's laughter in the background. Both sides create a confused state of fear mixed with relief; hence the insomnia.

After being convinced that Aleppo is still safe enough to visit, I embark on a massive "Arab Spring" digital cleaning of my Twitter, Facebook, and email accounts. I unfollow, defriend, untag, and block. I send harmless documents and photos to the "cloud," uninstall apps on my phone, and pack an old-fashioned blank notebook in my suitcase. I purge and delete, attempting to erase every trace of recent history that could incriminate—an email, a forwarded joke, a controversial article—anything that could expose a line of thought that does not fully align with the regime's convoluted, conspiracy-driven account of the "demonstrations."

225

The minuscule chance of being questioned at the airport, given what "questioning" currently means, terrifies my non-thrill-seeking nature. Prepared statements of loyalty are mentally stored, composed from blocks of Baathist text memorized years ago at school. I naively convince myself that detaining an American citizen after giving a speech on reform would not be the smartest publicity move for Asad.

On the full flight, somewhere over Eastern Europe, before stepping onto Syrian soil, I finally face the obvious question: why do I have this need to go? Because the gap between being a Syrian in Syria and being a Syrian in America is becoming an uncrossable chasm. Each side has declared the other completely delusional. In a way, the trip itself is my personal protest, an attempt to bridge the gap between the separate selves we have created over the years: Syrian selves built on foundations of fear and repression and American selves that have become dependent on standards of freedom that do not exist in our homeland. I need to go because my silence has become unbearable to myself. I need to go to reclaim my place, my city, my identity. Because after watching Tunisia and Egypt from afar, there is a need to be closer; to be a small part of history unfolding; to witness a dream emerging from a nightmare.

The Syrian landscape, a black surface dotted with lights, comes into view. As the wheels touch down, I breathe in the now familiar mix of relief and guilt. A long, winding, sickly light green corridor connects the plane to Aleppo International Airport and we are greeted with a large glossy poster on the wall screaming with bold print: *Natrinak 'ala nar!* "We are 'on fire' waiting for you." The inappropriate advertisement is courtesy of Syria Duty Free, "formerly" owned by Mr Rami Makhlouf, ex-businessman extraordinaire (and still first cousin of the president). A tired lady hands out a brochure with all the "offers" or special deals on perfumes, cigarettes, and alcohol. My eye catches the bottom of the page, "Only available in Damascus, Aleppo & Daraa." Daraa, the spark of the revolution, a city under siege for two months, internationally known for the recent bloodshed on its streets, has access to Bleu de Chanel but not bread for its people. Welcome to Syria.

At the airport, everything is "normal," no extra searches or excessive questioning, but we take special care to avoid the gaze of the men who watch and listen from chairs and doorways. I pull out my camera as we walk outside and my relative hisses, "Not now!" Through the car window I capture one quick shot of the airport, proof that I am finally here. The streets are calm, exactly the way

I left them one year ago. There is an uneasy feeling of everything being at once the same and completely different.

On my first night, I sleep for ten uninterrupted, dreamless hours. I wake up clear-headed, the white noise is finally silenced. There is no gap between where I am and who I am. Fear is left behind, forgotten...For now.

WAITING FOR A VOLCANO? DON'T HOLD YOUR BREATH   2 July 2011

In the universe of Revolution 2.0, Facebook is the reigning capital, and The Syrian Revolution 2011 page (with over 218,000 "official" followers) is considered prime real estate. Earlier this week, the page boldly dedicated Thursday, 30 June to the "Aleppo Volcano," but disappointment and low expectations began to appear days before, as the fiery graphic shrunk slowly, from proudly occupying the entire profile picture to sharing half the space with "Burn your Bills Wednesday," and downgraded to a scant third after declaring the weekly national demonstration on 1 July as "Leave! Friday."

Still, on the morning of the eruption, we woke up not knowing what to expect. Though the call for Aleppo's supposed uprising had become a Facebook footnote, people were tense, carefully arranging their day to avoid "tripping" by accident into a demonstration. Pool parties and evening outings were postponed as everyone waited for the news.

At noon, there was still no sign of lava anywhere. I had stayed home all morning, too nervous to drive. My friends called, complaining about the unjust media pressuring the city to join the revolution. They told me the circulating Facebook jokes about crude ways the men of Aleppo imagined putting out the flames of the volcano. We heard that the opposition had called on nearby villages to "march" into the city. All major roads entering Aleppo were shut down and blocked by security forces the night before with large trucks and sand bags. Every car entering the city was searched. Aleppo is being protected by the army from the rest of Syria. For obvious yet delusional reasons, this makes the loyalists proud.

After one o'clock, I was bored with the non-existent news on Facebook, Twitter, and satellite channels, and decided to go out. A quick #aleppo search revealed an innocent mix of sarcastic and hopeful tweets, but none from inside the city. I passed by Sa'd allah al-Jabri Square, a central square in Aleppo named after the revolutionary hero who fought against the French occupation, the prime location the protesters have not been able to reach. Other than a few, watchful policemen positioned at each corner under the burning sun, the square looked normal, from the light pedestrian traffic moving across and the double lanes of cars wrapping around it.

Later in the afternoon, back at home, my cell phone rang. The relative I was driving with earlier whispered, "the volcano has erupted." My Twitter and Facebook accounts were overflowing with news of small protests emerging from the Old City and the University Square. Protesters gathered in the narrow streets of Bab al-Hadid, Bab al-Nasr and later al-Jamiliyyeh, but because the 3G network had been cut off months ago and internet service had become impossibly slow, there was a breakdown in communication between the groups who were supposed to meet at al-Jabri Square. Instead they were outnumbered by pro-regime locals who violently beat them with sticks and knives. Police followed closely behind arresting the wounded while the lucky ones ran away. Soon after, internet connections choked across the city and the updates ended abruptly, but not before we knew that the volcano was a failure.

That night, my friends, a mix of society girls married to prominent Sunni and Christian business owners, took me to a hotel terrace overlooking the city in a predominantly Christian neighborhood. The husbands expressed frustration at the weakened economy, with empty hotel rooms and idle factories. They enthusiastically defended the regime and said that the opposition was not giving the president enough time to implement reforms. They consider the messy, chaotic demonstrations as illegitimate, and the protesters as *mukharribeen*, "saboteurs," whereas they see the large, organized *maseerat*, "marches" loyal to the regime as perfectly civilized representations of patriotism.

Each man at the table claimed to have driven around the areas of unrest that afternoon. They insisted that the dozen protests across the city never had more than 25 people each (although we heard later that there were in fact hundreds of protesters who reached the square). They declared that the thugs on the street were "real" men, heroes, for protecting the city by brutally assaulting their neighbors. With each round, the stories were inflated, the numbers were fine-tuned, and the exact locations were agreed upon. I watched as rumors solidified into facts in front of my eyes.

Aleppo has become the symbol of convoluted Arab pride. The rich merchants and industrialists see themselves as the gatekeepers of Syria's economy: they know if Aleppo falls apart, the whole country will follow. The unique mix of wealth, religious diversity, and a dark political past, has created an urban society blinded to the rest of the country's opinion of the people of Aleppo as weak, selfish, regime-defenders who stand proud and silent, oblivious to the blood pooling around them.

A well-connected woman at the table told us how she traveled back by car from Damascus last week amid tanks and the rubble of destroyed statues of the late president Hafiz al-Asad along the main artery between Homs, Hama, and Aleppo. The highway was marked by black rings where the opposition torched large tires to keep tanks out of their cities. She said that stretch of road, felt "like a dream," that it didn't feel real compared to her life in Aleppo. I longed to tell her that the reality is exactly the opposite. She is living in the dream world of Aleppo, but soon she will have to wake up to the nightmare she has been protected from, because the sand bags and the illusions will not hold up much longer.

Aleppo did not erupt on Thursday (or even on Friday), but a small tremor exposed tears in the community's fabric. This ancient city, sitting on a seismic fault line, is not in danger of a volcano but an earthquake, one that is rumbling from within.

@TheSyrianRevolution2011: next time, get the name right...

THE CORRECTIONS   25 July 2011

By coincidence, I was reading Jonathan Franzen's *The Corrections* while in Aleppo, although it may not have been pure coincidence, as sometimes books seem to possess magically perfect timing. (Last year's *Freedom* may have been the more appropriate title for my trip, but I have a habit of reading books out of sequence.) Every afternoon, while the city paused under the oppressive July heat, I read pages (and pages), escaping my dysfunctional Syrian society, and entering the familiar but distant, dysfunction of suburban America. Both worlds could not have been more alien to each other. But as I came to this passage, I was reminded how fiction always finds a way to interject into reality:

Other people stopped being real enough to carry blame for how you felt. And like self-pity, or like the blood that filled your mouth when a tooth was pulled—the salty ferric juices that you swallowed and allowed yourself to savor—refusal had a flavor for which a taste could be acquired.

I read it over and over, trapped within the lines. I connected with every word, the blame, the pain, the pity, I was steeped in it, and I could taste it clearly in my daily interactions in Aleppo. We, as Syrians, over the past decades, have slowly acquired the deadening refusal of reality. We learned to refuse it with such force that some could no longer recognize reality even when it was right in front of them.

Franzen loves to hammer his titles into his narratives, so I was not surprised as I read *The Corrections* (as in *Freedom*), that he would dissect the idea of "correction," to discover its essential meaning. As I absorbed the word, my surroundings were colored with his "corrective" lens; for who wasn't speaking about *islah*, reform or correction? Everyone from the president to the opposition to taxi drivers were discussing reforms: What exactly were they? What would they change? Can we trust they would ever come? If everything is truly *bi kheir*, fine, why do we even need them?

Our past reads like a history book dedicated to corrections. Our modern Middle Eastern map was drawn by European colonialists as a landscape of "corrections" carved along divide and conquer boundaries; artificial boundaries that strove to rip apart our natural ethnic, religious, and cultural diversity into politicized factions that would define us for a century. For example, in Syria, minorities (Alawites, Druzes, Isma'ilis, Christians, and Kurds) were recruited to the *Troupes Spéciales de Levant*, the armed French forces, while Sunnis were discouraged to enlist. It is a simple concept: take a minority and grant it ruthless power over a majority. What happens when, inevitably, the majority rises? Declare them ethnic-cleansing-loving savages who wish to erase the minorities. For who would ever defend a majority?

These corrections now determine the outcome of Arab Spring uprisings in each country; they determine whether the army will stand with the dictator or with the people. Their corrections have become our destiny.

The Asad regime has portrayed the Sunni majority as vampires thirsty for Alawite (and sometimes Christian) blood, when the exact opposite is true. Sunnis (as well as minorities) are murdered, tortured, and imprisoned every day as they continue their non-violent resistance. (Yet, it is the regime's vampirish thugs who chant, "Bashar, don't worry, we are your men and we drink blood."[229]) Together, Christians,[230] Alawites,[231] Kurds,[232] and Sunnis have joined the uprising against the regime across the country. Yet, so many in Syria (and outside), even Sunnis, fear inevitable sectarian violence and recall the horrors of Iraq, Bahrain, Lebanon, and Libya. On the street, in cars, at cafés, you hear whispers of the threat of the Muslim Brotherhood[233] (you know, the really evil Sunnis) in order to defend the regime's brutality against protesters. And as if our diverse Syrian social fabric lacked divisions to evoke, (or provoke) the regime is set on inventing even more empty labels: the *salafis*, the *shabbiha*, the *mundasseen*, the *jaratheem*, etc. And when that fails, they strike the ultimate, defenseless fear into the hearts of the citizens: the fear of *al-majhoul*, the unknown, or the fear of the future. Masters of the taxonomy of fear, our dictators learned well from the handbooks of colonialism: divide, divide, divide, kill, torture, imprison, then conquer. And rule with fear—of the unknown. For who could ever defend the unknown?

The regime has convinced their followers that they are the only power able to uphold our precious secularism, to protect us from killing each other, to correct us from ourselves.

As a child, the first cliché you learn about history is that it repeats itself. So, to understand how Bashar might approach reform today, there is really no need to look back farther than his father. Hafez al-Asad's military coup of 1970, was named *al-Harakeh al-Tashihiyyeh* "The Corrective Movement." A scaffolding of corrections that covered his true desire: ultimate power. The movement had a dedicated chapter in every grade's *Qawmiyyeh* (National Education) textbook, and a delightful national holiday celebrated every 16 November. Someone once described it to me as Syria's Thanksgiving, but I was disappointed when I found out instead of a comforting family meal, you were forced to participate in a mandatory *maseera*, march across the cold, gray squares.

Asad resurrected (*baatha*) the Baath Party and aimed to fix our unstable political past, unite the Arabs, fight for Palestine, and live forever. His Corrective Movement, reinforced the greatest hits of the original Baath Party agenda: Unity, Liberty, Socialism, and (don't forget) our promise to fight Imperialism, Zionism, backwardness and, after dealing with an uprising of his own a decade into his rule, the oath was corrected to include the crushing of the evil forces of the treacherous Muslim Brotherhood. But al-Asad's Arabism proved insincere (remember Lebanon?) and his Socialism was even less so as he abandoned his original, loyal base of farmers and factory workers to forge powerful alliances with the prominent, urban, wealthy families of the private sector (capitalism, another correction?). But the Movement also buried the country in endless lists of detailed five-year plans and committees and bureaucracy, to chart his most revered outcome: Progress.

(Forty-one years later, may we, the people, assess your progress?)

Whenever I ask about the so-called progress, the usual response is that Syria has become a better country since Bashar took over eleven years ago; it has become more open, more modern, it has "flipped 180 degrees." After a few inquiries to define "better," the list is unsurprisingly materialistic: cell phones, satellite television, internet, sushi restaurants, Beirut-style nightclubs, and private schools, universities, and banks (how very socialist of them). Human rights, freedom of speech, and free elections obviously don't make the list.

Bashar has his own legacy of corrections that began in 1994 with the death of his older brother Basil in a car accident. The second son, the second choice, who was never meant to lead, had his first "official" correction when he ascended to power after the death of his father in 2000, with a hasty modification of the Syrian constitution. The same constitution, that the regime has been "studying" to change over the last five months to quell the uprising, was amended in one day, lowering the age requirement from forty to thirty-four to accommodate the young doctor and making Syria the only country with an inherited presidency.

In Syria, the name "Arab Spring" brings up unpleasant memories of another spring, the spring of 2001, when Syrians naively thought that our Westernized president would adopt true reforms. From his father's throne, he launched the "Damascus Spring," allowing for the first time, intellectuals and political dissidents to meet and speak freely in private salons. It was a trap to expose the "traitors" and many (including today's leading opposition figures such as Arif Daleela and Walid al-Bunni) paid for their opinions with many years in prison. That was the last word on free speech and reform, but we did have overpriced, mediocre sushi, and paid for our precious cell phone service directly to Rami Makhlouf[234] (the brilliant multi-tasker, who taps our phones and wallets at the same time). Damascus Spring wilted into a decade-long Syrian winter of unprecedented greed, corruption, and cronyism revealing a ruthless Bashar firmly set on his father's course with no corrections in sight.

For those who suffer from historical and political amnesia, do you still wonder why some are weary of "reform?"

But this history of events (crimes), skirts the main issue: what is the meaning of "correction?" In the novel, *The Corrections*, an obsessive, controlling matriarch tries and fails to correct every member of her family, only to realize in the end that it was she, not them who needed a heavy dose of correction. Syrians have been told, for forty-one years, by our eternal father and his son that we need correcting, we need to be reformed. Almost half a century of corrections...it can destroy a family, and it can destroy a country as well. For what kind of people constantly need to be corrected?

As any parent knows, insistent correcting has one sure outcome: rebellion. In our late adolescence, we rebel against the Leader: because the truth has become a lie, sincerity has become conspiracy, and trust in the *nizam* has eroded like the decomposed body of Hamza al-Khateeb. And unlike the Leader and his Party, we are not broken beyond repair.

Today in Homs, the killing continues as a hateful sectarian scenario is cemented into place, setting the stage for Hama 2.0. My relatives in Homs sleep in their hallways far from any windows, hoping to stay safe from the constant rain of bullets. Every hour brings more tweets of the dead as the "grandchildren" of Khaled bin al-Walid are being slaughtered. At the same time, I read that Bashar's first speech, almost four months ago, was dubbed as "The Second Corrective Movement"[235] as he offensively claimed to create a modern Syria based on human rights. Based on what? The blood that spills in streams across our streets, or the prison cells that overflow with our innocent men? According to the latest rumors,[236] Bashar will be giving a fourth speech by the end of July (before the beginning of a fateful Ramadan), "with a surprise that surpasses imagination!"[237] He supposedly plans to dissolve the Baath Party and hold democratic elections, confident that his widespread urban popularity (thank you, Aleppo and Damascus) will faithfully support him. His series of corrective speeches are like episodes of a bad *musalsal*, soap opera: (1) There is a conspiracy; (2) Look, I formed a new government; (3) *Hiwar* is the cornerstone of the next era; (4) Disregard the dead, the missing, disregard the past, we will start anew, we will Correct!

Dear President, you have not listened to your own Father's words, "The concept of 'homeland' loses its meaning if its citizens are not equal...If Syria had not always been above sectarianism, it would not now exist." We have been watching a different, wildly popular soap opera that was circulating in the region this spring, because even fresh history still repeats itself. In case you did not see it: (1) You kill; (2) You talk; (3) You beg; (4) You leave.[238]

Our blind Eye-Doctor-in-Chief refuses to acknowledge the only reform we are interested in: the people's desire to un-correct his family's corrections. For what is Arab Spring but the struggle to undo the sabotage and abuse of power, inflicted upon the people by their dictators? In the age of the people's corrections, the salty refusal to deny reality and the bloody refusal to fear the future, have become the strongest tastes on our palette, but we have an intense craving for another, sweeter taste.

The Syrian Revolution is a massive red, reset button for justice, equality, and liberty. We are the corrections, united in our history, diversity, and even dysfunctionality. And like Franzen intended, we come first, then comes freedom.

Section VIII

Regional Reverberations of the Arab Uprisings

The 2011 Arab uprisings and ongoing mass mobilizations have been largely confined to such countries as Tunisia, Egypt, Bahrain, Libya, Yemen, and Syria. Their effects have nonetheless reverberated across the Arab world, from the Atlantic Ocean to the Persian Gulf. These have taken multiple shapes, modes of expression, and consistencies, leading to differing outcomes, at least in the first half of 2011. Early revolutionary hope and optimism were largely contagious, crossed national boundaries, and produced a sense of popular solidarity not felt since Nasserist Arab nationalism united the majority of Arab masses. For the first time in decades, the future did not seem as foreclosed as it had long been, and new political imaginaries were suddenly possible. This hope and sense of empowerment even reached the heart of the current counter-revolution on the Arabian Peninsula, with different forms of protestation marking the Saudi Arabian, Emirati, and Kuwaiti oppositional, anti-status quo horizon.

In Morocco and Jordan, some sporadic mass protests demanding changes within government as well as serious reform managed to secure certain concessions, such as parliamentary elections, the permission to assemble, economic subsidies, and constitutional amendments. Although most of the concessions were largely cosmetic, at least in the first six months of the Arab uprisings, they demonstrated that these regimes, if not willing to concede some of their power, at least were threatened enough by the potential consequences of not trying to appease opposition forces. In Iraq and Palestine, on the other hand, local officials and their American and Israeli imperial/colonial masters, respectively, collaborated to either suppress the emerging protest movements or to co-opt them altogether. Neither could afford the solidarity protests, the threats posed by a unified, cross-sectarian and cross-political party front calling for the end of occupation and political corruption, which threaten to expose the illegitimacy of both regimes. Further west, in Algeria, Jasmine Revolution protesters were met with indiscriminate levels of state violence even after the Algerian regime lifted the decades-long state of emergency on 24 February 2011. The empty gesture has not signified real changes in the daily lives of people, and superficial reforms such as economic subsidies and easing of taxation on certain foods did nothing in the way of pacifying Algerians, who for decades bore the brunt of Abdelaziz Bouteflika's violent regime.

The hope and feelings of empowerment inspired by the Tunisian, Egyptian, and other revolutionaries, did not spare places such as Lebanon, although historical and regional particularities led to somewhat short-lived manifestations there, as Mikdashi demonstrates in the following pages. As with the case of Iraq, political sectarianism is regularly deployed to impede the possibility of national solidarity. The "wall of fear" in the Arab world has largely been broken, as has been reiterated constantly. But the violence and unrelenting intimidation tactics meted out by the counter-revolutionary forces—spearheaded by Saudi Arabia, Qatar, and to a large extent, the United States— has chilled the revolutionary enthusiasm and the specter of an open, egalitarian, and democratic future that does not include the callous regimes of the last few decades. Calls for regime change in these states have been few and far between, but what they all have in common is the realization that the status quo is simply no longer sustainable.

30
The Political Status Quo, Economic Development, and Protests in Jordan

Ziad Abu-Rish[239]

10 May 2011

In the wake of the "Arab Spring," Jordan witnessed nine consecutive weeks of Friday protests as well as numerous sit-ins calling for political and economic reforms. But as NATO's intervention in Libya deepened, civil society in Bahrain was brutalized, protests in Syria expanded, and struggles over the limits of regime change in Egypt and Tunisia continued, a tense calm eventually prevailed in Jordan. Whatever protests exist today thus far do not carry the threat of a mass-based anti-regime uprising.

REFORM vs. REVOLUTION

Protests in Jordan were different from those that took place in Bahrain, Egypt, and Tunisia, or those that are currently taking place in Syria and Yemen. All these states, including Jordan, are governed by authoritarian systems of rule that offer little in the way of accountability and civil liberties, as well as increasingly neoliberal economic policies that erode the ability of the average citizen to meet their basic needs. However, the number of citizens that took to the streets in Jordan stood relatively small in comparison to the mass numbers seen in other countries. Setting Jordan even further apart was the nature of the protesters' demands, which centered on changes in the regime-appointed government and a diverse set of political and economic reforms. In other words, these mobilizations were never about regime change.

The difference between protesters in Tahrir Square and average Jordanians is not in their aspirations for real meaningful change. The fact that Jordanians are not choosing revolution, openly calling for the abolition of the monarchy, or turning out in significantly large numbers is not the same as them not wanting change that is real and meaningful. Rather, it is simply a reflection of the fact that many elements inform the actions which people choose to undertake in their quest for freedom, including a diversity of positions in between the dichotomous poles of allegiance to the monarchy and calls for its abolition. In other words, most segments of society continue to be committed to the status quo, even if only for short- to medium-term reasons. At the same time, there are those who are committed to the status quo for the long haul. In considering these dynamics, as opposed to those attained in, for example, Tunisia, Egypt, Bahrain, or Yemen, it would be wise to consider the legacies animating each society, the strategic calculations within these contexts, and the unforeseen contingencies (like the murder of Khalid Said in Egypt or the self-immolation of Mohamed Bouazizi in Tunisia) that radicalize public demands. While they are not the only reasons, the following dynamics are important insofar as they help us understand the structural and strategic constraints on the possibility of anti-regime (mass) mobilizations in Jordan:

(1) There has been an effective rhetorical separation between the monarchy (that is, the regime) and the government (that is, the royally-appointed cabinet). In other words, political discourse in Jordan has represented contemporary politics (whether the government, the formal opposition, or any of the state institutions) in the Kingdom as separate from the role of the monarchy. This is partly a function of the particular legitimacy structures of the monarchy. It is also a function of the fact that law and violence have enforced this separation. Equally important, the monarchy has in many ways set itself up as the vanguard of reform in the Kingdom, claiming to both plot the course of reform and manage its dangers. Barring some type of radicalization of the public, this separation and the legal violence that underpins it will continue to have a real effect on the nature of political demands being advanced.

(2) The dynamic of top-down regime-managed political reform has offered several controlled outlets for public frustration (for example, organized demonstrations, new media forums, and parliamentary elections), while maintaining the concentrated and unaccountable nature of power in both the polity and the economy. This strategy has sometimes responded to public demands (for example, the sacking of the cabinet of Samir al-Rifa'i) while at others has pre-empted them (for example, calling for national consensus on a new election law). Thus, unlike

in Tunisia and Egypt, the "reform game" is still playing itself out in Jordan with little indication of what *Jadaliyya* Co-Editor Hesham Sallam described in the Egyptian case as "a rebellion against orthodox Egyptian politics, which includes the ruling party and the ineffective and mostly co-opted formal opposition parties it surrounded itself with for decades." One need only read the statements by Jordanian Islamist, leftist, and centrist parties in order to appreciate the persistence of their reformist positions on the Kingdom.

(3) There are important socio-political legacies of intergroup relations in Jordan. For several decades, the monarchy has played the role of mediator between rival tribes in Jordan. This has caused a broad spectrum of Trans-Jordanian tribes to maintain their loyalty to the King and his ability to "keep the peace" among competing tribes and factions therein. Furthermore, the monarchy's historical strategy of constructing a social base by privileging Jordanians of East Bank origin over those of Palestinian origin has buttressed the regime. Given that Jordanians of Palestinian origin represent a majority of the population, East Bankers would lose whatever privileges they currently have in an alternative system of rule. At the same time, the selective incorporation of members of the Palestinian–Jordanian business community into the ruling coalition through particular neoliberal policies has given a potentially powerful anti-regime constituency a stake in the status quo. Finally, with a history of repressing and co-opting secular and leftist opposition figures/movements, the primarily-of-Palestinian-origin Muslim Brotherhood (MB) and its political wing—the Islamic Action Front (IAF)—have emerged as the leading opposition group on the Jordanian political scene. Thus, the existing alternative to the regime (that is, an IAF-dominated government) presently poses significant problems for parties that stand to lose the most from a redistribution of power (not to mention that various segments of the Jordanian population that are weary of the IAF). This is perhaps most evident in the statements by a coalition of centrist parties that "only when there emerge two strong parties running for elections," would it become appropriate to enact the type of reforms that would allow for a prime minister (PM) and cabinet to be selected by the parliament—as opposed to the existing practice of a royally-appointed PM whose cabinet is selected from outside the parliament. These legacies combine to create formidable obstacles to the formation of broad-based mass

mobilizations necessary for either revolution or genuine reform. In effect, they have created variations of what Eva Bellin (in a different yet related context) calls "contingent democrats" (i.e., supportive of democracy only given certain guarantees of what the power-distribution in that democracy would look like).

(4) The regime has a consolidated command of all branches of the armed forces, intelligence services, and police agencies. The Jordanian regime effectively adapted to the regional series of military coups that occurred between the 1940s and 1960s to consolidate its rule and "coup proof" itself. As Hesham Sallam and Paul Amar have argued, fissures between the different coercive institutions of the state—as well as that between the army and the regime—are central dynamics that structure the strategic calculations of both formal opposition groups as well as those activists interested in contentious politics. There is little doubt that all coercive institutions of the Jordanian state would be effectively mobilized in defense of the monarchy.

REGIME RESPONSES

The Jordanian regime responded to the protests that erupted in a variety of ways. First, it allowed the protests to take place, in some instances going so far as to have police officers disperse water and juice to demonstrators. Second, the regime implemented several measures designed to offer short-term economic relief for the rising cost of living. These included the elimination of fuel taxes, easing hiring requirements within the public sector, subsidizing the price of basic foods at the military and civilian cooperatives, and a twenty Jordanian dinars (approximately thirty dollars) increase in the monthly salary and pension payments for both civilian and military public sector employees and retirees. Finally, the regime acquiesced to what was perhaps the central demand of the protesters by sacking the cabinet of then Prime Minister Samir al-Rifa'i and appointing Ma'rouf al-Bakhit to take his place. The outgoing cabinet had been appointed in an attempt to bolster the legitimacy of the existing political system in the wake of the November 2010 parliamentary elections, which were marked by the boycott of the leading opposition party—the Islamic Action Front (IAF)—and various allegations of voting fraud and electoral gerrymandering. None of these measures, however, offered anything structurally different than was the case prior to the emergence of protests, neither politically nor economically.

The dismissal of the government in Jordan is part and parcel of the existing repertoire of governance in Jordan. Nevertheless, the formation of al-Bakhit's cabinet proved a turning point for the protests in Jordan. As the regime met the central demand around which protesters had initially mobilized, the task of collectively defining more specifically what exactly political and economic reform would look like splintered the diverse forces that had previously come together. Beyond calling for the downfall of the al-Rifa'i cabinet there was little consensus about what reforms to call for let alone what reforms were necessary. Some were satisfied with the change in government and what measures had been taken thus far. Others, though skeptical, stated that the al-Bakhit government should be given a chance. The Islamic Action Front, the dominant opposition group, called for the right of the political party with the most seats in parliament to select the next prime minister, rather than the current practice of appointing someone to the position by royal decree. Still, others called for constitutional changes, most notably a return to the constitution of 1952, the amendments to which are viewed by some as the foundation for the current system of authoritarian rule. Despite consensus on the fact that political and economic reforms were necessary, little agreement was made on the institutional mechanism through which to tackle them. The only theme unifying these disparate voices for reform was an anti-corruption sentiment, which itself was subject to competing definitions. By late March, the mobilizations that started in January fizzled out.

It would be problematic to view the trajectory of this brief spate of contentious politics as simply the function of the dilemmas of consensus building and collective action. Rather, one must also consider what appears to have been a multi-pronged strategy by the regime within the context of Jordan's structural constraints to mass-based cross-sectoral anti-regime mobilization. Beyond the short-term fixes that provided immediate alleviation of some economic pressures as well as the tried and true practice of sacrificing the prime minister at the alter of the regime, there was a series of steps taken to bolster the new government of Ma'rouf al-Bakhit. One such step was King Abdullah II's "Letter of Designation" to al-Bakhit. The letter stated that forces whose interests would be threatened by change had stalled the reform process and there would be no tolerance for that this time around. There was also the announcement by al-Bakhit of a new public gathering law that would now only require forty-eight hours notice for demonstrations rather than permission from the governor. Finally, the regime also acquiescced to the demand for a national teacher's union—notwithstanding the yet-to-be-defined nature of said union.

If the above measures represented minor and immediate attempts at bolstering the new government, there were other more publicized steps that soon followed. Most discussed was the establishment in March of a fifty-two-member National Dialogue Committee (NDC) to secure a "consensus" around the reform process within the framework of national unity. The NDC has since become the lynchpin of the regime's domestic and international campaigns to prove its alleged now-serious approach to reform. That the president of the royally-appointed Senate (that is, the upper house of parliament), however, is also the official chair of the NDC, has made several opposition groups question its independence. The Islamic Action Front, for example, has refused to participate without assurances that constitutional reform would be included on the agenda and that the committee's conclusions would be binding in one way or another. Other opposition groups have also taken issue with the membership of the NDC, accusing it of being inadequately representative, especially when it comes to women, who make up only four of the fifty-two members.

Despite these dynamics, the NDC has taken center stage in public discussions of reform in Jordan as its deliberations have coalesced around three sub-committees, each with its own specific topic: the definition of a "New Jordan"; laws regulating the formation and operation of political parties; and an election law. These issues, though consistently part of the formal opposition's grievances, are grounded in debates and grievances that pre-date the emergence of regional uprisings and thus represent business as usual vis-à-vis the reform game. Any serious redistribution of power, independent methods for holding public figures accountable, and the removal of pre-existing red lines of political speech remain absent. What many observers—both local and international—seem to miss, or rather choose to ignore, is that this is not the first time a national committee has been established to undertake consultative deliberations on reform (e.g., the National Charter Committee). It is unlikely that the results of the NDC will differ much from their predecessors in their recommendations or their implementation, which raises questions about the utility of the NDC in bringing about fundamental change. Still though, the vast majority of opposition groups (formal and alternative) as well as civil society organizations have legitimated the NDC through either their participation or their statements of support.

If the regime in Jordan had temporarily lost control of the discourse on reform to demonstrators on the street, it has since reconsolidated its image as the vanguard of change and progress in the Kingdom, claiming to both plot the course of reform and manage its dangers. If anything, the NDC and other regime-sponsored measures represent the continuation of top-down political reform that offers controlled outlets for public frustration while maintaining the concentration of power in both the polity and the economy. Unlike Syria and Yemen, the "reform game" is still playing itself out in Jordan with little indication of a rejection of orthodox politics.

This regaining of the momentum by the regime should come as no surprise given that the starting point of the demonstrations was something quite different from those of Egypt, Syria, Tunisia and Yemen. The level of polarization between the regime and the general Jordanian population was never close to the zero-sum game it reached elsewhere, and it was never allowed to reach that level. This is partially the result of the multi-pronged strategy of the regime in the wake of the regional outbreak of demonstrations, as well as several complex historical factors specific to Jordan and alluded to above.

While the types of confrontations between protesters and the regime that characterized Bahrain, Egypt, Libya, Syria, Tunisia, and Yemen were nowhere to be seen, the Jordanian regime's strategy was not void of coercive measures. The nature of protesters' demands and the numbers of those mobilized were manageable independent of violent dispersal, especially in light of extra-coercive strategies. However, three particular instances—beyond the general fact of continuing authoritarian rule—reminded the population of the potential/reality of violence and other forms of coercive action without radicalizing existing or would-be protests. The first took place during one of the weekly Friday protests (18 February 2011), when plain-clothed assailants attacked demonstrators with sticks, stones, and makeshift whips. Despite the usual police and gendarmerie presence, not one of the assailants was apprehended during the attack. While the government publically denounced the assailants, discussion of an official inquiry and prosecution of those responsible eventually faded. The second instance was when the 24–25 March sit-in at the Dakhiliyyah Roundabout was first attacked by "loyalist counter-protesters" and then violently dispersed by the gendarmerie. Here too, vigilante acts were denounced but little was done in the way of accountability against the plain-clothed assailants or the gendarmerie despite over one hundred reported injuries and one confirmed death. This incident, perhaps more than that of 18 February, has echoed loud and clear throughout the Jordanian news media and blogosphere. It is one thing to hold weekly demonstrations with generic calls for reform, it is quite another to hold an indefinite sit-in, articulate specific demands, and do so in a space that offered a Tahrir Square-like feel with respect to its public visibility and potential numerical increase. Finally, there was the reintroduction of the requirement of all male citizens between the ages of eighteen and thirty-four to update their military service deferment status. While details of this particular policy merit their own article, suffice it to say that the regime demonstrated its will to engage in population control tactics that a majority of the affected citizens possibly found too costly as a price for participating in or supporting reform-oriented public agitation.

The Polity

The combination of regime strategies implemented as a response to the protests transformed an already small and limited disruption in the just over twenty-year-old regime-dominated discourse of reform into another example of the benevolence and exceptionality of Jordan's authoritarian system of rule. There is yet to be any structurally different organization of power in terms of civil liberties, representation, or accountability. This is to say nothing about the economic development strategy underway in Jordan, which is briefly addressed below. A baseline minimum with respect to real political reforms, according to the demands that have been made by various groups in Jordan, would include:

A Representative Election Law: There are three major problems with the existing Election Law that governs the election of the Lower House of Parliament. First, the electoral districts are currently uneven and allot more seats to certain traditional regime-supporting constituencies than is the general basis for seat-allotment. This effectively compensates for a perceived demographic disadvantage of the regime (that is, its electoral social base is much smaller than those voters that would cast ballots in favor of opposition candidates). Second, while seats are typically allotted on the basis of the population residing in a district and its sub-districts, voters are free to register in whichever district they subsequently choose and in any sub-district therein. This allows regime-protected socio-political formations (whether tribes or co-opted opposition parties) to mobilize voters across districts and sub-districts in favor of regime-friendly candidates. Finally, the Single Non-Transferable Vote System (of which Jordan is one of only three countries to implement) means voters cast a single ballot in favor of a single seat despite voting in a sub-district and district that is allotted several seats. This discourages individuals to vote for parties or policies given that they typically use their only vote for a personal contact of some sort (i.e., a relative or a member of their tribe). Any meaningful change to the representativeness of the Parliament would require that these three aspects of the Election Law be amended in line with even and fair districting, voting within the districts and sub-districts one was counted in for purposes of seat allotment, and a bloc or party-list voting system.

An Empowered Parliament: Currently, the regime's authority pervades the structure of parliament. Legislation is first introduced through a royally appointed prime minister (who selects his cabinet), must also be approved by the royally-appointed Upper House, and is subject to ultimate approval or rejection by the King. While few opposition groups have dared to publically call for an elected Upper House or the removal of the King's prerogative to reject legislation, a growing number of groups are calling for the right of the party with the largest number of seats in the Lower House to select the prime minister and that cabinet appointments be drawn from the Lower House. Such changes, in addition to those of the election law, would begin the process of transforming the role of parliament from that of legitimizing decrees to one of legislating policies. Still remaining would be for the cabinet and parliament to no longer require the approval of the King for the implementation of new legislation.

The Economy

When protests first emerged in Jordan, their demands focused on rising prices. But as the protests persisted, they became much more direct in decrying "policies that impoverish and starve" the citizens of Jordan. To be clear, the heart of the problem in Jordan's economy is the nexus of poverty, unemployment, and weak purchasing power on the part of the majority of its citizens. This nexus has been produced by the emphasis on investment in non-productive sectors and enterprises that offer little real added value to the economy while providing quick and large returns to those select Jordanians with privileged access to such investment arrangements. This has been accompanied by a misplaced faith in the alleged trickle-down effects of the market (that is, when the market economy grows, everybody benefits), which in turn justifies the exclusive concern with growth rates. Such principles and policies of economic development have been decided and implemented by those at the commanding heights of both the polity and the economy.

The existing economic development model in Jordan has failed to provide adequate employment, income, and purchasing power to the average citizen. While both the regime and the government have taken steps to alleviate some of the most immediate symptoms of the problem, there has been little indication that the principles underlying these symptoms are being subject to serious reconsideration. However, the failure to engage in such reconsideration should not point to an inevitable challenge to the existing political economy. While protesters have sharpened their criticisms of the economic conditions in Jordan, the discursive separation between government and regime—as well as between economic conditions and the development model—persist.

While medium- to long-term solutions might not necessarily be found in a continuation and/or increase in state subsidies, it makes little sense to abandon such protections against the vagaries of the "free market" in the short-run. Absent a genuine reconsideration of the existing development model underway in Jordan, such suggestions are simply justifications for wealth disparities, exclusionary economics, and discursive elitism. A genuine reconsideration of Jordan's economic development strategy would require the regime, the government, and commentators to move away from self-congratulatory celebrations of issues such as Jordan's rankings in The Heritage Foundation's 2010 Economic Freedom Report. Indices such as "Business Freedom," "Financial Freedom," and "Trade Freedom" ultimately measure the ability of capital to move in and out of the borders of Jordan and to circulate amongst its economic elites. It makes no difference to the average citizen that Jordan's economy is ranked the thirty-eighth freest in the world and fourth freest in the Middle East and North Africa. Such rankings (and their celebration) render invisible the daily experiences of the average Jordanian. Alternatively, it would do us all some good to consider that Jordan ranks in the bottom thirty percent globally, in terms of both poverty and unemployment—meaning that seventy percent of the countries in the world have lower rates of poverty and unemployment than Jordan does. According to official government statistics, the average rates of poverty and unemployment in

Jordan over the past few years are approximately thirteen percent each. Unofficial estimations of poverty and unemployment are a good five to ten percent higher. Irrespective of these conflicting estimations, such statistics are especially striking given that poverty and unemployment are not correlated in Jordan–meaning that most of the poor are employed and most of the unemployed are not poor.

CONCLUSION

While the thrust of explicitly political cross-sectoral mobilizations have dissipated, regime-protester dynamics seem to be taking a more diffuse nature in the form of a combination of disparate public sector employee strikes, university campus violence, and confrontations between security personnel and either tribal or Islamist members. However, rather than planting the seeds of an inevitable "Jordanian Spring," such tensions—for now at least—are better viewed as the traces of Jordan's authoritarian system of rule, its neoliberal policies, and the always present tensions therein; independent of any sense of an inevitable radicalization and spread of regime-protesters dynamics.

31
Dissent and its Discontents: Protesting the Saudi State

Rosie Bsheer[240]

SAUDI ARABIA'S SILENT PROTESTS   29 January 2011

Riyadh feels a little less stale in the few weeks since the Tunisian people toppled their dictator-president Zine El Abidine Ben Ali on 14 January 2011. In cafés, restaurants, and salons [*majalis*], friends and colleagues greet me with a smug smile, congratulations, and a *'u'balna kulna* (may we all be next). Everywhere I go, people are hypothesizing on whether the same could happen to "them," referring to the possibility of a Saudi Arabia not headed by the Al Sauds. Although most concur that it is highly unlikely, they are nonetheless more convinced than ever of the power of the people to bring about change.

It is not surprising that Saudis are jumping on the bandwagon of optimism that has swept the Arab world in the last two weeks. That they are expressing their discontent and criticism of the Saudi regime in public spaces, however, is. In the week of 26 January, several "gatherings" took place at government institutions in several Saudi cities. Groups of seventy to one hundred Saudi men peacefully stood in front of different municipalities as well as the ministries of Education, Labor, and the Interior. The men were silently protesting their deteriorating living conditions, rising unemployment (in one of the strongest economies in the world), and increasingly corrupt and stagnant bureaucracy. These public protests have received little press coverage, but the fact that they have occurred for several days speaks volumes as to the increasing willingness of Saudi citizens to challenge the status quo.

At the Ministry of Labor, the protesters demanded solutions to the discrimination against Saudi nationals in the hiring practices of private companies and called for the serious implementation of Saudization in the private sector. Begun in the mid-1990s, Saudization is a policy that aims to increase the numbers of Saudi men and women in the workforce. By law, private sector companies are required to hire thirty percent of their employees from the Saudi labor market. Most, however, have found legal loopholes to evade this law and continue to have very few Saudis on board, and mostly in low-paying jobs. Saudi Arabia today has a fifteen to twenty percent unemployment rate yet it is host to eight million foreign employees. At the protests in front of the Ministry of Education, Saudi teachers demanded their long-awaited raises, salaries that matched their grade qualifications, and a freeze on the closing of educational programs. Finally, those who gathered at the municipalities were tired of years of waiting for their land grants to be processed and demanded more efficient case processing and communication. In all three instances, the Saudi men (always men) called for transparency and accountability in dealing with their cases and an end to the very pervasive problem of *wasta* (favoritism and nepotism) within the Saudi Arabian private and public sectors. These are in addition to the ongoing weekly silent protests at the Ministry of the Interior, where families have protested the illegal detention of loved ones as prisoners of conscience without charge or trial.

Saudi law prohibits all public gatherings and punishes them by lashings and a prison term that ranges from several months to two years. Saudi media outlets usually report on public gatherings in ways that focus on their consequences in order to deter further acts of protestation. In the last few days, Saudi media have reported on two of the four Saudi nationals who have immolated themselves in the Eastern and Southern regions of the Kingdom in protest of economic and political corruption. However, they have remained largely silent on last week's "gatherings." But if the past ten days of regime-controlled Saudi media is any indication, the Al Saud regime is very nervous. So far, the ruling members of Al Saud have issued different excuses for hosting Ben Ali despite the continued protestation of Saudi citizens and citizens of other Arab states. In the beginning, newspapers justified hosting Ben Ali by stressing the Kingdom's long tradition of hospitality, claiming that the government is obligated to welcome everyone (completely evading the fact that Saudi Arabia has the strictest travel requirements in the world). When that was not enough, Foreign Minister Saud Al-Faisal added that during his tenure in Saudi Arabia, Ben Ali would not be allowed to partake in any political or other activities that could harm the Tunisian people. This part of his speech was repeatedly aired on local Saudi channels for days. More recently, the government announced that they hosted Ben Ali to spare the

Tunisian people further harm and violence. In other words, by agreeing to welcome him in the Royal Guest Palace in Jeddah, they saved the Tunisian people from their dictator. The irony of this narrative has not escaped most Saudis, who continue to be ashamed of their authoritarian government's unabashed support for one of the most brutal oppressors in the region.

Since 19 January 2011, Saudi newspapers have been obsessively relaying news of reform, namely economic plans and policies that will allegedly solve the problems of rising unemployment, inflation, and poverty. Saudi Minister of Labor Adel al Faqih went so far as to promise to eradicate all restrictions on women's employment, something he later had to rescind due to opposition from many sectors of society. His speeches were full of promises of reform and change that he claimed will actually improve the lives of all Saudis. King Abdullah's New York speech last week was even more inflated. In it, he referred to the Saudi people as his bloodline, again positing himself as the benevolent father of the nation. In this role, he comforted his children that he will return home soon to serve them. In what sounded more like satire, King Abdullah promised prosperity, development, gender equality, and peace, all reforms that will, this time, really touch the lives of all Saudis. The regime's performance of these empty promises, which are too little, too late, will most likely become more amplified as more Saudis join silent protests, write critical opinion editorials, immolate themselves, and proudly watch as days of public anger spread from Tunis, to Cairo, to Sanaa.

Saudi Arabia might be far from having its own "day of anger," let alone a revolution, but it takes so much less to trigger the anxieties of the Saudi dictators. The latter are not concerned with being overthrown anytime soon, although the fact that local acts of opposition coincide with internal family struggles over succession is slightly inconvenient. That said, the Al Sauds are extremely allergic to any kind of public criticism and action against their rule, persons, or what they consider to be *their* country. They would rather deal with such incidents on an individual basis and behind closed doors, mainly through coercion. The ruling members often convey this stance through the media they control tightly. In the last few days, there have been several articles on the "open door policy" of the ruling family, what many so-called experts refer to as "Saudi democracy." It is true that many of the top ruling members of the Al Saud family receive people in their offices (*diwans*) on a daily basis, listen to their complaints, and in many cases, provide financial or moral support. But for the most part, only those who already have some connections (*wasta*) can actually make it to these royal *diwans*. The remaining twenty million Saudis, clearly, cannot access this avenue of "democracy." The Saudi regime has also resorted to other means to deter Saudi citizens from organizing protests. Local talk shows, for example, have hosted several prominent Saudi sociologists from the King Saud University in Riyadh, all of whom spoke against the "phenomenon of gatherings," denigrating it as "uncivilized," negative, and above all, illegal. These experts posed public gatherings as even more of an affront in light of the fact that the regime has a so-called "open door" policy that in reality is very much tightly shut in the face of those who need it most.

AGENCY AND ITS DISCONTENTS   25 February 2011

Saudi Arabia woke up on 23 February 2011—dubbed "Bright Wednesday"[241] by Saudi media—to the announcement of thirteen Royal Orders[242] that preceded the much-anticipated return of Abdullah by a few hours. The King's "gift to the nation"[243] signaled a major push for the improvement of everyday life of all Saudis by pumping thirty-five billion[244] dollars into comprehensive development projects in every region and corner of the Kingdom. The financial boost promises to cut across sectors, from higher education and social security to real estate loans and immediate aid to the unemployed and the needy. Abdullah, nearing the end of his eighth decade, proved to *his* people that he has been listening to *some* of their demands despite his three-month absence from home. In line with other kings before him, Abdullah has shown the world that his petro-regime, like those in the recent past, will continue to deal with calls for serious reforms and signs of criticism or opposition by yet again throwing money at growing internal challenges.

Surely, the King's latest batch of band-aid solutions is a welcome relief to the millions of Saudis struggling[245] under the weight of soaring unemployment,[246] inflation, and bureaucratic corruption, not to mention the millions of citizens living under the poverty[247] line. But for Saudis, who are constantly being told to be patient, it is no longer acceptable to simply treat the symptoms of their country's pressing troubles. Such short-term solutions[248] are publicly known to be failed strategies that have led to the state of under-development in the Kingdom. Citizens now expect their government to come up with real, long term solutions to what they see as the most endemic problems: (1) corruption, which has not spared any aspect of the private or public sector; (2) lack of accountability and transparency, both of which are the lifeline of corrupt practices; and (3) the absence of human rights, the right to gather and organize, and freedom of expression.

For the last year, calls for such major structural reform have surfaced across the Kingdom, whether in its state censored and controlled media or in royal courts and private and public salons. Some of these have culminated in the fledgling movements for change that were made public in the last two weeks, such as the Islamic Omma Party[249] (the first so-called political party in Saudi Arabia), the March 11 "Thawrat Hanin" (the Revolution of Longing), and "Saudi Revolution 20 March."[250] Despite the massive turnout of Saudis celebrating the king's return on the streets of Riyadh yesterday, citizens remain hopeful that the King's orders are the first step in a larger, more serious reform project. Many Saudis have already voiced their disappointment that the King did not address any of their calls for political reform, improving women's rights, and launching an exhaustive inquiry into corruption. Most have expressed their discontent in the letters[251] that were sent to the King since he returned from a medical trip abroad. The letters were signed by citizens from all walks of life and have been circulating online. They are calling for more serious structural reforms,[252] lifting all economic, legal, and social restrictions on women[253] as well as an overhaul of the political system.

Wednesday's kingdom-wide celebrations should not undermine[254] the reality and seriousness of calls for change here. Yes, Saudis respect and have faith in King Abdullah. After all, he is less corrupt than his late brother Fahd and his clan, and much more reliable and forgiving than his less popular, ruthless brothers who are second and third in line for succession. To support the King does not foreclose the very real democratic aspirations of a people whose political, social, economic, and human rights have been trampled on for almost a century. That said, we should not ignore the fact that Saudi municipalities and state media issued a call to all Saudis to go out on the streets and show their king that they love him. Accordingly, several universities, schools, orphanages, and other organizations commissioned buses to transport thousands of young Saudis to the airport road so the King can see them on his way home. Municipalities have also allotted several public spaces in each city where people can gather and express their support for the ailing king. In a country where social policing is stringent and the law forbids gatherings and any public celebration, it is not surprising that young Saudis were singing and dancing on the streets until late hours of the night. This was hijacked by Saudi state media and portrayed as an "exceptional youth phenomenon" in the Arab world, where the young often "hate" and want to overthrow their governments. Not surprisingly, as I was being driven around Riyadh last night, I saw many of the young men who chose to continue these public celebrations on the streets for a second night in a row being pulled over and either ticketed or arrested.

Many Saudis are ideologically opposed to monarchical rule and want to see an end to the Al Saud monopoly over power. Yet their calls for change fall short of demanding an overthrow of the regime. So far, proponents of change are hoping the King will realize that the Saudi Arabia he left in November for treatment in New York is not the same as the one he just returned to. They thus continue to demand that the current regime implement the political, economic, and social changes that the majority of Saudis want to see happen, contrary to regime arguments to the opposite. That Saudis are still seeking reform within the established political system is not proof of their love for the so-called benevolent "King of Humanity" (Abdullah's favorite nickname), as is being portrayed in Arab and international media. It also does not indicate their deep support for an authoritarian form of governance. If anything, it is a clear indication of people's fear of: (1) the current regime's oppressive reactions to attempts to protest against it, let alone to overthrow it; and (2) the bloody struggle over power that will ensue.

As is, the future here looks very ambiguous, with the Al Saud ruling members struggling over succession policies in light of the deteriorating health of Abdullah and his brothers. Further, Saudis know too intimately the consequences of even trying to oppose the US-fortified petro-regime that has as of late provided symbolic and material support to brutal Arab dictators who have zero legitimacy or popularity in their countries. This week alone, four of the founders of the Islamic Omma Party were imprisoned, and were given the ultimatum[255] of either giving up their calls for political organizing or remaining in prison. All four chose the latter. The Facebook page of Thawrat Haneen has also been blocked and completely erased from the social networking site. Tens of Saudis who dared to publicly protest the corruption that has led to the flooding of Jeddah for a second year in a row have also been arrested. Not to mention the hundreds of Saudis each year who go missing, are placed under house arrest, or are banned from travel, because of their political opinions. Saudis are also too aware of how their internal problems—

from regionalism and the wide spectrum of religious (in)tolerance to political/economic feuds and sectarianism—might explode in the absence of the only regime they have ever known.

Seventy percent of the population in Saudi Arabia is below the age of thirty-five. Along with citizens in their forties, they are becoming increasingly more confident in their own agency in affecting change within their own societies. For now, it seems that those who are calling for reforms are giving their dying king a chance before they start to seriously consider other options. How they will do it, in the face of one of the strongest petro-states in the world, remains to be seen. What happens next in Bahrain, the "Gulf's Guinea Pig Society,"[256] in the aftermath of King Hamad's meeting with King Abdullah two days ago, is sure to have a huge impact on Saudi political and revolutionary imaginaries.

SAUDI ARABIA'S WEEK OF SHAME   18 March 2011

Since King Abdullah returned to Riyadh on 23 February 2011, members of his ruling family have resorted to myriad political, economic,[257] and personal measures to prevent public expressions of dissent against the Al Saud. The Ministry of the Interior issued a statement[258] warning that any act of public protest is prohibited in Saudi Arabia and punishable by law. The country's senior ulema were quick to legitimize this criminalization of protest with religious justifications,[259] reminding everyone that "conspiring" against the political leadership is an unIslamic act akin to conspiring against God. The ulema then issued an official memorandum requesting that preachers at mosques discuss the importance of loyalty to the Al Saud during Friday sermons and to discourage people from calling for or joining protests. Minister of Foreign Affairs Saud al-Faisal then held a press conference[260] in which he threatened against any foreign interference—mainly implying that of Iran—and called for national dialogue and the importance of peacefully continuing the state-led project of reform.

Reminiscent of his father, King Abdullah sent his representatives to every corner of the Kingdom in the last three weeks to garner support from tribal and business leaders, political families and power brokers, and youth representatives, to name a few. Some tribal leaders from the southern and eastern parts of the country—areas historically accused of having secessionist tendencies—came to the King last week to renew their allegiance to him in person. The Ministries of the Interior and Defense also contacted all their retired personnel via telephone to secure their loyalty and that of their children and grandchildren. However, measures to mitigate potentially explosive tensions go beyond orthodox diplomacy and religio-legal maneuvers. According to a source in the Interior Ministry, hundreds of arrests have been made across the Kingdom in the last two weeks alone, all in relation to online organizing for popular protests that called for comprehensive reforms. In the beginning of the month, rumors were circulating that the founder of the Facebook page that called for a "Day of Rage" on 11 March 2011 in Saudi Arabia was murdered[261] in Riyadh. Although still unconfirmed, the rumor has succeeded in making people think twice about, if not completely deterring them from, getting involved in any sort of political organizing.

Even more alarming is the blatant anti-Iran, anti-Shi'a rhetoric that the Saudi state-owned media has been propagating for the last two weeks on behalf of the Al Saud ruling family. Raising the specter of an Iran-manufactured "Day of Rage" in Saudi Arabia turned support for legitimate and popular demands into a crime against national security. This was exacerbated by unofficial alerts that were circulated via text messages. Some warned that joining the protests was punishable by five years in prison and several hundred thousands of Saudi Riyals in fines. Others incriminated anyone who was caught taking photographs of any possible protest. The punishment for such a crime was stated to be three years in prison and tens of thousands of Saudi Riyals. Still more text and email messages announced that the 11 March protest was orchestrated by al-Qaeda and/or other unpopular figures such as the hated Islamist opposition leader Saad al-Faqih[262] or the feminist scholar Hatoon al-Fassi.[263] While the source of the alerts that circulated widely remains unknown, they nonetheless had the impact of shifting the mood, in Riyadh at least, from one of excitement, possibility, and hope for bringing about change to one of suspicion, fear, and doubt of the motives of the planned "Day of Rage."

The 11 March protest started as a popular call for serious political, economic, and social reforms, undergirded by demands for the establishment of a constitutional monarchy and the building of a vibrant and free civil society. The call started to gain momentum as larger segments of society were making their demands for reform public (see examples here[264] and here[265]). But many of those who had considered joining the demonstration gradually felt that the 11 March protest was being hijacked by Islamists whose goal was primarily to overthrow the Al Saud monarchy, and not necessarily to protest the lack of real political, economic, social, and human rights. That some later referred to the protest as the "Hunain Revolution," a reference to a battle[266] in the early history of Islam, is perhaps indicative of that. To say the least, the demonstrations, whose original organizers remain unknown, were badly planned and their goals were largely ambiguous. This made it easy for one insignificant opposition group, in this case a group of staunch anti-Al Saud Islamists, to hijack the "Day of Rage" as their own, thus enabling proponents of the status quo to summarily discredit the whole movement for reforms. Regardless, on the eve of 11 March, in the aftermath of the Saudi security forces' use of live ammunition to disperse[267] a protest in the Eastern Province, it was becoming clearer that public demands for reform and the institution of a constitutional monarchy would have to be delayed. This was especially the case when the United States refrained[268] from condemning the security forces' violence against unarmed, peaceful demonstrators. What had started as a month of public discussions and debates on the possibility of forcing political, social, and economic reforms were silenced overnight in the name of national security.

What little hope was left for the possibility of protests taking place was shattered by the heightened security that was deployed in all major Saudi cities on Friday 11 March. As many foreign reporters have already described[269] elsewhere, Riyadh felt and looked like a police state. A police vehicle was parked every fifty meters, and in some neighborhoods, every ten. In some areas, a mixture of police, undercover intelligence cars, and Interior Ministry trucks, was positioned every couple of hundred meters, especially between the Faisaliya and Kingdom towers. Anti-riot police were also stationed at designated locations in every neighborhood in central Riyadh, with a huge presence in front of Jareer bookstore on Olaya street, close to the protest's planned point of departure. Sirens went off all day and late into the night. And in the event that this was not enough to make the point, helicopters hovered low over Riyadh's homes until midnight to scare off potential dissenters, if any had remained.

Despite regime claims to the contrary, hope and possibility were very much in the air in the weeks prior to the "Friday of Rage." Saudis from all walks of life were expressing their lack of faith in a regime that for decades has done nothing but talk and make empty promises of reform. In newspapers, online blogs and chat rooms, salons and cafés, many expressed their willingness to take to the streets and protest for their rights on condition that the pro-reform movement allow for diversity in political, religious, and ideological views. While the latter did not happen, the fate of the 11 March protests was nonetheless never as done a deal as the Al Saud regime would like its people and the world to think. Prior to the planned protest, the regime exhibited great signs of fear and insecurity. The ruling members of the Al Saud were and still are more anxious than they have been in decades, their media and online censors more vigilant than ever. If anything, the last four days' hyper-glorified depictions of "the people's love for their Al Saud rulers" and the "unbreakable bond that has united them since the great founding father, Ibn Saud" only goes to show Al Saud's state of uncertainty. The ruling family may not lose sleep over sharing the same fate as Ben Ali or Mubarak any time soon. But as already mentioned, it takes much less to keep the antiquated Saudi ruling members on their guarded toes.

The Al Saud rulers, however, are resilient, and although they know that the status quo is unsustainable, resist change they will. The "reforms"[270] announced by King Abdullah today, the majority of which bolster the power of his family's two main constituencies, the security forces and the religious clerics, indicate just how concerned the Al Sauds are over their future, and the extent to which they will fight political and social reforms. The way the regime's discourse shifted when calls for demonstrations failed to materialize is most telling of this "old guard" mentality within the family. The Ministry of Culture, for example, went from completely banning any mention of the day of rage in Saudi media to pressuring all writers to congratulate the ruling family in light of the "failure" of the previously unmentionable protests. The few ethical Saudi newspaper writers who have refrained from taking a celebratory and self-congratulating stance are being pressured[271] into taking sides: the right, pro-government side, that is. Especially superficial analyses and state propaganda have dominated Saudi television and its printed press since the Saturday after the supposed "Day of Rage." These moves indicate a great sense of Al Saud relief that security forces have managed to suppress all calls for anti-government protests.

Well, almost all calls. The little matter of ongoing protests in the Eastern Province for over two months, mostly calling for the release of political prisoners, does not really count. These are usually framed by the Saudi regime as anti-patriotic expressions of disloyal (Shi'a) citizens heeding the orders of their Iranian coreligionist lords. The Al Saud regime, with its pervasive institutionalized sectarianism, has yet to recognize the Shi'a citizens of the Eastern Province as anything but second-class citizens. It denies them their religious, political, social, and economic rights even more so than it does their Sunni counterparts. It also enables discrimination against the Shi'a in schools, hospitals, and employment. And when these disenfranchised citizens publicly demand the rights they are systematically denied, they are labeled "agents" of Iran while simultaneously being expected to act as loyal Saudi subjects. Despite the continuation of a long history of institutional and popular discrimination against them, Saudi Shi'a protesters in the Eastern Province have taken great care in the last few years to show their allegiance to the Saudi crown and have raised the Saudi flag in their months-long demonstrations.

Yet, the Saudi regime continues to employ its Shi'a citizens as tools in its competition with its regional nemesis, Iran. It is perhaps one of the reasons that we often hear about protests in Saudi Arabia's eastern (Shi'a) cities, but not, for example, the several[272] ones that have taken place in Riyadh,[273] Jeddah, and other parts of the Kingdom. While all the protests seem to demand the release of political prisoners, bureaucratic reforms, and an end to corruption, Saudi media singles out the protests in the Eastern Province to show that they are the only ones creating chaos in the Kingdom. In recent weeks, this rhetoric was also used as a premise for Saudi troops to invade[274] Bahrain under the guise of the GCC's Peninsula Shield Troops. The Saudi regime, fearful of "uprising contagion," argues that the Bahraini government has failed to quell what both countries' royal families have portrayed[275] as a Shi'a uprising against the Sunni monarchy. The Saudi regime thus had to take matters into its own hands in order to safeguard regional stability and protect its own national security. And despite US Defense Secretary Robert Gates' assurance that his government found no evidence of Iranian interference in Bahrain, the Saudi regime has escalated its propaganda condemning Iran's meddling in Bahrain's internal affairs. After the Saudi regime sent in its troops to reshape Bahraini affairs, using Iran as a scarecrow, the King issued a second warning[276] on 14 March against any international interference in Saudi affairs.

As UN Security Council Resolution 1973 gave broad backing[277] to military action against Muammar al-Qaddafi this morning, it seems like an empty call to ponder the hypocrisy of supporting democratic opposition forces in some places, and not others.[278] But at a time of tragic double standards, it might be worth asking what is so different about al-Qaddafi—whose Libya is an integral part of the African Union—requesting support from neighboring African countries against internal opposition to his rule, and Bahrain's supposed[279] appeal for help from its GCC big sister, Saudi Arabia? It is quiet again in Saudi cities, after Saudi Arabia's deplorable regional role foreclosed the short-lived sense of empowerment and possibility we felt here in the Kingdom over the last month. To speak would entail condemning one's own complicity in what so many people here are very quietly calling their government's "invasion of Bahrain," despite the White House's 14 March claims to the opposite.[280] Except for the few brave shows of solidarity in Qatif and Seyhat,[281] it has been very quiet indeed. For many citizens of the Arab world, this moment, with its specificity, is all too reminiscent of the 1990–01 Gulf War. It is a very traumatic one, more so because it comes on the heels of the success of other Arab revolutions and the hope they gave birth to. This week has been a historic one. But unlike the revolutions of Tunisia and Egypt, it will go down in Saudi Arabia's long history of shame, one that has much blood on its sleeves, and in which the West as well as other Arab countries are deeply complicit.

32
The Never Ending Story:
Protests and Constitutions in Morocco

Emanuela Dalmasso and Francesco Cavatorta[282]

12 August 2011

On 1 July 2011, Moroccans went to the polls in a referendum promoted by King Mohammed VI to approve a new constitution to replace that of 1996. A vote of over ninety-eight percent, in an official turnout of over seventy-two percent, unsurprisingly approved the new text.

The new constitution supposedly represents a further step in the direction of establishing a liberal-democratic system and does indeed contain provisions to that effect. For instance there is now the explicit recognition that Morocco is a "parliamentary constitutional monarchy," that national identity is pluralistic and not simply Arab and Muslim, and that, crucially, the figure of the King is no longer "sacred," but simply inviolable. In addition, the Parliament's powers have been increased.

There is no doubt that the new constitution represents a concession to the Moroccan protest movement that emerged during the Arab Spring. Yet, this should not obscure the fact that the monarch strictly controlled and managed the whole reform process. In order to avoid further challenges to his authority and public role, Mohammed VI decided to pre-empt the most radical demands of the demonstrators such as the end to the monarchy's executive role. He wanted to offer Moroccans a new charter that indicated the country was moving toward the establishment of democratic governance. With the vast majority of Moroccans approving the new constitution despite the 20 February Movement's calls to boycott the referendum, it seems that the monarchy has been able to end the debate about its primacy in the country's institutional set up. Sectors of civil society, the vast majority of political parties, the trade unions and both the national and international press all supported the "yes" camp in the referendum, clearly suggesting that they still trust the

260

monarchy to lead the reform initiative. While the provisions of the new constitution do represent a considerable change, critics have outlined that they are in no way radical or "democratic."

At no point does the new constitution call the principle of an executive monarchy into question. This is really the heart of the matter for those Moroccans who claim that tinkering at the edges of the system without dealing with the primary role of the monarch as an executive and ultimate decision-maker makes a mockery of the country's supposed democratic transition. Furthermore, some within the "yes" camp such as Ali Bouabid, leading member of the Socialist Party, questioned the administration of the referendum. He argued that the real turnout was probably only around fifty percent and suggested that ballot boxes were stuffed to boost the official turnout and mask the real strength of the boycott camp. It is very difficult to substantiate claims of vote rigging, but this is a practice that the *makhzen* (the ruling elite of Morocco centered around the monarchy and composed of high-ranking military officials and bureaucrats, local notables, and rich businessmen) has often used in the past to manage elections. Another point that challenges the referendum's legitimacy is the fact that most media outlets heavily campaigned for a "yes" vote.

However, unlike the past patterns of protest and reform, the approval of a new constitution did not in fact end the protest and political debate on the monarchy's role in democratizing the country. Since independence, Morocco has had a number of constitutions, born of the monarch's proposals for change in response to negotiations with political parties. These negotiations never undermined the monarchy's pre-eminence; they were intended to appease opponents who were grateful for having been partly listened to. This strategy of "constitutionalizing" political and institutional reforms under the guidance of the monarchy and relying on the advice of committees and commissions appointed by the King was also a feature of Hassan's reign. It allowed him to remain the central figure of the reformist effort. Mohammed VI has applied this logic to the 2011 constitutional changes: re-configure governing institutions by giving the impression of change while holding on to executive prerogatives. In any case, the approval of each new constitution coincided with the end of discontent and turmoil. This is not the case today.

The protest movement has continued to demand genuine reforms and even the end of the monarchy's executive powers. Street demonstrations persist and despite the fact that the crowds are never larger than a few thousand, they constitute a nuisance for the monarchy. This is a political rupture for Morocco, testifying to the durability of the protest movement and to the erosion of monarchical legitimacy.

The regime has met the ongoing street protests through a dual strategy. On the one hand there is a concerted media campaign to either ignore the protesters or to point to the heterogeneity and extremism of their movement. The media represents the protesters as both divided, between Islamists and leftists, and ideologically unable to offer a genuine alternative because of their extremism. Thus the monarchy claims to represent the middle-ground with its mix of religious legitimacy and attachment to modern values.

On the other hand, the protesters are met with a degree of violence. Civilian militias attack and disrupt the marches of the 20 February Movement without any intervention from the security forces and the police. While there is no evidence that the *makhzen* and, crucially, the monarchy have organized such militias, it is apparent that they enjoy significant financial and material means and benefit from the security forces' "neutrality." The vast network of military officials, bureaucrats, local notables, and business people linked to the state who have a keen interest in the persistence of current forms of rule can mobilize counter-protest movements in support of the King through patronage channels. The monarch does not have to necessarily or directly sanction such counter-protests. Crucially, the security forces have to be seen to remain above the fray. While they do not intervene to protect the 20 February Movement demonstrators against civilian violence from counter-demonstrators, they are not directly repressing anti-regime demonstrations. This allows the state to present itself as neutral. The dual strategy of ignoring protests and allowing for violence against them by the *baltaga* (thugs) allows the monarchy to continue playing its self-ascribed role: the arbiter of Moroccan politics and society. The regime is today replicating the traditional "divide and conquer" strategies that it has recurrently mobilized to contain dissent, allowing the monarch to remain above the fray and supposedly settle societal differences.

What we seem to be witnessing is another re-run of the "never-ending Moroccan democratization" which does not deliver meaningful democratic change or a system of elected representatives accountable to citizens. It simply reinforces the role of the King as the ultimate arbiter of the political system. The two novel elements that have emerged today are the resilience of the protest movement and the arrival of the *baltaga*, but the overall strategy of the monarchy to remain at the core of the political system follows a familiar path.

The Arab Spring of 2011 has forced Mohammed VI to make some concessions to the Moroccan protest movement, but these concessions should not be seen as a necessary step towards radical change. The Moroccan monarchy has a long tradition of and experience in managing political contestation. This management has been consistently couched in the rhetoric of a democratization, which has yet to ever materialize. At the moment, the rhetorical embrace of democracy and constitutional changes do not satisfy the 20 February Movement. Street protests continue and the movement is delivering an important and perhaps unprecedented challenge to the monarchy.

The monarchy and the *makhzen* are not in danger of collapsing and the constitutional changes have proved satisfactory for political parties and ordinary citizens alike because they still believe in "democratic gradualism." Yet, for the first time there is today a movement of citizens coming together from different ideological currents that all refuse to accept such gradualism even after the regime has met some of its demands. The Arab Spring in Morocco is set to continue, as the 20 February Movement wishes to be the one writing the final word of the never-ending Moroccan democratization.

The departure of Tunisian leader Zine El Abidine Ben Ali in January 2011 and Egyptian President Husni Mubarak's resignation on 11 February sparked conjectures about Algeria as the next country in the Arab world to attempt to rid itself of authoritarian leadership. While Egyptians have lived under "state of emergency" laws since Mubarak came to power after Sadat's assassination in 1981, Algeria's version, also prohibiting any public demonstrations, was enacted in 1992 after the country's first national multiparty elections and runoff set for 16 January 1992 were suspended. A military coup d'etat deposed then President Chadli Benjedid who had ruled since 1979.

By 21 January 2011 a network of Algerian oppositional movements had formed under the organizational umbrella of the "National Coordination for Change and Democracy," made up of labor unions as well as human rights, feminist, and student associations from civil society. When they called for a demonstration on Saturday 12 February for the main 1 May Square in Algiers the capital, some two to three thousand participants met violence at the hands of a force of thirty thousand police. A second peaceful march a week later on 19 February never reached the square impeded again by police force, all amply documented by videos and images posted on YouTube and Facebook. In Oran, Algeria's second largest city, organizers had to content themselves with calling for a meeting on Saturday 19 February in a public hall absent the requisite permit to march or demonstrate in public space.

Patterns of Algerian civil unrest differ from Tunisian and Egyptian versions not only in frequency of protests over the past few years but also in the composition of participants and the spaces they temporarily and respectively occupy. On the one hand, low figures of intellectuals, political parties members and civil society groups have turned out for peaceful takeovers of the main squares in Algeria's larger cities or in front of government buildings throughout the country as they unfurl banners and shout slogans to make clear demands. At the same time, much larger numbers of youth protests occur often concentrating within their own poorer and crowded neighborhoods such as Algiers' densest urban neighborhood of Bab el Oued. These are young men acting against an all encompassing *hogra* (oppression) in ways that have been termed rampages, looting parties, and bread riots regardless of the diverse precipitating causes—rising prices for basic foodstuffs, bad housing, no jobs, and government clampdowns on the informal economy.

So-called bread riots and food protests are not mere "rebellions of the belly," argues Edward P. Thompson's classic study, but best viewed as a "highly complex form of direct popular action, disciplined and with clear objectives." Thompson's formulations about the eighteenth-century English crowd offer one description about Algeria where years of large-scale urban anti-government revolts play out his concept of a "moral economy of protest."* These latter uprisings are examples of power and resistance in which the strategies and inchoate language of demands for justice articulated by protesters are dynamic evidence of social claims for greater equity. Specific acts by young male crowds target banks, shops, and cars for destruction and looting as symbols of economic injustice and evoke widespread fears of a return to the violence of the bloody decade of the 1990s that is said to have claimed two hundred thousand Algerian lives.

However, unlike Tunisia and Egypt, the Algerian economy posted 160 billion dollars in foreign currency reserves. Due to immense natural gas and oil resources that account for two-thirds of the

---

* E. P. Thompson, "The Moral Economy of the English Crowd in the Eighteenth Century," *Past and Present* 50 (1971): 76–78.

country's revenues, one-third of the GDP (gross domestic product), and more than ninety-five percent of export earnings, Algeria's hydrocarbon sector has assured a low external debt hovering at one percent of the GDP. Sporadic government moves towards a market-based economy means that state spending and state-created employment have shrunk. Nonetheless, the populace accurately perceives the government as the principal engine for job creation. Fueling the population's demands is the knowledge of growing hydrocarbon revenues that barely trickle down to make a dent in low living standards and high rates of youth unemployment.

"Mubarak chased from power: Egypt one, Algeria zero" is a recent cartoon tagline by acerbic Algerian cartoonist Ali Dilem that depicts a demonstrator waving the flag and urging current President Abdelaziz Bouteflika to leave so that Algeria may even the score. By 2009 as Bouteflika approached the limit of two presidential mandates, he initiated a third one after swiftly pushing through a constitutional amendment to allow the president to run for office indefinitely. Echoing the Algerian soccer team's elimination of Egypt from the 2010 World Cup matches in which Algeria scored one and Egypt zero, Dilem's cartoon image acknowledges Algeria's pre-eminent position as the country in the Arab world with the highest number of political demonstrations and marches, local violent protests and street riots. In the year 2010 alone, estimates range from one hundred to thousands of discrete, newsworthy incidents that made and will continue to make the constant eruptions of turmoil and unrest, peaceful and violent, as the principle strategy for sectors of Algerian society to direct their grievances vociferously and en masse to their government leaders.

33
Emergencies and Economics:
Algeria and the Politics of Memory

Muriam Haleh Davis[283]

1 March 2011

On 24 February the Algerian government lifted the state of emergency that has been operative in Algeria for almost two decades. Undoubtedly, this was a response to the changing political tides in the Middle East, as well as popular unrest in Algeria itself. While localized riots have been a common occurrence in the country since 2005, the start of 2011 has witnessed a wave of simultaneous protests in Algeria. On 8 January, the regime announced it would temporarily cut taxes on sugar and cooking oil in an attempt to quell the protests. But that was before the Jasmine Revolution. After watching events in Tunisia, and then Egypt, Algerians were emboldened, taking to the streets even as the president, Abdelaziz Bouteflika, refused permission for the protests and made sure that water cannons and police helicopters were readily available.

The seventy-one-year-old Bouteflika, who is widely believed to be in remission from cancer, has responded by lifting the state of emergency that had curbed freedom of expression and had been justified by the specter of political Islamism in the 1990s. This threat crystallized around the 1991 elections, in which the FIS emerged victorious and the military responded by annulling the results, dissolving parliament, banning the FIS, and brutally cracking down on all stripes of Islamists. By most accounts, Bouteflika's decision to end the state of emergency represents a minor victory in the wake of the confrontation between Islamic radicalism and authoritarian governance.

Yet in a recent editorial,[284] journalist Azzeddine Bensouiah wrote that "the lifting of the state of emergency signifies absolutely nothing, in terms of action, for most Algerians." Perhaps this is not surprising, given that Interior Minister Dahou Ould Kabila announced that marches would continue to be banned in the capital.

And yet protests are set to continue. A different, but equally cynical, take on the uprisings was captured in a cartoon[285] that ran in Liberté, and which depicted Bouteflika standing above a crowd, bound by ropes holding a gun at protesters trying to pull him down. Under the heading "international community asks Bouteflika for restraint," Bouteflika remarks: "I don't give a damn! If they pull, I'll shoot."

While much has been written on the bloody war between the state and political Islamists, the role of foreign capital is much more opaque. The Islamists have received much press in recent weeks (no matter that there are important differences among these groups), but another kind of emergency has gone practically unmentioned: the 2001 Emergency Reconstruction Plan, which enacted economic reforms overseen by the IMF and stimulated significant foreign investment in Algeria (most of which occurred in the hydrocarbon industry). This "emergency" has been largely forgotten, but it goes a long way in explaining the recent cartoon as well as the political trajectory of Algeria in the last decade.

The act was certainly not Algeria's first foray into the annals of the Washington Consensus. During the 1990s Algeria became dependent on foreign loans and adopted austerity measures that worsened unemployment. As a result, there was violent backlash by Algeria's main labor union, the UGTA (General Union of Algerian Workers), which staged numerous strikes and protests. This was largely in response to the dual economy that had emerged between the oil and gas companies, on one hand, and the Algerian population, on the other. As one historian of Algeria has written,[286] the government helped foster the "creation of veritable dual economies, with the oil and gas companies being physically shielded and isolated from the hostilities, while the general population went largely unprotected by security forces."

Yet the attempt to attract foreign capital amid a bloody civil war, which was spurred on by the polarizing logic of the first Gulf War and socioeconomic unrest, posed considerable challenges. In an attempt to gloss over the deep political cleavages, some of which dated back to the war of independence, Bouteflika enacted a legalized form of political forgetting: the 2005 Charter for Peace and National Reconciliation.

On a model that departed from South Africa's Truth and Reconciliation Committee, Bouteflika provided amnesty to members of FIS who committed acts of terror as well as agents of the state—which included the military and state officials. Officially, it stated that "Anyone who, by speech, writing, or any other act, uses or exploits the wounds of the National Treaty to harm the instructions of the Democratic and Popular Republic of Algeria, to weaken the state, or to undermine the good relation of its agents who honorably served it, or to tarnish the image of Algeria internationally, shall be punished by three to five years in prison and the fine of 250,000 to 500,000 dinars." Three years later, in October 2008, Bouteflika asked for the suspension of the constitution's article seventy-seven, which allowed him to stand for a third term. Once again, national security, political stability, and the specter of Islamism were used to justify the deepening of authoritarian rule.

And yet, to view authoritarianism and Islamism as a zero-sum game is to overlook the ways in which Algeria was imbricated in the global economy of oil and terror in the 1990s. The "dark decade," which killed approximately two hundred thousand people was not simply a struggle between the state and the Islamists. Spurred by the concerns of foreign investors who were eager to see signs of political stability and the eradication of Islamism, the state had concrete incentives to radicalize the FIS rather than engage them in the democratic process. Moreover, FIS' own internal divisions were deepened as the Salafists, trained in Afghanistan and hostile to any form of democratic participation, emerged on the scene. Eventually, these anti-democratic Islamists formed the GIA (Islamic Armed Group), which was initially funded by Osama Bin-Laden. The split between national Islamists groups committed to some form of political participation and transnational groups insisting on the destruction of the state has continued in Algeria, with the GIA eventually giving rise to the GSPC (Salafist Group for Call and Combat) and the AQMI (Al Qaeda in the Islamic Maghreb). In the early 1990s, while the regime was busy with FIS, more seditious enemies were emerging elsewhere, ironically funded by some of the same foreign interests that were investing in hydrocarbons. Foreign investment in Algeria has continued in the past decade—US direct investment in Algeria, for example, totaled 5.45 billion dollars in 2007, most of which went to the hydrocarbon sector.

Both the Algerian state and radical Islamists were involved in transnational networks of terrorism and capitalism, which made the bitterest of enemies into occasional bedfellows. This peculiar combination of forces led to the mystery surrounding the murder of seven French Trappist Monks of Notre Dame de l'Atlas, who were kidnapped and killed in March of 1996. (It also happens to be the subject of the movie *Des Hommes et Des Dieux*, which recently won the award for best film at "French Oscars" last week.) While the GIA initially took responsibility for the killings, it later emerged that the GIA had undertaken the actions with the knowledge and potential complicity of the Algerian intelligence service (DIS). Thus, while the story of the showdown between the Algerian state and Islamists is not without validity, clearly the interests of the regime have been considerably more complex. As Algeria has emerged as a key ally on the "war on terror," receiving financial and technical assistance in exchange for cooperation in matters of security, North Africa and the Sahel have become important locations for the security economy of the United States, with Halliburton and their subsidiary, Kellog, Brown & Root, playing starring roles. Indeed, these events point to a recent history and political landscape that cannot be reduced to the corruption of local political elites, economic "mismanagement," or the threat of radical Islam.

The divisive history of the War of Independence (1954–1962) as well as the violence of the 1990s continues to impact Algeria's political landscape in important ways. The various groups that formed the National Coordination for Change and Democracy (CNCD) in January, which initiated the recent protests in Algeria, are undoubtedly diverse. They include the secular RCD (Movement for Democracy in Algeria), the communist MDS (Democratic and Social Movement), and the NGO, Algerian League for Human Rights (LADDH). Yet despite the 2005 attempts at reconciliation, and the lifting of emergency rule, things once forgotten are visible in the constitution of this group. For example, the fact that the participation of RCD, a mainly Kabyle party, has caused hostility, exposes the Berber unrest that continues to haunt Algerian national identity. Moreover, it is significant that the FIS' recent request to join the coalition was denied, despite its considerable popular support. Lastly, while Hocine Ait Ahmed's socialist party, the Socialist Forces Front (FFS) was initially involved in the coalition, it ultimately refused to join. Yet despite this fragmentation, the collective frustration is both palpable and undeniable. Indeed, the FFS responded to the lowering of prices in January with a statement that remains prescient for Algeria and beyond: "The government cannot buy Algerian's silence."

34
Iraq and its Tahrir Square

Zainab Saleh[287]

17 February 2011

Iraq's absence from the "Egypt Today, Tomorrow the World" map,[288] published a week after the massive demonstration in Egypt on 25 January and which included the dates of planned demonstrations in different Arab capitals, was striking. The absence was not limited to the dates listed. Iraq as a country was not included. It is as if the absence of protests indicated the absence of the country itself. As if Iraq was not affected by the recent events in Tunisia[289] and Egypt.[290] This conspicuous absence is due to the nature of the present political regime in Iraq, which adopted and institutionalized a sectarian discourse after the fall of Saddam Hussein. Iraq is reminiscent of Lebanon:[291] the sectarian quota system has paralyzed political life. How is it possible to create a united popular initiative when markers like Kurd, Shi'a, Sunni, and Christian are in circulation and when the word Iraqi does not count?

One of the comments on Facebook about the abovementioned map was: "Why isn't Iraq on that map???" The reply to this comment read: "A sad question with so many answers." What makes this question especially sad is Iraq's secular political history up until Saddam Hussein's rise to power in 1979. Saddam Hussein banned all open political activity and as a result many groups (for example, the Dawa Party and the Kurdish parties) were driven underground or flourished in exile (that is, the UK, Iran, and Syria). The return of opposition members from exile with the American troops after 2003 has had a devastating impact on Iraqi political life. These figures' sectarian discourse and their thirst for government positions have led to the marginalization of independent and alternative voices. Given the nature of the political game in Lebanon, a reader may ask "When is such a revolution going to happen in Lebanon?" But not "Where is Lebanon?" However, the story of Iraq is different and its absence from the map cannot be overlooked. For instance, how can a reader not feel sad when she remembers the protest history of Iraq, including the 1920 Revolt, the demonstration that brought down the Portsmouth Treaty and the government in 1948, and the uprisings in the north and the south in 1991?

Iraq is now seen as beyond the pale of the Egyptian Revolution. Demonstrations have happened in Bahrain, Jordan,[292] Libya, Syria, and Yemen. The Yemeni President, Ali Abdullah Saleh announced that he would not seek another term. The Jordanian King Abdullah bin Hussein II sacked[293] the Jordanian prime minister and his cabinet. However, Iraq remained distant from these events until 5 February when Iraqi Prime Minister Nouri al-Maliki announced he would not seek a third term after his mandate expires in 2014. He also promised[294] "to donate half of his salary to the treasury in a gesture of solidarity with the poor of Iraq." Al-Maliki stated that his decisions stem from his commitment to democracy. However, it is not hard to read the effects of the Egyptian Revolution in al-Maliki's sudden recollection of democracy. The day following al-Maliki's announcement, demonstrations were held in different cities across Iraq. The people protested[295] against unemployment, high prices, and corruption. It seems like word of al-Maliki's generous donation did not resonate much with Iraqis. However, these demonstrations remained limited to a few hundred people at most. They were followed by a demonstration in the city of Diwaniyya on 3 February, during which the police opened fire on the demonstrators and killed three of them. These events received little attention even in the Iraqi press.

On 7 February, announcements that[296] "Tahrir Square in Baghdad is getting ready for huge demonstrations" were circulated on many Iraqi websites and Facebook pages. The announcement invited Iraqis to join demonstrations on 25 February in Baghdad's Tahrir Square. Some of the slogans included in the announcement were:

Haven't we had enough silence??
Haven't we had enough of patience??
Don't you know we're like a mule who carries gold but eats
    thorns??...
Death to a democracy that turns things from bad to worse!!...
Death to the democracy of death and beheading!!...
Death to a democracy that assassinates the rival pen and the
    true word!!
Death to the democracy of cancerous walls that have torn apart
    the body of my beloved Baghdad.

The announcement ends by addressing the army and the police:

> We address this call to the military and police. We ask them to
> protect the homeland and the people...We ask them to be like
> their brethren in Tunisia and Egypt. We are no longer living in
> a time of demagogy and fatal weapons but in a time of the pen
> and the true word that defends the poor. Tell everyone about the
> day of 'The Revolution of Iraqi Wrath' for the sake of change,
> freedom and true democracy. Change...Change...Change.

This announcement reflects the bankruptcy of the discourse of
democracy amid corruption, nepotism, sectarianism, assassinations,
murder, separation walls, and dictatorship. Clearly, the political
developments in Tunisia and Egypt were an incentive to write this
announcement and to call for protests. Addressing the army and the
police reflects an awareness of what happened in Tunisia and Egypt.
Moreover, the choice of Tahrir Square (*sahat al-tahrir*) in Baghdad
indicates the writers' identification with Egypt. Midan al-Tahrir in
Cairo has become a symbol of the struggle and unity of the people,[297]
beyond any political, gender, class, and religious divisions.

However, the significance of Tahrir Square in Baghdad is more
than simply the identification with Egypt as it draws on Iraqi
history as well. Baghdad's Tahrir Square includes The Monument
of Freedom designed by the prominent Iraqi sculptor, Jawad Salim.
The first Iraqi President, Abdul-Karim Qasim, commissioned Salim
to build the monument after the 14 July 1958 Revolution, which
ended the monarchy and British rule in Iraq. The monument
consists of fourteen bronze pieces. Each piece represents a story in
the history of Iraq. These stories are organized into three distinct
periods:[298] one before the 14 July Revolution, the second the day
of the Revolution, and third after the Revolution. The first set
of pieces portrays the suffering of the poor oppressed people in
Iraq and hope amid darkness. The second set includes a political
prisoner who is trying to break the bars of a prison, as well as the
famous depiction of a solider bursting out chains. This part of the
monument refers to the 14 July Revolution. Finally, the third set
of stories revolves around prosperity, freedom, and coexistence in
Iraq. Hence, the monument has clear symbolic significance since
it conveys the suffering of the Iraqis throughout history. However,
this suffering is brought to an end by the prevailing will and unity
of the Iraqi people. By including Sumerian and Babylonian symbols,
the Tigris and Euphrates, a date palm tree, Arabs and Kurds, Salim

stresses the unity of Iraqis and their common history. The selection of Tahrir Square thus has implications beyond the similarity of the name with Midan al-Tahrir in Cairo. The Monument of Freedom emphasizes all Iraqis' belonging to Iraq regardless of their religious, ethnic, and political differences.

The story of the monument (that is, the prevalence of the people's will and the downfall of the monarchy along with the end of the British rule) has direct implications for the current situation in Iraq. Today, Iraq has been under US occupation for over eight years (irrespective of the nominal withdrawal of the US "combat forces"), and the current government takes its orders from Washington. Political sectarianism has rendered any independent political activity nearly impossible. The paradox of demonstrating under the Monument of Freedom will not be lost on Iraqi demonstrators. While the monument was erected in commemoration of the independence of Iraq and the end of colonial rule in the 1950s, the upcoming demonstration in the square will take place in a divided and occupied Iraq. Still, this call shows a desire to create an inclusive Iraqi political space, dedicated to Iraq and its people, akin to what is being formed in Tunisia and Egypt today.

Over the past several days, however, Iraq has begun to appear on the landscape of demonstrations, particularly in the aftermath of the Egyptian rage over Husni Mubarak's refusal to step down on 10 February. Students, professors, and intellectuals held a demonstration in Bagdad's al-Mutanabi Street (the historical street of bookstores) against corruption and the deterioration of public services. The anger of the people seems to have been sensed by the Iraqi government, which closed down one of the bridges that lead to Tahrir Square in an attempt to prevent the protesters from reaching it from the eastern part of the Tigris. Demonstrators from the western part of the Tigris, demanding the release of detained people and calling for the respect of human rights, managed to reach the square.[299]

Most recently, the news of Husni Mubarak's resignation has re-kindled hope among Iraqis. Calls for huge demonstrations in Iraq this Friday (18 February), instead of 25 February, are increasing.

Let us wait and see what Iraq's Tahrir Square holds for the coming days!

Postscript: Developments are unfolding rapidly as of the translation of this article. Anti-government protests have taken place in Sulaimaniyah, Nassiriyya, and Kut. Some people were killed and wounded during clashes with security forces.

35
Tahrir's Other Sky

Noura Erakat and Sherene Seikaly[300]

9 February 2011

> The Earth is closing on us
> pushing us through the last passage
> and we tear off our limbs to pass through.
> Where should we go after the last frontiers?
> Where should the birds fly after the last sky?
> — *Mahmoud Darwish*

Egypt's exhilarating call for freedom, as Elliott Colla[301] recently noted is an astonishing moment of poetry. The refrain, "*Ish-sha'b/ yu-rîd/is-qât/in-ni-zâm,*" (The People Want the Fall of the Regime) resoundingly rings for millions in the Arab world and beyond. With all eyes on Liberation Square, many are wrestling with what Maya Mikdashi aptly called the unfamiliar restlessness of hope.[302] As the twists and turns of the 25 January Revolution quickly unfold, another extraordinary process is taking place. The relentless resilience of Egyptians risking life and limb for freedom has seared cracks in the sky and revealed another horizon of politics.

Since 1967, when defeat rang the death knell of the pan Arab anti-colonial project, the figure of the Palestinian revolutionary has been an icon of the liberation struggle, for her courage, resilience, and *sumud* (steadfastness). The model of the Palestinian *fida'i(ya)* itself drew from the anti-colonial struggles of Algeria and Cuba. At the center of a battle for land and life against Zionist colonial settlement, subject to expulsion and exile, Palestinian women and men forging forward against a better-funded and heavily-equipped enemy constituted an ideal type. This status is a result of systemic colonial oppression and the now century long denial of self-determination. It also flows from the work of generations dedicated to a struggle that indelibly marked Palestine as a spring of freedom fighters.

Palestinians too have understood themselves as exceptional. After the revolution, they believed that their nation-state would be a

274

democratic one based on freedoms of movement, expression, and association. Since the onset of Zionist settlement in the nineteenth century, the political, cultural, and intellectual work of Palestinians has resisted the unyielding attempt to make them invisible. The late 1960s and 1970s were a time of intensive cultural production and political work that squarely located Palestine at the center of Arab leftism and anti-colonialism. The first intifada (1987–1993) shook the Arab, Israeli, and international public. It was a broad mass uprising that transcended generational, sectarian, and class divides. Through demonstrations, strikes, refusing to pay taxes, boycotts, stone-throwing, and underground schools, men, women, youth, and children united in a collective demand for self-determination. Together these, and many more, registers of Palestinian resistance embodied a different kind of politics.

At the same time, since its inception in 1964 (originally as a moderate organization that Gamal Abdel Nasser hoped would stem the tide of Fatah's guerilla struggle), the PLO has also been squarely located, and at times complicit, in the corridors of Middle East power. The Palestinian movement formed an exception to the rapidly consolidating rule of military officers in Egypt, Syria, and Iraq. Yet the movement's political structures were alternately targeted, shunned, used, and funded by these regimes. The organization's Beirut years (1970–1982) were ensconced in confessional politics. The state-in-exile period (1982–1993) in Tunisia distanced the movement from the hardships and demands of Palestinians under occupation. The PLO's stance in the early 1990s was a reaction to, not an instigator of, the grassroots call to end the occupation that was the first intifada. But it was perhaps Yassir Arafat's donkey ride into Jericho in a clumsy echo of Che Guevarra and Fidel Castro that was the final rupture.

The writing on the wall was clear to many in that moment of flimsy and ephemeral triumph. The utterance of "a Palestinian state" was unequivocally tied to its very impossibility on the ground. Oslo did not initiate peace and equality; it was the birth of what Jeff Halper has called Israel's "matrix of control."[303]

One of Tahrir Square's many lessons is that the Palestinian Authority has solidified itself as a version of a broader anti-democratic structure, rather than the leadership of an exceptional polity and struggle. Palestinians gathered in occupied Ramallah in solidarity with the Egyptian people chanting "Down with Oslo" delivered that very message this week when the Palestinian Authority violently suppressed[304] them. In an eerie echo of the

Mubarak regime, plainclothes police forcefully infiltrated, punched, kicked, and detained participants and journalists. This course of action confirms what we already know: since Oslo, a self-ordained leadership has worked to steadily eviscerate the Palestine of post and anti-colonial resistance movements in the folds of a (not so) "new Middle East."

The US invasion and occupation of Iraq in 2003 and its subsequent support for Israel's 2006 onslaught of Lebanon were the devastating markers of the Bush administration's reconfigured "new Middle East."[305] The Fatah-dominated Palestinian Authority has neatly fitted within the US-camp. This now fully delivered configuration situates US allies: Jordan, Egypt, Saudi Arabia, Lebanon's March 14th Coalition, and Fatah at odds with Iran, Syria, Hamas, and Hizbollah. Accordingly, the Mubarak regime and the PA have worked in lock-step to cater to US prerogatives earning them, along with Jordan, the moniker of Israel's "strategic allies in the region."[306]

The PA's policies have included colluding with the US and Israel to target Hamas at the expense of the 1.5 million Palestinians in Gaza. Mubarak's regime has been part and parcel of Israel's debilitating blockade regime by sealing the Rafah border[307] while the PA turned a blind eye to Israel's atrocities against Gazans during its twenty-two day aerial and ground offensive, Operation Cast Lead.[308]

The Mubarak regime has taken on Fatah's power struggle with Hamas as its own given the latter's ties to the Muslim Brotherhood, long deemed a threat to domestic order.[309] The Brotherhood and Hamas represent both domestic opposition and the regional discontent with a status quo that guards the interests of an exclusive and intransigent political elite. The fortitude of the Mubarak-Abbas alliance is also the result of a profound and vested investment in maintaining US hegemony in the Middle East. The ouster of Mubarak would tip this balance and have broad ramifications throughout the Middle East as captured by Michael Hudson[310] and Bassam Haddad.[311]

The PA's thwarting of solidarity protests is a gesture of support for the Mubarak regime. It also exposes the PA's fear that a people's revolution, first courageously realized by the Tunisian people, will spill into the Occupied Territories. Abbas's presidential mandate has long expired and notwithstanding external support, so too has its legitimacy.[312] If anything, what Abbas and the PA have successfully orchestrated is the consolidation of their political structure as an accomplice of empire.

The Palestine Papers seem for many to have added flame to this incendiary formulation. So much so, that *Al Jazeera*'s Arabic station, in the midst of its three-day exposé on the leaked documents, neglected to cover the momentous events in Egypt on the very day of 25 January. For those following the Oslo process, the Palestine Papers were not news. We have long known that the PA is more than willing to accept a land swap; to effectively abandon the right of return of Palestinian refugees; and to accept a de-militarized "state" and a truncated East Jerusalem in the midst of a territorial archipelago of mutually exclusive Bantustans. The PA has declared these positions as necessary concessions in a "pragmatic approach"[313] to conflict-resolution.[314] Perhaps the PA breathed a sigh of relief when the 25 January Revolution got the Palestine Papers off the air; it dimmed the necessary, if long overdue, light searing through their version of pragmatism. But this winter of discontent that began in Tunisia and spread to Egypt is of far deeper consequence than any leaked document.

The century long battle with a colonial settler project shows no sign of abating. For this very reason, the time has come to transcend icons and borders and make politics anew. A politics that continues to call for an end to the occupation and apartheid. A politics that envisions a new horizon beyond the dead end of Oslo's "matrix of control." A politics that moves beyond the status of exception. A politics that understands itself as one critical part of a broader struggle that refuses authoritarianism and calls for self-determination. The revolutionaries in Tahrir, Alexandria, Mahalla, Suez, Minya, and throughout Egypt have shown us that we are not, after all, under the last sky.

36
What is [the] Left?

Maya Mikdashi[315]

29 June 2011

Lebanon has been without a government for months. Finally, a thirty-member cabinet was formed two weeks ago. With a revolutionary uprising in Syria[316] and the brutal response by the Syrian regime intensifying, there is now a Lebanese government whose sole function, it seems, is to weather the storm at the country's northern border, the increasing instability of its border to the south, and the Special Tribunal for Lebanon's[317] indictment that approaches the country with the unstoppable velocity of a train wreck.[318] What this constellation of forces will bring is unknown, but it is certain that when the floodgates open, we will either sink or swim in a tide of violence and further instability. Sitting at my desk in Beirut, I can confidently say to critics abroad that yes, it can get even more unstable. However, as analysts, journalists, and activists question this muscular "macro-picture" we must not lose sight of all the daily struggles[319] that form our lives as humans, citizens, refugees, migrants, and political beings. Yes, it is true that the coming months will be critical to the fate of the Arab-Israeli, and Palestinian-Israeli, struggle. It is true that in Lebanon, we must be concerned with the fate of the resistance and with it, our geopolitical placement in this new Middle East. But is this where the struggle for social justice begins and ends?

I have been reading accounts of the demise of the Lebanese left with some ambivalence.[320] After all, has the word "left" come to only mean supporting the resistance? Is supporting Hizbollah, the group that is only the most recent incarnation of Lebanese resistance to Israel (and an incarnation with troubling economic policies, at that), all it takes to win your "leftist" credentials in Lebanon today? What about other historically progressive issues, such as questions of gender and economic equity, or political rights and the freedom of expression? Since the protests began in Syria, many Lebanese activists who consider themselves part of "the left" (you can see many of them, chain smoking their way through cups of coffee in cafes) have been wringing their hands over the fate of the Syrian regime while self-proclaimed "leftist parties" have been chest pounding their way through Ras Beirut. I recently told a friend of mine that I was working on a piece for *Jadaliyya*[321] about the *fatwa*[322] issued by Lebanon's Mufti "analyzing" a proposed civil law to protect women and children (but not, it seems, men) against domestic violence. This particular "leftist" patiently explained to me that now is not the time write about these "micro" issues, not while the "greater good" is at stake. My friend was telling me that my time and intellect were better spent writing about "the big picture." But what exactly is this bigger picture if not an intricate mosaic of interconnected inequalities, and what is the "greater good" if not a silent prayer for those people that will be sacrificed in order to achieve it?

A week ago I was walking with another friend on Hamra street, and I was confronted by a group of male protestors waving SSNP[323] flags and pictures of Bashar al-Asad. Watching this almost pornographic show of support for a regime that has always been most effective when repressing its own people, I was reminded of the invasion of Kuwait. Back then, I watched the television as Scud Missiles unleashed by "the Great Arab leader" Saddam Hussein landed on Tel Aviv. At the time, Saddam was said to be Salahuddin incarnate. Never mind the fact that Salahuddin was a Kurd, and Saddam Hussein's Anfal campaign killed, displaced, and maimed hundreds of thousands of Iraqi Kurds. More than a decade later, in July of 2003, I was sitting in a Baghdad hotel room in the middle of the US-occupied city. I was watching a dear friend and colleague say that in 1991, Saddam had bought the Arab world with a few ineffectual Scud Missiles, leaving him free to intensify his necrophilic regime and call himself the defender of the Arabs against US-Israeli interests. I felt small then, watching these words fall from my colleague's mouth like a stone into my chest. I now know that in fact power is always allied to power, and that Saddam's regime, like Husni Mubarak's, Ben Ali's, and Asad's was, and is, tied to a complex knot of alliances and counter-alliances with US-Israeli-Saudi interests. Power moves in a current through multiple registers and it is expressed by different actors through different technologies, but it always leaves and exploits a bruised vulnerability. It is this current of power put into action when a dictator gives an order to shoot at protestors, when an Israeli soldier makes a Palestinian wait in the sun, or when a Lebanese husband knows that he can legally[324] enter his wife's vagina with his penis with or without her consent. These expressions of power are structurally different, but they are all united in their purpose to protect and extend unequally distributed power relations. Similarly, while the injustices of foreign occupation and dispossession, domestic authoritarianism, and sexual violence should not be uncritically equated and thus amalgamated into some vague cry about the state of the world, we should also not accept the political fragmentation and alienation that comes with parsing out injuries and oppressions and weighing them to see which deserves our attention. We should not look at "the big picture" and forget that it is painted with the brushes of many injustices, and many injuries.

Writing this lament from Beirut while a revolution is being brutally oppressed in Syria and while Israel continues to threaten the next invasion, I think of Iraq in 2003. Sitting in that Baghdad hotel room one month after the US-led invasion and destruction of most of that country, and remembering the posters of Saddam Hussein hastily pasted on the streets of Beirut following those Scud Missiles in 1991, I felt cheap. Just as I feel cheap today, arguing with some self-proclaimed "leftists" that we can be against authoritarianism and against US-Israeli interests. That we can be both pro-democracy and pro-Palestine, both pro-revolution and anti-Zionist. That we should not allow our fear of what might come after stop us from acting with our principles, now.

Epilogue
Parting Thoughts

Madawi Al-Rasheed

As the famous first year of Arab popular uprisings comes to a close, many observers in the Arab world and beyond will turn their attention to four concerns. First, the common conditions that precipitated mass protests across countries with apparently different histories and trajectories. Second, the specificity of each location and the outcomes this has generated. Third, in a region where foreign powers continue to meddle with internal affairs, the role of regional and international players in supporting or thwarting uprisings will continue to be a controversial dimension. And fourth, where next in the Arab world such uprisings are more likely to gather momentum in the future. This edited archival record of the events on the ground and commentaries written by established scholars and young academics is a window of opportunity that allows a future generation to get to the debates, controversies, and conflicts that shook the Arab world and astonished outside observers. It is an early witness, called upon to narrate great transformations to future audiences. As such, the book fulfils an important function as it draws attention to specific events and voices, actions and reactions that defined the early moments of the unprecedented mass protests. The multiple voices in this volume document important aspects of the revolutionary "moment," thus highlighting the supremacy of defiance over silence, change over the status quo, hope over despair, multiple trajectories over a single reality. This volume will help future generations of scholars focus their mind on the four concerns that emerged out of the Arab uprisings.

Regardless of individual histories, by January 2011, all Arab countries appeared to have reached an advanced stage of entrenched authoritarian rule. In republics and monarchies, one common thread was easily detected. Corrupt dynastic family rule was the norm. Highly visible old autocrats enjoyed a sacrosanct status. They developed networks of economic privileges, financial monopolies, corruption rings, and death squads. In addition to the autocrats themselves, wives, sons, distant relatives, and close beneficiaries controlled economies, intimidated activists, and spread fear and terror. These common features experienced across the Arab region were at the heart of the Arab uprisings from Tunisia to Yemen. By the end of 2011, all Arab countries experienced protests of one kind or another but only a few had succeeded in overthrowing their autocrats.

Another common feature that united Arab autocracies was their intimate relation with Western governments. While enjoying special relations with Western powers that continued to see them as the only available security against a range of real and imagined threats, Arab autocrats were strengthened by Western economic, military, and political support. Even autocrats who had antagonized the West for decades had been brought back into the fold on the eve of the Arab uprisings. Muammar al-Qaddafi and Bashar al-Asad were good examples.

While important common political grievances, rampant corruption, and economic marginalization were behind the mass protests, events proved to take a very local turn when demonstrations gathered momentum in each country. The swift demise of Zine El Abidine Bin Ali and Husni Mubarak proved to be exceptional. In Tunisia and Egypt, the overthrow of regimes was accompanied by little blood shed, if compared with other countries such as Libya, where foreign military intervention was provided to assist rebels against the Qaddafi regime. In Bahrain, Gulf Cooperation Council countries, mainly Saudi Arabia, intervened not on behalf of the rebels but on behalf of the ruling Al Khalifa family to supress the pro-democracy movement there. Similarly in Yemen, Gulf countries intervened to guarantee the safe exit of Ali Abdullah Saleh. In Syria, the Arab League struggled to arrange a similar exit for Bashar al-Asad but the outcome at the time of writing remains unknown. Syria is quickly moving towards an uncertain future with the threat of civil war looming large over a multi-ethnic and multi-sectarian population. Even Iraq, supposedly a democratic country since its occupation by the United States in 2003, became part of the Arab uprisings when sections of the population staged demonstrations demanding better living conditions, employment, and an end to corruption. On the far periphery of the Arab world, quiet Oman joined the protests and witnessed bloodshed as a result of security forces shooting peaceful protestors demanding employment and an end to corruption. Wealthy Saudi Arabia saw the death of six Shi'a protestors and heavy security control to thwart the possibility of the Arab uprisings blossoming inside the country among the disenfranchized Shi'a population. Equally wealthy Kuwait was shocked by young opposition forces storming its parliament in an attempt to end the premiership of a member of the Al Sabah ruling dynasty.

The diversity of the so-called Arab Spring is as important as the common threads that led to the region becoming the focus of local and international attention as its population struggled to free itself from decades of authoritarian rule. While protests and activism were visible everywhere, the demands that protestors voiced differed across the region. People demanding "the downfall of the regimes" may have become the prism through which the protests could be understood in some countries but this demand was not voiced everywhere. If people in Arab republics strove to overthrow their oppressive regimes altogether, it seems that people in wealthy Gulf countries, together with those in heavily subsidised monarchies (Jordan and Morocco), tried to improve the conditions of servitude and authoritarianism. This volume is, therefore, important as it highlights a case study approach, documenting the nature of mobilization—ranging from mass demonstrations to mere digital activism—and regime responses, equally diverse. As future generations of scholars try to write the history of the first months of 2011, they will no doubt find in this volume's short archival/analytical pieces, written by an interdisciplinary team of commentators, a wealth of opinions, arguments, and rich analysis, all inspired by a *longue duree* knowledge of the region. The volume makes the early events that sparked the Arab uprisings so lively in their interconnections and domino effects in the region.

What complicates the emerging picture of revolt is the fact that the Arab world is no peripheral or remote corner of the world. In fact, it continues to be at the heart of international relations, as it remains the seat of the unresolved Palestinian displacement by the state of Israel. Moreover, certain Arab countries are a vital source of oil and gas energy that is important to the whole world. Internally, the Arab world has an incredible youth bulge feared by its northern European neighbors and beyond. Moreover, the Arab world is a rich mosaic of languages, ethnicities, sectarian identities, tribal affiliations, ideologies, and old and new social classes upon which authoritarian rule survived and thrived. As such, the Arab uprisings are no simple local events promising a straightforward bright future in which democracy, human rights, political participation, transparency, and equitable economic opportunities will easily and automatically follow after a year of protests and upheaval.

Regional rivalries, nourished by the decline of the old core of the Arab world (Egypt) and the rise of the Arab nouveaux riches (GCC states) and other regional powers (Turkey and Iran), promise to further complicate the picture. What started as a pro-democracy uprising in places like Bahrain and Syria could easily turn into a nasty sectarian civil war as a result of external intervention and internal dynamics. As such the Arab uprisings have meant different things to different actors at the regional and international levels. One of the paradoxes of the protests in countries like Tunisia, Egypt, and Libya is its endorsement by the most undemocratic Gulf countries, namely Qatar, while Saudi Arabia adopted a wait-and-see strategy with plans to co-opt the outcomes, Bahrain notwithstanding. Iran's Islamic Republic claimed the protests as an Islamic awakening, thus overlooking the non-Islamist dimension of the protests in places like Tunis and Cairo. The West framed Turkey as a model of an Islamic democracy that can be exported, but Arab audiences remain sceptical. In some corners, the economic decline of countries like Egypt makes the Turkish success an appealing option to emulate.

A year after the Arab protests began, regional rivalries continue to be played out with international players. The United States, the European Union, Russia, and China, for example, have indeed joined the race to carve a place for themselves on the new political and ideological maps of the region. The Arab world is now an open arena for multiple powerful players. It remains to be seen whether the collective charisma of the masses that dismantled the old personality cults around dictators will succeed in safeguarding revolutions against co-optation and hijacking.

While this volume offers an invaluable insight into the events that dominated 2011, the coming months or perhaps years will no doubt unveil a new Arab world. Alarmed by bloodshed, pessimists may see the current protests as a prelude to redrawing old maps of the colonial era, thus paving the way for the consolidation of sectarian enclaves and cantons and possibly prolonged turmoil if not civil wars. Optimists, on the other hand, would like to see all encompassing civil democratic states emerging across the region while keeping the old colonial maps in place. In between lies the reality that major historical transformations come with high human, economic, and political cost. The Arab uprisings proved that neither velvet and quiet revolutions nor evolutionary top down reforms were capable of dismantling decades of entrenched autocratic and corrupt rule. If 2011 was an exceptional year, it certainly confirmed that Arabs were ready to pay the price of revolution and re-enter world history as people who can make their own destiny.

Entrenched Arab authoritarianism survived because it had put in place security structures, social forces, and even religious groups that acted as safeguards against the kind of democracy that many young people in the Arab world aspire to. Like other world revolutions, the Arab Spring will be no different in the way it may be derailed and even hijacked internally, regionally, and internationally. But one of the major achievements of the Arab revolutions so far is the paradigm shift it generated. After decades of simply succumbing to what the autocrat wants, Arab masses are inscribing their wish in the public sphere. As peaceful protests become the language of the masses, it seems that there is no return to the *status quo ante*. Revolutions are often dangerous liminal phases and the Arab ones are no exception.

Notes

Go to www.daurefs.com to access the links in this book by note number.

1. www.youtube.com/watch?v=Fgw_zfLLvh8
2. www.jadaliyya.com/pages/contributors/327
3. www.jadaliyya.com/pages/contributors/13843
4. www.jadaliyya.com/pages/contributors/5450
5. www.jadaliyya.com/pages/index/1252/on-the-re-mythification-of-the-arab
6. http://books.google.com/books?id=nQ9jXXJV-vgC&printsec=frontcove
   r&dq=imagined+communities+benedict+anderson&hl=en&ei=QurRTe_
   FDZC3tgevjMGYCg&sa=X&oi=book_result&ct=result&resnum=1&ved=
   0CDMQ6AEwAA#v=onepage&q&f=true
7. http://books.google.com/books?id=8UamWMisjtkC&printsec=frontcover&
   dq=Comparative+Perspectives+on+Social+Movements;+Political+Opportun
   ities,+Mobilizing+Structures,+and+Cultural+Framings&hl=en&src=bmrr&
   ei=k-rRTdSUFcOatwespKWmCg&sa=X&oi=book_result&ct=result&resn
   um=1&ved=0CCoQ6AEwAA#v=onepage&q&f=false
8. www.youtube.com/watch?v=jH5v-g-qM4o
9. www.jadaliyya.com/pages/index/577/revolutionary-contagion_morocco-and-
   a-plea-for-spe
10. www.jadaliyya.com/pages/index/1469/what-happened-to-protests-in-jordan
11. www.jadaliyya.com/pages/contributors/7739
12. www.jadaliyya.com/pages/contributors/8829
13. www.jadaliyya.com/pages/contributors/24307
14. http://thecable.foreignpolicy.com/posts/2011/05/19/full_text_of_obamas_
    middle_east_speech
15. www.guardian.co.uk/commentisfree/2011/may/25/imf-arab-spring-loans-
    egypt-tunisia?CMP=twt_gu
16. http://wikileaks.ch/cable/2008/12/08CAIRO2543.html
17. www.aljazeera.com/focus/2011/02/201121165427186924.html
18. http://dawn.com/2011/02/04/1989-and-the-arab-world/
19. http://online.wsj.com/article/SB10001424052748704132204576135773161
    623018.html
20. www.jadaliyya.com/pages/index/1214/orientalising-the-egyptian-uprising
21. www.jadaliyya.com/pages/index/1387/english-translation-of-interview-with-
    hossam-el-ha
22. http://muse.jhu.edu/journals/journal_of_democracy/v018/18.3mansfield.html
23. www.jadaliyya.com/pages/contributors/4687
24. www.jadaliyya.com/pages/index/460/jordans-day-of-anger
25. www.jadaliyya.com/pages/index/346/rigging-the-egyptian-elections_the-
    organizing-narrative-%28why-the-wafd-has-to-participate-in-the-upcoming-
    elections-part-1%29
26. www.jadaliyya.com/pages/index/378/liberal-elite-discourse-and-the-realities-
    of-jordan

27. www.jadaliyya.com/pages/index/295/jordan-liberalism-and-the-question-of-boycott
28. www.jadaliyya.com/pages/index/427/neoliberal-pregnancy-and-zero-sum-elitism-in-the-arab-world-%28part-4%29
29. www.jadaliyya.com/pages/index/164/mubaraks-mubarak-%28part-1%29
30. www.jadaliyya.com/pages/contributors/4905
31. www.jadaliyya.com/pages/contributors/5123
32. www.jadaliyya.com/pages/contributors/5123
33. www.jadaliyya.com/pages/contributors/3379
34. www.jadaliyya.com/pages/contributors/5341
35. www.jadaliyya.com/pages/contributors/7957
36. www.nickburcher.com/2010/07/facebook-usage-statistics-by-country.html
37. www.jadaliyya.com/pages/contributors/6322
38. www.jadaliyya.com/pages/index/561/the-egyptian-revolution_first-impressions-from-the-field-
39. www.jadaliyya.com/pages/index/516/why-mubarak-is-out-
40. www.jadaliyya.com/pages/contributors/8720
41. http://mideast.foreignpolicy.com/posts/2011/01/31/egypt_at_the_tipping_point
42. www.arabawy.org/2010/10/31/something-in-the-air/
43. http://blogs.ssrc.org/tif/2011/02/09/the-road-to-tahrir/
44. www.democracynow.org/2011/2/7/protests_demanding_mubarak_to_resign_grow
45. www.democracynow.org/2011/2/7/protests_demanding_mubarak_to_resign_grow
46. www.jadaliyya.com/pages/contributors/10682
47. www.facebook.com/ElShaheeed
48. http://today.almasryalyoum.com/article2.aspx?ArticleID=287064&IssueID=2037
49. www.nytimes.com/2011/02/13/world/middleeast/13wealth.html?_r=3&pagewanted=1
50. www.merip.org/mer/mer210/mitchell.html
51. www.independent.co.uk/opinion/commentators/fisk/robert-fisk-as-mubarak-clings-on-what-now-for-egypt-2211287.html
52. www.egyptindependent.com/news/young-revolutionaries-call-military-form-technocratic-interim-govt
53. www.nytimes.com/2011/02/18/world/middleeast/18military.html?_r=1
54. www.jadaliyya.com/pages/contributors/23108
55. www.whitehouse.gov/the-press-office/2011/05/19/remarks-president-middle-east-and-north-africa
56. www.g20-g8.com/g8-g20/g8/english/live/news/declaration-of-the-g8-on-the-arab-springs.1316.html
57. www.whitehouse.gov/the-press-office/2011/02/01/remarks-president-situation-egypt
58. www.imf.org/external/np/g8/pdf/052711.pdf
59. htt www.imf.org/external/np/g8/pdf/052711.pdf
60. www.iif.com/download.php?id=OkBUBnljqeU=
61. http://web.worldbank.org/WBSITE/EXTERNAL/COUNTRIES/MENAEXT/EGYPTEXTN/0,,contentMDK:22888974~menuPK:50003484~pagePK:2865066~piPK:2865079~theSitePK:256307,00.html

62. www.socialistproject.ca/bullet/462.php
63. www.jadaliyya.com/pages/index/1711/data.worldbank.org
64. www.whitehouse.gov/the-press-office/2011/05/19/remarks-president-middle-east-and-north-africa
65. www.whitehouse.gov/the-press-office/2011/05/19/remarks-president-middle-east-and-north-africa
66. www.imf.org/external/np/sec/pr/2011/pr11174.htm
67. http://weekly.ahram.org.eg/2011/1048/ec1.htm
68. www.worldbank.org/en/country/egypt
69. http://commdocs.house.gov/committees/intlrel/hfa87675.000/hfa87675_0f.htm
70. www.opic.gov/
71. http://commdocs.house.gov/committees/intlrel/hfa87675.000/hfa87675_0f.htm
72. www.opic.gov/sites/default/files/OPICfactsheetegypt.pdf
73. http://uk.reuters.com/article/2011/02/15/uk-egypt-ebrd-idUKTRE71E4OB20110215
74. www.ebrd.com/pages/research/publications/flagships/transition.shtml
75. http://bankwatch.org/
76. http://bankwatch.org/sites/default/files/Are-we-nearly-there-yet-EBRD.pdf
77. www.ebrd.com/pages/news/events/am_astana/speeches/AM015e-X.pdf
78. www.kharafinational.com/kn/index.html
79. www.kharafinational.com/kn/index.html
80. www.ameinfo.com/265102.html
81. www.jadaliyya.com/pages/contributors/11772
82. www.abdolian.com/thoughts/?p=4769
83. www.unwatch.org/site/apps/nlnet/content2.aspx?c=bdKKISNqEmG&b=1313923&ct=8411733
84. www.jadaliyya.com/pages/contributors/17985
85. www.guardian.co.uk/world/2011/apr/24/libya-tribal-leaders-talks-misrata
86. www.youtube.com/watch?v=eL6I5hktEs0
87. http://books.google.com/books?id=rhuWHwAACAAJ&dq=libya%27s+qaddafi+mansour+el-kikhia&hl=en&ei=dOy9TY2-DYyasAP_nJjBBQ&sa=X&oi=book_result&ct=result&resnum=1&ved=0CCwQ6AEwAA
88. www.youtube.com/watch?v=eL6I5hktEs0
89. www.guardian.co.uk/world/2011/apr/24/libya-tribal-leaders-talks-misrata
90. www.nytimes.com/2011/03/22/world/africa/22tripoli.html?_r=2&hp=&pagewanted=all
91. www.france24.com/en/20110222-lending-support-libya-tribal-chiefs-legitimise-uprising-gaddafi
92. www.france24.com/en/20110222-lending-support-libya-tribal-chiefs-legitimise-uprising-gaddafi
93. www.guardian.co.uk/world/2011/apr/29/misrata-rebel-leader-pleads-help
94. www.guardian.co.uk/world/2011/apr/29/misrata-rebel-leader-pleads-help
95. www.reuters.com/article/2011/02/22/us-libya-protests-tribes-idUKTRE71L7N220110222
96. www.meforum.org/1813/the-middle-easts-tribal-dna
97. www.foreignpolicy.com/articles/2011/03/07/understanding_libyas_michael_corleone?page=full

98. www.huffingtonpost.com/benjamin-r-barber/libya-gadhafi-future_b_826718.html

99. http://books.google.com/books?id=LO4xG-bH1CQC&pg=PA175&lpg=PA175&dq=samuel+huntington+tribal+libya&source=bl&ots=rhQ2JiZiQe&sig=5exGqnZeLlws7zV0cD6s5epBeIM&hl=en&ei=aDW7-TaKyKpSusAPnsZHJBQ&sa=X&oi=book_result&ct=result&resnum=1&sqi=2&ved=0CBoQ6AEwAA#v=onepage&q&f=false

100. www.foreignpolicy.com/articles/2011/03/07/understanding_libyas_michael_corleone?page=full

101. www.foreignpolicy.com/articles/2011/03/07/understanding_libyas_michael_corleone?page=full

102. www.huffingtonpost.com/benjamin-r-barber/libya-gadhafi-future_b_826718.html

103. www.nytimes.com/2011/03/22/world/africa/22tripoli.html?_r=2&hp=&pagewanted=all

104. www.guardian.co.uk/world/2011/apr/24/libya-tribal-leaders-talks-misrata

105. www.nytimes.com/2011/03/22/world/africa/22tripoli.html?_r=1&hp=&pagewanted=all

106. www.motherjones.com/mojo/2011/02/whats-happening-libya-explained

107. www.jadaliyya.com/pages/contributors/10791

108. www.jadaliyya.com/pages/index/725/on-international-intervention-and-the-dire-situation-in-libya

109. www.un.org/News/Press/docs/2011/sc10187.doc.htm

110. www.reuters.com/article/2011/03/12/us-libya-arabs-idUSTRE72B1FI20110312

111. www.nytimes.com/2011/03/14/opinion/14slaughter.html?_r=1

112. www.foreignpolicy.com/articles/2011/03/11/america_has_beaten_qaddafi_before

113. www.jadaliyya.com/pages/index/725/on-international-intervention-and-the-dire-situation-in-libya

114. http://mideast.foreignpolicy.com/posts/2011/03/10/as_the_us_considers_intervention_in_libya_it_should_look_to_history

115. http://mideast.foreignpolicy.com/posts/2011/02/26/libya_and_the_new_international_disorder

116. www.foreignpolicy.com/articles/2011/02/24/act_now

117. http://af.reuters.com/article/libyaNews/idAFLDE71N0MV20110224?sp=true

118. www.reuters.com/article/2011/02/25/us-obama-libya-idUSTRE71O5P520110225

119. www.nytimes.com/2011/03/14/opinion/14douthat.html?_r=2&ref=rossdouthat

120. www.jadaliyya.com/pages/index/725/on-international-intervention-and-the-dire-situation-in-libya

121. www.iiss.org/whats-new/iiss-in-the-press/march-2011/no-fly-zone-may-not-halt-gadhafi-offensive/

122. www.google.com/hostednews/afp/article/ALeqM5iM8urGyDnPgcNd4Qf7O7GUDqeIWg?docId=CNG.6f3d9b4e1c1a20150f12d52ade851682.441

123. www.afrika.no/Detailed/20311.html

124. www.reuters.com/article/2011/02/21/libya-energy-idUSLDE71K0RV20110221?pageNumber=1

125. www.fpif.org/articles/a_new_us_relationship_with_libya

126. http://mondoweiss.net/2011/03/is-libya-already-lost.html
127. www.jadaliyya.com/pages/contributors/11118
128. www.nytimes.com/2011/02/23/world/middleeast/23bahrain.html?_r=1
129. www.google.com/search?sclient=psy&hl=en&client=firefox-a&hs=XVM&rls=org.mozilla:en-US:official&tbs=nws:1&q=sectarian+bahrain&aq=f&aqi=&aql=&oq=&pbx=1&cad=h
130. www.state.gov/r/pa/ei/bgn/26414.htm
131. www.miamiherald.com/2011/02/21/2078376/huge-bahraini-counterprotest-reflects.html
132. www.bbc.co.uk/news/world-middle-east-12502820
133. http://twitter.com/#%21/emoodz
134. http://twitter.com/#%21/emoodz
135. http://twitter.com/#!/search?q=%23fateh
136. www.opendemocracy.net/alaa-shehabi/bahrain-from-national-celebration-to-day-of-rage
137. www.youtube.com/watch?v=fDfVo_Noino
138. www.migrant-rights.org/2010/12/17/the-unrecognised-life-of-migrant-workers-in-bahrain's-construction-industry/
139. www.smi.uib.no/pao/khalaf.html
140. www.state.gov/r/pa/ei/bgn/26414.htm
141. http://countrystudies.us/persian-gulf-states/42.htm
142. www.enhg.org/resources/articles/belgrave/belgrave.htm
143. www.time.com/time/world/article/0,8599,2053107,00.html?xid=tweetbut
144. http://video.google.com/videoplay?docid=-991981630797627023
145. www.economist.com/node/10979869
146. www.counterpunch.org/2010/09/03/monarchy-v-democracy/
147. www.alarabiya.net/articles/2010/09/04/118499.html
148. http://articles.cnn.com/2010-09-04/world/bahrain.arrests_1_bahrain-news-agency-bahraini-bna?_s=PM:WORLD
149. www.guardian.co.uk/commentisfree/2011/feb/13/bahrain-valentines-day-gulf-arab-states
150. www.twitlonger.com/show/8v50hn
151. www.reuters.com/article/2011/02/17/bahrain-minister-idUSLDE71G24K20110217
152. www.jadaliyya.com/pages/contributors/11118
153. www.reuters.com/article/2011/02/21/us-usa-bahrain-saudi-idUSTRE71K06Q20110221
154. www.gulf-daily-news.com/NewsDetails.aspx?storyid=300977
155. www.bna.bh/portal/en/news/448953
156. www.thenational.ae/thenationalconversation/comment/the-community-at-pearl-roundabout-is-at-the-centre?pageCount=0
157. http://books.google.com/books?id=iCmYhXoC0FMC&printsec=frontcover&dq=Rosemarie+Said+Zahlan+the+making+of+the+modern+gulf+states&source=bl&ots=Kkesx6ih-f&sig=msw1lRRVoR__4fsdiroGDcwlh60&hl=en&ei=rsF2Te_JBc_tsgbC4fT9BA&sa=X&oi=book_result&ct=result&resnum=1&ved=0CBQQ6AEwAA#v=onepage&q&f=false
158. http://en.wikipedia.org/wiki/National_Union_Committee
159. http://books.google.com/books?id=3gkHLMay35gC&pg=PA67&lpg=PA67&dq=Bahrain+demonstrations+1956&source=bl&ots=FQ-S1uyvQY&sig=4uGAB92TRTdQMnFnbFD9hFYCIek&hl=en&ei=TsR2TakKx-

M6zBuqYzPUE&sa=X&oi=book_result&ct=result&resnum=6&ved=0CE
EQ6AEwBQ#v=onepage&q=Bahrain%20demonstrations%201

160. http://docs.google.com/viewer?a=v&q=cache:-BzegIQKo_QJ:www.
stanford.edu/group/ethnic/Random+Narratives/BahrainRN1.1
.pdf+Bahrain+demonstrations+1965&hl=en&gl=us&pid=bl&
srcid=ADGEEShplJU-dFXCgIC1-AseCJErqHcLU1NobyDyMb
FkzkrEUt3ywN-dTyGgCegicdrldSKx0-yHi7ZMg34rbRBHi8_
WQoI16DNY7sgmNWAJqhTK2_24d-1br54WDHVTeVckJY8OW-
xY&sig=AHIEtbQ4aWT6gw6hpM-xhEgTS3JfA5JMrQ&pli=1

161. www.smi.uib.no/pao/khalaf.html

162. http://en.wikipedia.org/wiki/1981_Bahraini_coup_d%27%C3%A9tat_
attempt

163. www.hrw.org/legacy/reports/1997/bahrain/

164. www.foreignaffairs.com/articles/67553/jane-kinninmont/bahrains-re-reform-
movement

165. http://docs.google.com/viewer?a=v&q=cache:FT5WV4SctXoJ:www.upr.
bh/human_r/Bahrain_National_charter-En.pdf+Bahrain+National+AC
tion+Charter&hl=en&gl=us&pid=bl&srcid=ADGEESiDtQrRhNdFe_
VH329MEvaxflYxX_d5o3SZ6402j9PVvDI2RbcQsYbkm8fTkEhNLMO
usL4EZ6dQGTLJ3vRD2O8t-dtSLSh5nTR-6xxfnZpo-0B8rZXZm7tCe-
MleUlF7dkv0MWv&sig=AHIEtbRY_KZoBypqAdljiPBUWkDvFedbhA

166. http://temporaryartist.wordpress.com/2011/03/07/blind-eye-to-the-butcher-
2002-documentary/

167. http://temporaryartist.wordpress.com/2011/03/07/blind-eye-to-the-butcher-
2002-documentary/

168. www.aei.org/event/1460

169. www.scribd.com/doc/49888133/Bahrain-Opposition-Representation

170. www.economist.com/node/10979869

171. http://en.wikipedia.org/wiki/Al_Bandar_report

172. www.guardian.co.uk/world/2010/oct/22/bahrain-elections-overshadowed-
crackdown

173. www.economist.com/node/17254432

174. http://articles.latimes.com/2010/sep/07/world/la-fg-bahrain-crackdown-
20100907

175. www.reuters.com/article/2010/10/23/us-bahrain-elections-fb-idUSTRE
69M0TO20101023

176. www.facebook.com/TrueRoyalDemocracy

177. www.msnbc.msn.com/id/41638606/ns/world_news-mideast/n_africa/

178. www.gulf-daily-news.com/NewsDetails.aspx?storyid=301280

179. www.gulf-daily-news.com/NewsDetails.aspx?storyid=301237

180. https://www.zawya.com/Story.cfm/sidZAWYA20110227042247/Oman and
Bahrain shuffle cabinets

181. www.arabtimesonline.com/NewsDetails/tabid/96/smid/414/ArticleID/
166316/t/Gulf-satisfied-with-steps-to-solve-Bahrain-impasse/Default.aspx

182. http://online.wsj.com/article/SB100014240527487035800004576180522653
787198.html?mod=googlenews_wsj

183. www.ft.com/cms/s/a1e266c6-3d20-11e0-bbff-00144feabdc0,
Authorised=false.html?_i_location=http%3A%2F%2Fwww.ft.com%2
Fcms%2Fs%2F0%2Fa1e266c6-3d20-11e0-bbff-00144feabdc0.html&_i_
referer=

184. www.jadaliyya.com/pages/contributors/13734
185. http://bna.bh/portal/en/news/450193
186. www.youtube.com/watch?v=d5BLzidTD1o&feature=related
187. www.youtube.com/watch?v=7Lf-BuO_j04
188. www.asharq-e.com/news.asp?section=1&id=24509
189. www.amnesty.org/ar/news-and-updates/report/evidence-bahraini-security-forces%E2%80%99-brutality-revealed-2011-03-16
190. http://184.105.232.115/48/7e/487ef5af7148af84686d26206ae63510/ba648 07/152011_487e_w_2.3gp?c=276258722&u=362689378&s=BLruW7%D9 %88%D9%84%D8%B9%D9%86
191. www.cbsnews.com/8301-503543_162-20044298-503543.html
192. www.youtube.com/watch?v=pNH1OGUcaBM&feature=player_embedded
193. http://14febbah.wordpress.com/2011/03/16/live-shooting-at-people-in-sitra-village-in-bahrain-%D9%82%D9%88%D8%A7%D8%AA-%D8%A7%D 9%84%D8%B4%D8%B1%D8%B7%D8%A9-%D8%AA%D9%82% D8%AA%D9%84-%D8%A7%D9%84%D9%86%D8%A7%D8%B3- %D9%81%D9%8A-%D9%82%D8%B1/
194. www.youtube.com/watch?v=vWI5aJOPeG4&feature=related
195. http://m.timesofindia.com/india/Stray-bullets-kill-Indian-in-Bahrain/articleshow/7732246.cms
196. www.ft.com/cms/s/0/8089a7c8-521a-11e0-8a31-00144feab49a. html#axzz1GtmJFwyB
197. http://alwasatnews.com/mobile/news-532864.html
198. http://freemohammedsaeed.files.wordpress.com/2010/09/44462_154635071 218357_154634604551737_517616_7849677_n14.jpg
199. http://14febbah.wordpress.com/2011/03/13/bahraini-police-men-with-thugs-attacking-protesters/
200. http://gulfnews.com/news/gulf/bahrain/bahrain-remains-committed-to-dialogue-but-stability-top-priority-1.779304
201. www.jadaliyya.com/pages/index/846/distortions-of-dialogue
202. http://af.reuters.com/article/worldNews/idAFTRE72J0VH20110320
203. www.alwasatnews.com/mobile/news-532723.html
204. www.bbc.co.uk/arabic/middleeast/2011/03/110319_bahrain_latest.shtml
205. http://manamavoice.com/news-news_read-6695-0.html
206. www.ifex.org/bahrain/2011/03/18/alsingace_rearrested/
207. http://blog.indexoncensorship.org/2011/03/18/bahraini-blog-father-goes-missing-police-raid-familys-home/
208. www.youtube.com/watch?v=OOb0yS92jxs
209. www.amnesty.org/en/library/info/MDE11/014/2011/en
210. www.hrw.org/en/news/2011/03/18/bahrain-protest-leaders-arbitrarily-detained
211. http://14febbah.wordpress.com/2011/03/17/bahrain-police-beat-drivers-in-the-unrest/
212. http://mahmood.tv/2011/03/19/just-bahraini-not-welcome-at-checkpoints/
213. www.washingtonpost.com/opinions/high-stakes-over-bahrain/2011/03/15/AB7ykyZ_story.html
214. www.jadaliyya.com/pages/index/956/pearl-no-more_demolishing-the-infrastructure-of-revolution
215. www.bbc.co.uk/news/world-middle-east-12794593?utm_source=twitterfeed &utm_medium=twitter

216. www.thenational.ae/news/worldwide/middle-east/bahrain-king-defends-state-of-emergency-as-pearl-monument-torn-down?pageCount=0
217. www.jadaliyya.com/pages/index/926/its-official_in-2006-the-lebanese-government-was-hoping-israel-would-disarm-hezbollah-for-them-
218. http://english.aljazeera.net/news/middleeast/2011/03/201131855056179376.html
219. www.ft.com/cms/s/0/8089a7c8-521a-11e0-8a31-00144feab49a.html #axzz1GtmJFwyB
220. http://twitpic.com/4ay0hy
221. www.jadaliyya.com/pages/contributors/9701
222. www.jadaliyya.com/pages/index/935/how-it-started-in-yemen_from-tahrir-to-taghyir
223. www.jadaliyya.com/pages/contributors/1744
224. www.jadaliyya.com/pages/contributors/545
225. www.jadaliyya.com/pages/index/668/litmus-test-rowdiness-in-damascus-today-%28video%29
226. http://online.wsj.com/article/SB10001424052748703833204576114712441122894.html
227. www.jadaliyya.com/pages/contributors/32373
228. www.jadaliyya.com/pages/contributors/27141
229. www.youtube.com/watch?v=6dOUQOXQcMg
230. www.jadaliyya.com/pages/index/2181/statement-of-syrian-christians-in-support-of-the-r
231. www.guardian.co.uk/commentisfree/2011/may/28/syrian-alawites-protests
232. http://weekly.ahram.org.eg/2011/1055/re141.htm
233. www.ft.com/cms/s/70a48c08-b2c1-11e0-bc28-00144feabdc0, Authorised=false.html?_i_location=http%3A%2F%2Fwww.ft.com%2Fcms%2Fs%2F0%2F70a48c08-b2c1-11e0-bc28-00144feabdc0.html&_i_referer=
234. www.nytimes.com/2011/05/01/world/asia/01makhlouf.html?_r=2&pagewanted=1&sq=anthonyshadid&st=cse&scp=21
235. www.nowlebanon.com/NewsArchiveDetails.aspx?ID=256081
236. www.nowlebanon.com/NewsArchiveDetails.aspx?ID=256081
237. http://syriarevolts.wordpress.com/2011/07/21/an-impending-speech-by-bashar-al-assad/
238. http://www.nytimes.com/2011/07/22/world/middleeast/22poet.html?_r=2&hp
239. www.jadaliyya.com/pages/contributors/1744
240. www.jadaliyya.com/pages/contributors/1635
241. www.alwatan.com.sa/Caricature/Detail.aspx?CaricaturesID=1506
242. www.alriyadh.com/net/article/607473
243. www.saudigazette.com.sa/index.cfm?method=home.regcon&contentID=2011022494505
244. http://gulfnews.com/news/gulf/saudi-arabia/king-abdulla-announces-35b-aid-for-saudis-1.766444
245. www.jadaliyya.com/pages/index/495/saudi-arabias-silent-protests
246. http://alasmari.wordpress.com/2011/01/24/b1/
247. www.jadaliyya.com/pages/index/202/poverty-in-the-oil-kingdom_an-introduction
248. www.ysoof.com/blog/?p=242

249. www.islamicommaparty.com/Portals/Content/?info=TkRreEpsTjFZbEJoWj
     JVbU1TWmhjbUk9K3U=.jsp
250. www.facebook.com/K.S.A.Revolution
251. www.alwahabi.com/?p=520
252. www.alwahabi.com/?p=553
253. www.facebook.com/profile.php?id=100001987518427
254. http://m.cnbc.com/id/41743620
255. www.islamicommaparty.com/Portals/Content/?info=TlRBekpsTjFZbEJoWjJ
     VbU1TWmhjbUk9K3U=.jsp
256. www.islamicommaparty.com/Portals/Content/?info=TlRBekpsTjFZbEJoWjJ
     VbU1TWmhjbUk9K3U=.jsp
257. www.jadaliyya.com/pages/index/737/agency-and-its-discontents_between-al-
     sauds-paternalism-and-the-awakening-of-saudi-youth
258. www.jadaliyya.com/pages/index/799/saudi-government-forbids-media-from-
     reporting-yesterdays-protests-issues-warning
259. www.assakina.com/fatwa/6834.html
260. www.mofa.gov.sa/sites/mofaen/servicesandinformation/news/ministrynews/
     pages/newsarticleid121046.aspx
261. www.monstersandcritics.com/news/middleeast/news/article_1623088.php/
     Report-Saudi-Facebook-activist-planning-protest-shot-dead
262. http://en.wikipedia.org/wiki/Sa%27ad_Al-Faqih
263. www.pbs.org/wgbh/pages/frontline/shows/saud/interviews/alfassi.html
264. www.jadaliyya.com/pages/index/818/demands-of-saudi-youth-for-the-future-
     of-the-nation
265. www.jadaliyya.com/pages/index/753/a-call-from-saudi-intellectuals-to-the-
     political-leadership
266. http://en.wikipedia.org/wiki/Battle_of_Hunayn
267. www.jadaliyya.com/pages/index/860/meeting-slogans-with-gunfire_saudi-
     security-forces-use-live-ammunition-against-protesters-%28video%29
268. http://af.reuters.com/article/energyOilNews/idAFWNA329320110310
269. http://hala1.wordpress.com/2011/03/12/days-of-rage-in-saudi-arabia/
270. www.alarabiya.net/articles/2011/03/18/142067.html
271. www.alwatan.com.sa/Articles/Detail.aspx?ArticleId=4847
272. www.jadaliyya.com/pages/index/495/saudi-arabias-silent-protests
273. http://saudidream.net/citizen-sufferings/%D8%A7%D9%84%D8%B
     3%D8%AC%D9%86%D8%A7%D8%A1-%D8%A7%D9%84%D
     8%B3%D9%8A%D8%A7%D8%B3%D9%8A%D9%8A%D9%86-
     %D9%81%D9%8A-%D8%A7%D9%84%D8%B3%D8%B9%D9%88
     %D8%AF%D9%8A%D8%A9/?utm_source=feedburner&utm_medium=
     feed&utm_campaign=Feed%3A+saudidream+%28%D8%AD%D9%84%
     D9%85+%D8%B3%D8%B9%D9%88%D8%AF%D9%8A%29
274. www.jadaliyya.com/pages/index/906/different-kinds-of-intervention_groups-
     respond-to-gcc-troops-entering-bahrain
275. www.jadaliyya.com/pages/index/733/lets-talk-about-sect
276. www.alwatan.com.sa/Local/News_Detail.aspx?ArticleID=45524&Category
     ID=5
277. www.bbc.co.uk/news/world-africa-12787739
278. www.guardian.co.uk/commentisfree/2011/mar/15/no-call-for-reform-saudi-oil
279. www.jadaliyya.com/pages/index/906/different-kinds-of-intervention_groups-
     respond-to-gcc-troops-entering-bahrain

280. www.reuters.com/article/2011/03/14/us-bahrain-usa-invasion-idUSTRE 72D6RB20110314
281. www.youtube.com/watch?v=LZK7I8r3BjE
282. www.jadaliyya.com/pages/contributors/32918
283. www.jadaliyya.com/pages/contributors/9374
284. www.presse-dz.com/revue-de-presse/17078-bouteflika-refuse-l-ouverture-politique.html
285. www.liberte-algerie.com/dilem.php?id=2645
286. http://books.google.com/books?id=ONWPQwAACAAJ&dq=between+terror+and+democracy&hl=en&ei=Dh5tTY3IBYiW8QO8w52MBQ&sa=X&oi=book_result&ct=result&resnum=2&ved=0CDEQ6AEwAQ
287. www.jadaliyya.com/pages/contributors/8284
288. www.crimethinc.com/blog/2011/02/02/egypt-today-tomorrow-the-world/#map
289. www.jadaliyya.com/pages/index/500/lets-not-forget-about-tunisia
290. www.jadaliyya.com/pages/index/645/the-architects-of-the-egyptian-uprising-and-the-challenges-ahead-
291. www.jadaliyya.com/pages/index/648/tunisia-egypt-lebanon
292. www.jadaliyya.com/pages/index/625/five-questions-on-jordan
293. www.jadaliyya.com/pages/index/519/jordan_the-limits-of-comparison
294. www.bbc.co.uk/news/world-middle-east-12373767
295. www.elaph.com/Web/news/2011/2/630015.html
296. http://irq4all.com/ShowNews.php?id=36932
297. www.jadaliyya.com/pages/index/561/the-egyptian-revolution_first-impressions-from-the-field_updated-
298. www.aregy.com/forums/showthread.php?t=29860
299. www.elaph.com/Web/news/2011/2/631131.html
300. www.jadaliyya.com/pages/contributors/7303
301. www.jadaliyya.com/pages/index/506/the-poetry-of-revolt
302. www.jadaliyya.com/pages/index/541/looking-to-egypt-again
303. http://merip.org/mero/mero091109.html
304. www.hrw.org/en/news/2011/02/03/palestinian-authority-end-violence-against-egypt-demonstrators
305. www.time.com/time/world/article/0,8599,1219325,00.html
306. www.haaretz.com/news/diplomacy-defense/without-egypt-israel-will-be-left-with-no-friends-in-mideast-1.339926
307. www.ynetnews.com/articles/0,7340,L-3501747,00.html
308. http://english.aljazeera.net/palestinepapers/2011/01/2011126123125167974.html
309. http://topics.nytimes.com/top/reference/timestopics/organizations/m/muslim_brotherhood_egypt/index.html
310. www.jadaliyya.com/pages/index/518/egypt-on-the-brink_the-arab-world-at-a-tipping-point
311. http://english.aljazeera.net/indepth/opinion/2011/02/201122102119350863.html
312. http://al-shabaka.org/policy-brief/politics/unmet-potential-un-committee-palestine#fn:8
313. www.nytimes.com/2011/01/26/world/middleeast/26mideast.html
314. www.economist.com/node/17046738
315. www.jadaliyya.com/pages/contributors/654

316. www.jadaliyya.com/pages/index/Syria
317. www.al-akhbar.com/node/15679
318. www.dailystar.com.lb/News/Politics/2011/Jun-29/Agreement-reached-on-STL-policy-statement-article.ashx#axzz1QeWKJVyR
319. www.al-akhbar.com/node/15632
320. http://english.aljazeera.net/indepth/features/2011/06/201162695034941634.html
321. www.jadaliyya.com/
322. www.darfatwa.gov.lb/content.aspx?kalima=1
323. http://en.wikipedia.org/wiki/Syrian_Social_Nationalist_Party
324. www.google.com/hostednews/afp/article/ALeqM5ijlItfJUz6OTsTFkL_26-z4cI9Fw?docId=CNG.7529f04e4c90d375e355a15d0a9e1ff2.d31

Index